The Adjustment Experience of Chinese Immigrant Children in New York City

The Adjustment Experience of Chinese Immigrant Children in New York City

Betty Lee Sung

1987
Center for Migration Studies
New York

The Center for Migration Studies is an educational,
non-profit institute founded in New York in 1964
to encourage and facilitate the study of socio-demographic,
economic, political, historical, legislative and pastoral
aspects of human migration and refugee movements.
The opinions expressed in this work are those of the author.

The Adjustment Experience of
Chinese Immigrant Children in
New York City

First Edition
Copyright 1987 by
The Center for Migration Studies

CENTER FOR MIGRATION STUDIES
209 Flagg Place, Staten Island, New York 10304-1148

Library of Congress Cataloging in Publication Data

Sung, Betty Lee

The Adjustment Experience of
Chinese Immigrant Children in New York City.

Bibliography: p. 260
Includes index.

1. Chinese American children — New York (N.Y.)

2. Chinese Americans — New York (N.Y.) — Cultural assimilation.

3. New York (N.Y.) — Foreign population.

I. Title

F128.9.C5C86 1987   305.8'951'07471   85-47914

ISBN 0-913256-89-7   ISBN 0-913256-96-X (paper)

Printed in the United States of America.

Table of Contents

List of Tables

List of Maps

List of Figures

Acknowledgments

First and foremost, my respect, thanks and acknowledgment go to Professors Aubrey Bonnett, Bogdan Denitch and William Kornblum, my mentors and advisors at the Graduate Center of the City University of New York, who gave me much valued scholarly direction and guidance, but even more important, boundless moral support and encouragement. Special thanks also go to Professor Lucie Saunders of Lehman College.

I might never have attempted to write this book if I had not already done a major portion of the research and fieldwork under a generous grant from the Administration for Children, Youth and Family, Department of Health, Education and Welfare (now known as the Department of Health and Human Services). My consultants under this grant were prestigious and renown scholars and educators. They were Professor Francis L.K. Hsu, director of the Multi-Cultural Program, University of San Francisco, past president of the American Anthropological Association, and prolific author; Dr. William Liu, director of the Asian American Mental Health Research Center and professor of sociology at the University of Illinois, Chicago Circle; Mr. Richard Kramer, principal of P.S. 130 in New York City; Professor Eva Sandis of the Department of Sociology at Fordham University, New York; and Professor Stanley Sue of the Department of Psychology at the University of California, Los Angeles. This team brought a wide interdisciplinary perspective to the research.

In my fieldwork, I was the beneficiary of hundreds of pairs of helping hands. The most important of these belonged to my research associate, Dr. Rose Chao, former college guidance counselor, mother of four, and Very Knowledgeable Person about the Chinatown community, having grown up in the neighborhood. Special thanks to Fay Loo, Annie Wang, Margaret Pan Loo and Susan Hsu for the supportive services and invaluable information that they provided. I am constrained by the Board of Education against identifying by name all the principals, deans and teachers in the schools where we did our research. I do want them to know, however, that there is gratitude in my heart for their time, their cooperation and their sharing of first-hand experiences with me. Thanks also to all the people we interviewed.

How shall I express appreciation to my long-suffering husband, Charles Chia Mou Chung, who put up with a wife whose every spare moment was spent chasing after data and banging away at the typewriter night after night? Finally, to my four children and four stepchildren, who provided me with plenty of insight and practical experience in child-rearing, and to all children everywhere, I dedicate this work.

Betty Lee Sung

I
Introduction

In 1983, 41 percent of the immigrants admitted to the United States were from Asia. This is not taking into account the thousands more who were admitted as refugees, of which 70 percent were Asians. Leon Bouvier of the Population Reference Bureau and former senior demographer for the Census Bureau said, "The United States is on the verge of being transformed ethnically and racially". The staff of the Select Commission on Immigration and Refugee Reform, created by Congress in 1978 to consider immigration reform legislation, decided that the topic they were studying was nothing less than "the future character of the United States itself" (Siegel, 1983:3).

Among Asian immigrants, the Chinese form one of the largest ethnic groups. Those from China and Hong Kong range from 30,000 to 35,000 each year, and this number does not reflect the separate 20,000 quota given to Taiwan in 1981. In addition, many ethnic Chinese immigrants and refugees from other Asian countries gravitate toward the Chinese communities after they enter this country. Approximately one-fourth of the Chinese immigrants and refugees are children and youths under 19 years of age.

OBJECTIVES

This study focuses on these young people, although it is necessary to place them against the backdrop of the total Chinese immigrant experience. A review of the literature reveals almost a total vacuum of studies on how children weather the immigrant experience. Often they are not viewed in a separate light; children are considered appendages of adults. They go where their parents take them. They live where their parents decide. They eat what their parents can provide. Yet children do have concerns of their own and do react differently. Being young, they are more flexible and adaptable. They do not have the responsibilities of adults and their activities are confined more to the world of school and play. Yet, their experiences deserve to be delineated and considered separately—especially when they exhibit unusual characteristics.

When the prestigious Westinghouse Scholarships were announced for 1983, three out of the top ten awards went to Chinese teenagers from New York City, and two of these were foreign-born. Among the nation's forty finalists, nine were Chinese, with seven of them immigrants. What has become increasingly evident in educational circles is that Asians, particularly the immigrants, have chalked up an impressive record of scholastic achievement (*Asian Week*, 1983:1). In California, where no more than 15 percent of the state's high school graduates are eligible for admission to the University of California system, 40 percent of Asian Americans qualify. Ten percent of Harvard's freshmen class is Asian (*Time*, 1983:52). The percentages are comparable for Yale and MIT (Massachusetts Institute of Technology).

Gerald Lesser, noted child psychologist, and his associates have done comparative studies on the mental abilities of children from various ethnic backgrounds, and they have found that Chinese children score highest except in verbal skills (here they score even lower than blacks). In reasoning ability, in numbers and in spatial relationships, their performance is exceptional. Even when controlling for class differences, the ethnic patterns persist, except that lower class Asians invariably score much lower than those of the middle class (Lesser, Fifer and Clark, 1965).

Since these achievements are not isolated phenomena, questions have arisen as to the reasons. Some attribute the academic success to genetic superiority, while others urge that it is more nurture than nature. Sociologist William Liu, who directs the University of Illinois Asian American Mental Health Research Center, stresses the importance of cultural conditioning: "Reverence and respect for education permeates Asian cultures. Children are motivated to do well to bring honor to the family name" (*Time*, 1983:52). Recently, social scientists have advanced the theory that cultural traits can be transmitted. If this is so, Chinese children can draw upon thousands of years of rich cultural heritage.

When things go awry, when accidents occur, when strategies do not work, we ask why and we look for the causes of failure. Conversely, when things go well and there are models of success, we try to emulate and learn from them. Therefore, why not look at Chinese immigrant children? These are children uprooted, set down in a foreign culture, generally at the lower end of the economic scale, experiencing problems of readjustment and undergoing rapid cultural change. Usually these are the conditions that bring about disorganization, alienation, juvenile delinquency, and behavioral and academic problems. How is it that Chinese immigrant children have surfaced above these conditions, or are their problems just unpublicized?

What happens in the lives of Chinese immigrant children and youth when they make that transoceanic leap from the Orient to American soil? More than geography is involved. The language, ways of thinking, behavior, responses, customs and fundamental beliefs of the two cultures are poles apart. The entire body of culture with which the immigrants are cloaked is called into question. The children must unlearn as well as learn. Even though they may find some aspects of the old culture obsolete, they are loath to give up that which is part of them. How much of the new must they take on to function adequately? How much are they handicapped at first? How long does it take to acquire some of the new ways? How much of their old culture do they retain? Which parts are universal and can be transferred? To answer these questions, information was sought along the following main topics:

- Historical perspective
- Accurate and detailed description of the family, school and community to identify institutional support or hindrance
- Problem areas such as bilingual education, bicultural conflict and youth gangs
- Support systems such as after-school programs and peer groups
- Change in status and roles
- Social and psychological adjustment

The first major thrust of this book is to study the immigrant experience of Chinese immigrant children and youth, and the second is to question whether the traditional beliefs associated with immigration in general apply to this group. Sociologists, in particular, associate the immigrant experience with pathological conditions such as culture shock, language barrier, lowered status, economic difficulties, psychological problems, prejudice and discrimination, concentration in ethnic ghettos, social conflict, breakdown of norms, and disorganization. Thomas Wheeler summed it up in the title of his book, *The Immigrant Experience: The Anguish of Becoming American* (1971). Louis Adamic cynically titled his book *Laughing in the Jungle* (1932), when he wrote of the tears and the heartaches, the sweat and toil of the Yugoslavian immigrants in the early part of the twentieth century. Reading the letters of *Polish Peasants* (1918) in William I. Thomas and Florian Znaniecki's monumental work, one cannot help but sense the pain of separation felt by family members and their intense desire to be reunited. In more factual tones, Oscar Handlin chronicled the debilitating social disorders that afflicted blacks and Puerto Ricans who migrated to New York City in *The Newcomers* (1962). Carlos Bulosan's accounts of his Filipino compatriots in *America Is In The Heart* (1943) revealed how a gentle, fun-loving people became insensitive and brutalized toward their own kind after coming to the United States. If the immigrant experience of these groups has been accompanied by so much pain and sorrow, hardship and dislocation, difficulties and conflict, it should be more so for a non-white, non-Occidental group who once encountered an extremely hostile reception in this country.

The bases upon which we question the traditional beliefs for children are that the children are more adaptable and that the structural or situational factors surrounding immigration today are quite different from those of the past. Changes have occurred in the political, judicial, international and social realms in recent years that have modified the process for the better. This book shows how structural factors condition and circumscribe the ethnic immigrant experience for the group as a whole, then looks at the process of how children fit into this scheme. The structural factors are covered in the chapters on immigration, ethnic communities, the school and the family. The process unfolds in the children's interrelationship and role within these social institutions.

METHODOLOGY

The study provides a broad overview rather than one that is narrowly focused. Children were observed in their daily activities and the significant others in their lives were interviewed. Some children were interviewed and others surveyed. Although the focus is on children and youth, the adult experience cannot entirely be ignored because it provides an important backdrop.

To study the impact of immigration on children, the Chinese may be one of the best groups to observe. They have had a long period of history in the United States, yet remain a first-generation immigrant population. They have suffered severe persecution and discrimination. They have a viable and cohesive ethnic community and distinct racial features. Their culture is radically different from the American one. Yet, they have maintained a hold on their own culture for more than a century in the United States. Finally, immigrant children far outnumber native-born Chinese American children.

New York City is the ideal place for a study of this type. Every year since the 1960s it has drawn from one-fifth to one-fourth of all Chinese immigrants to the United States. In 1970, New York City's Chinese population exceeded that of San Francisco, although the number one spot was reclaimed by San Francisco in 1980. Still, approximately 6,000 new immigrants arrive in the city annually, swelling the Chinese population of the New York SMSA to 138,000 in 1980 from 76,000 in 1970. The population had already doubled in the preceding decade, making it a fourfold increase within twenty years.

The increase came predominantly from immigration as the crude birth rate among the Chinese dropped to a low of 13.1 in 1980 (Chinatown Garment Industry, International Ladies Garment Workers Union, 1983:93). In essence, New York's Chinese population is a foreign-born immigrant group, undergoing transition from an Oriental culture to an American one. It is an ideal situation to study the process of adaptation, to note the problems encountered, and to see how they are resolved both collectively and individually.

Not only is the Chinese population in New York City concentrated within the urban center, it is highly concentrated in ethnic clusters of Chinatown and satellite Chinatowns. This study was confined to Manhattan and Queens since Manhattan contains the largest Chinatown along the eastern seaboard and Queens has one of the largest satellite Chinatowns.

The fieldwork for this study, undertaken in 1976 to 1979, was funded by a grant from the Department of Health, Education and Welfare, Administration for Children, Youth and Family.

The research was begun in the public schools, for that is where most of the Chinese immigrant children could be found. The schools chosen for the study had good-size Chinese student populations, but not disproportionately large ones. No attempt was made to study those Chinese children who were dispersed throughout the schools in the city. The schools would not have allowed individual records to be examined, and the logistics of the undertaking would have been impractical.

The subjects were selected from the three levels of public school: elementary, junior high and high school. Three schools were chosen from Manhattan's Chinatown area and three from the satellite Chinatown neighborhood (one from each level) for a total of six schools. Within these levels, the focus narrowed to the third and fifth grades in the elementary schools, the seventh grade in the junior highs and students in the bilingual programs in the pair of high schools.

Data were gathered by sitting in on classes, visiting the lunch rooms, roaming the schoolyards to watch the children at play, standing in front of schools to watch the children arrive and leave, staying for the after-school centers, and talking to teachers, security guards, deans, attendance officers, principals, guidance counselors and, of course, students. Visits were made to community agencies to speak with street workers, social workers and ministers. Policemen, a judge, and even gang members were interviewed.

The intent was to look for occurrences that were not just isolated incidents but rather fairly recurrent by observing, by listening, and by asking questions. Noted were the absence of parents from the homes, the long working hours of the pupils from elementary school through high school, the higher socioeconomic status of the residents of the satellite Chinese community over that of the Chinatown residents, and the fear that the gangs evoked among teenage boys.

A survey was administered to the students in the high school bilingual programs in both communities. The questionnaire was given under supervised conditions to about twenty to thirty students at a time. Two hundred students out of the 430 enrolled in the Chinatown high school bilingual programs answered the questionnaire, while seventy, or almost all, from the satellite Chinatown community high school bilingual program did so. Tabulation of the results from the survey provided revealing insights into the daily lives, outlook and attitudes of the teenagers and youths who could assess their feelings about their transplantation from one continent to another and from one culture to another.

Seeking information from a community that has always found it more discreet to reveal nothing is a task that calls for ingenuity and perseverance. The researchers must be familiar with the community and its undercurrents. They must be aware of the stance of each informant if they are to evaluate objectively the information obtained. For example, a social service worker may overstate a problem to justify his or her program. A teacher may attack bilingual education because his or her own job is threatened if he or she lacks bilingual skills. Adversaries may make comments against each other that are colored by their prejudices. The Chinese people are suspicious of outsiders, but they are careful not to offend. Consequently, they will provide "putoff" information contrary to fact, or they will provide favorable information but nothing adverse. They are concerned about "face" and are prone to bury their heads in the sand. Social science research is something foreign to their experiences. Hence, for them the unfamiliar is cause for suspicion.

Fortunately, in most schools, the teachers and staff were extremely cooperative. The teachers understood the importance of and the need for the research, although some thought we might uncover data unfavorable to their teaching performance and were a bit on the defensive side. Some schools kept excellent records, and these we could tap into immediately. To obtain comparable data, we would then have to construct the same data for the matched school, if at all possible. Obviously, at times this was impossible. Some records that could have thrown better light upon the situation were private, and we were not given access to them. In such instances, we relied upon what we could obtain. An example would be academic records—we could not match names with grades to see how any particular pupil was doing.

The most difficult part of our research was the home visits, undertaken to talk to parents or to see what the homes were like. The Chinatown community is no longer a safe one, and few people open their doors to strangers. However, the main difficulty was that the parents were rarely home, especially the fathers. Since we saw few fathers in the homes, this is a vacuum that must be taken into consideration.

Even when we gained access to respondents and managed to establish some trust and rapport, we found that many had very limited vocabularies and even more limited experience. They tended to answer in monosyllables, have no opinions, or speak in generalities rather than specifics. It took skillful prodding to elicit the type of information sought.

As mentioned earlier, immigration has generally been associated with and followed by pathological conditions. Yet, new contact between diverse groups, whether through conflict or cooperation, is one of the greatest stimuli for social and cultural change. Frederick J. Teggert (1955:22) maintained that the "collision" of cultures which follow migrations perform the constructive task of opening new avenues of progress by breaking the cake of custom and liberating new creative energies. Migration, therefore, is a dynamic force that compels change. It involves interaction between the host society and the immigrant group. If the immigrant group perceives the contact to be hostile, it will reinforce its identity and group cohesion by clinging more strongly to its own ways. If the reception is warmer, the immigrant group may react more positively and be more willing to respond to the overtures of the new culture (See, Mead, 1967). In other words, the immigrant defines the situation and adapts his response accordingly.

At first, immigrants define all their experiences within the context of their old culture and life experiences. Modification can only come about through subjective redefinition by the immigrants themselves (See, Thomas in Coser and Rosenberg, 1982). They do not and cannot cast aside the basic personality structure or value orientations acquired during childhood (Parsons, 1951:226-235). They build upon what is already ingrained (See, Hurh and Kim, 1980). However, the options opened to immigrants are greater because the group and cultural constraints of the past have been loosened and they are freer to construct new ways.

Unlike adults, children do not carry as much cultural baggage. Their absorption of the primary culture is not so deeply ingrained and can be relinquished or modified more readily. The lowering of the immigration barriers, the repeal of discriminatory laws, the improved relations between China and the United States, the establishment of special government programs to aid the immigrants, the ease of modern-day travel, the cushion of an ethnic community to enter and an economic base that provides ready employment, all combine to make the present-day transitional process smoother and easier.

Changes have taken place in the characteristics of the more recent immigrant families as well. Immigration laws now favor the educated and the skilled, so, unlike the earlier immigrants, those now coming to the United States are no longer confined to the laboring classes. The Chinese population has become better balanced with the presence of women, children and the elderly, as well as the rich, middle-class and poor.

In this type of research, the social scientist sees the data unfolding rather than fixed. Instead of beginning with preconceived notions of what to find, the researcher lets the continuous discovery of clues and data guide the study. It is in the analysis of the data that categories and concepts take shape and patterns begin to emerge. What is quite evident from our observations and interviews, as well as from the documentary evidence, is that the Chinese communities are undergoing rapid change. The underlying reason is the tremendous and continuous increase in immigration. Former institutions are being challenged. New ones pop up and shortly disappear. Movement into and out of the communities is at a rapid pace. Social relationships, attitudes, values, etiquette, customs and traditions are now altered in an attempt to adjust to the ways of the host country. The alterations are not always good fits. What we see happening in the Chinese community with the new influx of immigrants is social experimentation in a attempt to adjust in a trial-and-error manner, but of course drawing upon their cultural heritage and taking into account the new values dangled before them. By looking at what is actually happening, we may fathom the process of how people go about adapting. By examining some of the mechanisms that are supposedly helping the immigrants in their transition, such as bilingual education, we can come to some evaluation of their effectiveness. By identifying the levers that result in action, we can conjecture about causal relationships.

Most of our behavior is repetitive and stable. Most people know in advance how other people will react to certain situations or objects. Norms, rules, laws, values, tradition, customs specify how people should act. Of course, this assumes that people stay within their own culture or country. Under such conditions, there is less opportunity to see how the linkages between human behavior develop from actor to object, so that the process of interaction has been little studied or noted. Only when people, taken out of their familiar surroundings and social context, must adapt to new surroundings with new rules and different norms are we afforded an excellent opportunity to see the process in action. Studying the Chinese immigrant children offers this opportunity.

II
Immigration Networking

History shapes our destiny more than we realize. We inherit a body of circumstances often beyond individual control, and these are situational factors that set the parameters of our lives. In viewing the adjustment process of Chinese immigrant children, it is important to review briefly the history of Chinese immigration to the United States, for more than anything else American immigration laws circumscribed this history.

Although there is much evidence to suggest that persons from China touched the American continent as seafaring adventurers and left behind cultural relics and convincing evidence long before Columbus (Breur, 1972: 270-272), it was not until the cry of gold went up in California that the Chinese arrived in any numbers. By 1851, it was estimated that 25,000 Chinese were on the West coast engaged in placer mining or manual or domestic labor (Coolidge, 1909:17).

The first immigrants were able-bodied males whose aim was to earn money to take back to China. Mostly small farmers, fishermen and tradesmen, they came as *coolies*. Literally, coolie means "bitter strength", aptly describing the principal asset of these newcomers.

The only ones who ventured abroad to the new land in those days came from a small area in the southern province of Kwangtung near the mouth of the Pearl River. The provincial capital, Canton, was the only port in the entire empire open to foreign ships, and news of the Gold Rush reached there quickly. Although the *Laws and Precedents of the Ching Dynasty* stated that any person caught leaving the country illegally, whether to go to sea, to trade, to live or to farm, would have his head severed from his body by one stroke of the executioner's axe, the prospect of finding gold in California was a strong magnet that offered the promise of quick wealth (Sung, 1967:10).

The push factors were equally strong. China's veneer of invincibility had just been shattered by defeat in the Opium War. Hong Kong was ceded to Great Britain, and the threat of further European imperialism hung heavy over the weakened nation. The Manchu government, then in power, was decadent and corrupt. A wide-spread revolt, known as the Taiping Rebellion, led by Hung Hsiu Chuan, lasted from 1851 to 1864. Estimates of lives lost ran as high as 20 million (Lai and Choy, 1972:35). The country was ravaged and devastated. Bloodied and impoverished by war and rebellions, the discontented and more adventuresome looked beyond the oceans to a land that promised a better life.

It was difficult to distinguish whether the early Chinese immigrants were more coolies or pioneers. They had fled the intolerable conditions in their homeland, impelled by war, civil strife and population pressures, but they also came as free men with higher aspirations. One notable difference from other immigrants was that they had no intention of permanently settling abroad. As such, they did not truly fit into the mold as immigrants until recent years.

The saga of the early Chinese has already been chronicled elsewhere (See, Sung, 1967). Because they provided the much-needed muscle and hard labor in an expanding economy, they were welcomed at first and openly recruited. However, as their numbers increased and when economic reverses set in, they became convenient scapegoats and were blamed for taking away jobs from the "white man" by accepting lower wages. By 1882, sentiment had turned against them, and the first of many Chinese immigration laws was passed prohibiting their entry into the United States. Those who were here were allowed to stay, but they were continually plagued by harsh discriminatory laws that would not allow them to become citizens, to own land, to intermarry, or to enjoy the many rights guaranteed to other residents of the United States. Other convenants discriminated against them in housing and in public places. Special taxes targeted at the Chinese drove them out of mining and fishing. When the purge ended, they could do only those jobs the whites did not want, such as washing and ironing, cooking and serving food, and waiting on masters and mistresses—the kind of jobs that were labeled "women's work". The Chinese survived largely by operating laundries and restaurants.

Against this hostile backdrop, the immigrant experience for the Chinese was a totally devastating one. Those who managed to hoodwink the immigration inspectors or who sneaked into the country by extra-legal means lived in constant fear of detection. Only adult males undertook such risks. Since they could not bring their families with them and since they could not intermarry, they led lonely, celibate lives. As they could not become citizens, they did not have the vote, so naturally their interests and concerns were not heard. The phrase "not a Chinaman's chance" was coined during this period and simply meant no chance whatsoever. In short, the hostile environment encountered in this country was a negative situational factor that contributed immeasurably to a pathological immigrant experience. Even greater contributing factors were the migratory barriers.

THEORIES OF MIGRATION

Theorists on migration argue about population movement or why people migrate. One of the most common theories advanced is that migration is an equilibrating mechanism, redistributing population in response to inequalities in the distribution of social and economic opportunities (Meadows, 1980: 403 405). The world is viewed as an international economic system, and labor is viewed as human capital. Forces within the system become activated when equilibrium is disrupted setting up push-and-pull factors, such as the ones that sent the Chinese across the Pacific to California. In this structuralist approach, the migrant is merely an object acted upon by economic forces.

The early immigrants from China, in the period of free immigration in the United States, certainly fit this mold. The push factors of war, civil strife, poverty and population pressures were strong. The pull factors of gold and an overwhelming demand for labor were magnetic, and, like iron filaments, these immigrants were drawn to the American West to play out their destinies.

In this structuralist scheme, labor, like horsepower, in those days may have been measurable in constant units as so many men in response to so much demand for labor. Lost sight of, however, is the fact that men are human beings with feelings, sensitivities, attitudes, rationality, values, attachments and a cultural heritage as well as an historical heritage. In short, man is unique and behaves in a unique fashion. He interprets the world around him, and his response to the structural forces is a product of his socialization, his perception, his individuality, his survival and his economic condition. Under the same circumstances or impacting forces, most people stay put. Only a select few make the decision to pull up roots and migrate. Why some remain at home while others uproot themselves is not explained by the structuralist model. Increasingly the emphasis has shifted to the behavioral properties of the migrant as an actor. In this approach, the inner world of the migrant—his perceptions, motivations, values and attitudes—are taken into account. Migration is conceived of as a social process, having some aspects located in the culture system, some within the social system, and some within the personality system of the individual (Meadows, 1980:407).

Behavioralists contend that "migration is preceded by decision-making on the part of the migrants based upon a hierarchially ordered set of values or value ends", and that the decision is a "subjectively rational" one (Meadows, 1980:407. See also, Golant, 1971:203-219 and Simon, 1947).

In the case of the Chinese, however, a rational decision to leave one's homeland for the United States for the most intelligent and valid reasons would be futile if structural barriers prevented one from implementing that desire or that decision. However, as we shall later see, another component of the behavioralist theory— the social process of family linkage and networking—has engendered a momentum into which family members and relatives are fed into the migratory stream.

When the free movement of human beings across territorial boundaries is controlled, the political theory that migration is governed by international and national policies gains ascendancy. My contention is that Chinese migration to the United States has largely been governed and shaped by political obstructions and legal enactments. Table 2-1 shows how the Chinese and American borders have opened and shut since 1849. Most of the time, the gates have been shut on both sides of the Pacific Ocean. Either the emigrants are not allowed to leave or the immigrants are not allowed to enter, so that neither disequilibrium in the international labor market nor personal inclination to change one's country of residence could affect the movement of people to any perceptible degree. For example, the out-migration of Chinese in the 1850s undoubtedly would have been much greater had the imperial decree against emigration not been promulgated. The threat of decapitation certainly deterred many Chinese from leaving home, even while the undeveloped lands of the American West beckoned. It took daring and courage for those who defied the

Emperor in their surreptitious departure, but there will always be some who manage to circumvent the authorities.

TABLE 2-1

Political and Legal Obstacles to Chinese Migration Between China and the United States

CHINA	UNITED STATES
To 1860	To 1882
Imperial Decree Against Emigration	Free Immigration
(Doors Closed)	(Doors Open)
1860-1949	1882-1943
Few Impediments Against Emigration	Chinese Exclusion
(Doors Open)	(Doors Closed)
1949-1979	1943-1965
China's Borders Closed	105 Chinese Quota
(Doors Closed)	(Crack in Door)
1979-	1965-
More Exit Visas Issued	20,000 Chinese Quota
(Crack in Door)	(Doors Open)

The imperial ban was lifted in 1860. Chinese migration to the United States enjoyed a brief span of free movement until the passage of the first Chinese Exclusion Act in 1882. Subsequent exclusion acts such as the Scott Act of 1888, the Geary Act of 1892 and the Immigration Act of 1924 reinforced the thickness of the doors to the United States and made them almost impenetrable (Sung, 1967:50-56). The impediment had shifted to the other side of the Pacific Ocean.

So while the push factors for emigration in China grew stronger with foreign invasions, national humiliations, civil wars and reform movements (which eventually culminated in the Revolution of 1911) coupled with the intense desire of many Chinese to come to this country, the exclusion laws managed to keep them out. The gates were sealed against the Chinese until the Repeal Act of

1943. Repeal of exclusion did not result in the lowering of American barriers. The door was merely opened a tiny crack to permit an annual quota of 105 Chinese to enter. At that rate, only a handful squeezed through. In the 22 years that this quota was in force, a mere 5,891 quota immigrants of Chinese ancestry were admitted. Built-up pressure for increased Chinese immigration brought about a few temporary relief measures such as the War Brides Act of 1946 and the Refugee Relief Acts of 1953, 1957 and 1962, but these only permitted the entry of a few thousand Chinese. The political and legislative barriers held.

Meanwhile, the door on the other side of the Pacific clanged shut as well. When the Communist government came to power on the Mainland in 1949, China closed its borders to the outside world, neither allowing the people to leave nor others to enter. The Chinese barrier was almost impenetrable except for those who risked life and limb to try to cross the borders into Hong Kong. Thus the only ones who could take advantage of the tiny American admission quota were those already in Hong Kong or those who had escaped earlier to Taiwan.

LOWERING THE BARRIERS

In 1965, the United States decided to open her doors a little wider and to abolish the national-origins quotas, which gave preference to white Anglo-Saxon Protestants. Under the new law, the quota for any one country in any one year was set at 20,000 with an overall limitation of 170,000 from the Eastern Hemisphere. A quota of 105 to one of 20,000 was almost a two hundredfold increase. However, conditions on the sending side had not changed. Since the Chinese exit barriers were still in place, Chinese immigrants came primarily from the two islands of Hong Kong and Taiwan.

It was not until early 1979 that diplomatic relations were re-established between China and the United States. Since then, Chinese barriers have been lowered somewhat. It was reported that during Deng Xiaoping's state visit to the United States in January 1979, President Carter, ever concerned about human rights, appealed to the then premier to relax the ban on exit visas for relatives of Chinese Americans to allow them to join their families in this country. Much to President Carter's surprise, Premier Deng was amenable. "How many millions do you want?" he inquired. Even if China were to allow the mass departure of its people, the American quota would still act as an effective cork to large-scale immigration from China. Although perceptible improvement has been noted by recent immigrants in the number of exit visas issued by the People's Republic of China, such documents are still difficult to come by. At the time of this writing a new immigration bill, passed in 1987, may again restrict Chinese immigration. In sum, Chinese immigration is extremely vulnerable to the political winds.

Although it is simple to list these laws and barriers and show how they have prevented people from crossing national boundaries, it would be difficult to recount the toll in terms of human suffering, the pain of years of family separation, and the feelings of frustration, loneliness and anger. Can anything but bitterness arise out of a situation like this for those immigrants who had to endure? Not likely.

The immigration act that has been in effect for the past two decades was passed in 1965. The jump from a quota of 105 to 20,000 for the Chinese was a phenomenal improvement. Those applying for visas no longer had to wait ten years or more for that coveted piece of paper. The impatient ones who had preferred extralegal or illegal means of effecting entry into the United States no longer had to resort to devious and circumventing tactics. Legitimate means were at hand, so the burden of fear was removed. The Chinese were now at parity with other nationals, and the stigma of seventy-three years of discrimination was gone. What a sense of relief this law brought! Nothing has had a greater impact upon the lives of the Chinese in the United States than this single piece of legislation. It ushered in an era of expansion, liberalization and goodwill—an appropriate setting for a more positive immigration experience.

The 1965 Immigration and Nationality Act also sought to remedy some of the defects and blatantly discriminatory features of past legislation. Two of the main features of the act were concerned with the manpower needs of the country and the desirability to reunite families. Therefore, immigrants are admitted on the basis of occupational preference and relative preference. Those with special skills and education needed in this country had priority, but the law as written operates primarily in favor of family reunification. In fact, parents, spouses and minor children of U.S. citizens may now enter without regard to quota limitations. They are classified as non-quota immigrants and are not charged to the 20,000 quota permitted for any one country on a first-come, first-served basis with a cap or total admissions of 270,000 immigrants per year.

For quota immigrants, six preference categories were set up for priority issuance of immigrant visas; 80 percent were set aside for relatives, while only 20 percent were allocated for occupational preference. The preference categories are listed below:

1st Preference: Unmarried sons and daughters of U.S. citizens (20%)

2nd Preference: Spouses and unmarried sons and daughters of aliens lawfully admitted for permanent residence (26% plus any numbers not utilized for 1st preference)

3rd Preference: Members of the professions or persons of exceptional ability in the sciences and arts (10%)

4th Preference: Married sons and daughters of U.S. citizens (10% plus any numbers not utilized by first three preferences)

5th Preference: Brothers and sisters of U.S. citizens over 21 years of age (24% plus any numbers not utilized in first four categories)

6th Preference: Skilled and unskilled workers in short supply (10%)

Non-Preference: Numbers not used by the six preference categories (U.S. House of Representatives, 1980: 22-23)

Chinese immigration can theoretically increase at a geometric rate. A model for this process is shown in Fig. I. The model shows how an immigrant can rapidly rebuild his family network in the United States:

Immigrant (1) becomes citizen. He immediately sends for his wife (2) and his father and mother (3 and 4). If there are minor children, all of these are entitled to enter the country as non-quota immigrants. As soon as the parents arrive, they gain status as permanent residents and can file for their unmarried child (5) under second preference. Their married son and daughter-in-law (6 and 7) as well as any minor children of this couple (8 and 9) can apply for fourth preference visas. Or the citizen (1) can take an-

FIGURE I

Networking of Immigration to the United States under the Family Reunification Preference System

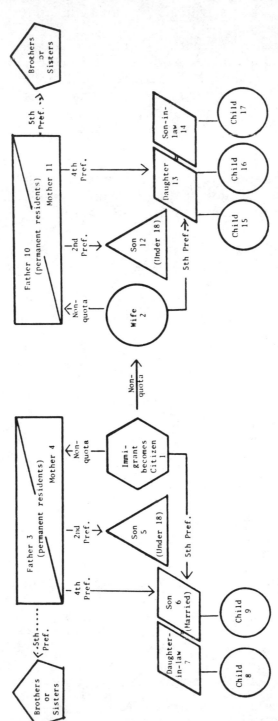

Source: U.S. Immigration and Nationality Act of 1965 as Amended.

other route by directly applying for his married brother's family under the fifth preference.

The wife of the citizen must wait three years before she obtains citizenship, but when she does she can duplicate the entire procedure that her husband went through to bring her side of the family to this country (*See*, right side of Figure I). A lateral move may also take place simultaneously by the parents applying for their brothers' and sisters' families utilizing the fifth preference category.

Of course there is a time sequence to this networking process. The Immigration and Naturalization Service is notoriously slow in processing the applications, and there are statutory waiting periods before one is eligible to become a citizen. The approximate time sequence is outlined in Table 2-2.

TABLE 2-2
Time Sequence of Immigration Networking

No. of Person in Model	Procedure	Waiting Period or Time Lapse
(1)	Enters U.S. as immigrant. Applies for citizenship. 5 years statutory wait.	5 to 6 years
(1)	Obtains citizenship. Sends for wife (2), mother & father (3 & 4) non-quota.	3 to 6 months
(3 & 4)	Enter as permanent residents. Send for minor son (5) under 2nd preference.	1 to 2 years
(3 & 4)	Simultaneously send for married son and his family (6 to 9) under 4th preference.	2 to 3 years
(2)	Wife applies for citizenship. Reduced waiting period of 3 years.	3 to 3½ years
(2)	Obtains citizenship, sends for parents (10 & 11) non-quota.	3 to 6 months
(10 & 11)	Wife's parents send for unmarried son (12) under 2nd preference.	1 to 2 years
(10 & 11)	Wife's parents simultaneously send for married daughter and her family (13 to 17)	2 to 3 years
(3 & 4) (10 & 11)	Both sets of parents may send for their respective siblings under 5th preference Eligibility has now branched out fourfold.	3 to 4 years

Notes: The time sequence may overlap and is not necessarily consecutive.

Assumption is made that immigrants will send for their immediate family members, but not all do. Size of the families will naturally affect the multiplication factor in the networking process and the number of people eligible to immigrate to this country.

In 1972, 15 percent of those admitted from China and Hong Kong were non-quota immigrants—close family members admitted without charge to the quota. By 1977, this had increased to 20 percent. As the immigrants obtain citizenship, they will increasingly take advantage of the non-quota provisions of the law to complete their family networking. Table 2-3 compares the number of Chinese admitted under relative preference, occupational preference and non-preference categories from 1968 to 1980. Non-quota immigrants are added to the relative category because they are, by legal definition, close family members. As is apparent, family networking was responsible for 85 percent whereas occupational preference was 13 percent and non-preference was only 2 percent of those admitted in 1980. The implications of family networking are several:

1. When families are reunited in this country, they will be permanent settlers and not sojourners as they were before.

2. The Chinese population will be more balanced with females as well as males, and children and elderly as well as mature adults. Formerly the Chinese population was predominantly adult male.

3. Chinese immigration will continue to increase substantially for some time to come. Slackening will come about, however, when the families are fairly well reunited and when native-born generations foresake the strong family obligation values which propelled the first generations to send for their kinfolk.

4. The Chinese population in the United States will be a predominantly first-generation group for some time to come. In New York City, three out of four Chinese are foreign-born. As such, the characteristics and needs of the group will be substantially different from a predominantly native-born one.

5. Ethnic communities will grow and expand to meet the needs of the newcomers.

6. The ethnic culture will be reinforced, but also altered to fit the American way of life.

7. The continual influx means that the Chinese communities must adapt to rapid growth, which means rapid change.

8. One could hypothesize that the strong sense of family ties that reassembled the family members through immigration might be rekindled in this country to provide an institutional base for a cohesive Chinese American society. Some of these bonds may operate to structure loose clan network clusters. If so, the Chinese

TABLE 2-3

Chinese Admitted Under Relative Preference, Occupational Preference, and Non-Preference Categories, 1968 to 1980

	Relative Preference & Non-quota[a]		Occupational Preference		Non-Preference		Total Quota & Non-quota[b]
	No.	%	No.	%	No.	%	No. = 100%
1968	8,998	.68	3,479	.26	773	.06	13,250
1969	13,976	.74	3,968	.21	1,032	.05	18,976
1970	8,795	.59	2,920	.20	3,181	.21	14,896
1971	9,563	.56	2,910	.17	4,454	.27	16,927
1972	9,893	.47	3,359	.16	7,917	.37	21,169
1973	12,756	.59	1,815	.08	7,027	.33	21,598
1974	15,025	.67	1,724	.08	5,656	.25	22,405
1975	16,396	.70	1,988	.08	5,174	.22	23,558
1976	20,830	.85	1,856	.08	1,741	.07	24,427
1976 qtr.	5,340	.82	835	.13	306	.05	6,481
1977	20,908	.84	2,733	.11	1,104	.05	24,745
1978	21,454	.84	3,237	.13	905	.03	25,596
1979	23,679	.86	2,839	.10	933	.03	27,451
1980	24,317	.85	3,836	.13	546	.02	28,699

Notes: [a] Relative preference includes those admitted as non-quota immigrants.
[b] Total figures may vary when Hong Kong figures are not available for inclusion.

Source: U.S. Immigration and Naturalization Service, *Annual Reports and Statistical Yearbook* (Washington, D.C. 1968-1980).

will have recreated an important aspect of their former culture in this country. However, strong American countercurrents emphasize the conjugal unit rather than the kinship one, and the prevailing American norms toward weaker family ties will operate to offset this tendency.

FUTURE IMMIGRATION

Figure II shows Chinese immigration to the United States from 1944 to 1980. Each spurt in numbers reflects immigration legislation. Since 1972, the Chinese have fully utilized the maximum quota of 20,000 permitted any one country. This quota was doubled by Congress in 1981 when it permitted Taiwan a separate 20,000 quota apart from Mainland China. Add to the double quota of 40,000 the non-quota immigrants and persons of Chinese ethnic origin from Vietnam, other Southeast Asian countries, and Latin America, and one can expect a steep climb in Chinese immigration to the United States for many years to come.

FIGURE II
Chinese Immigration to the United States, by Sex, 1944-1980

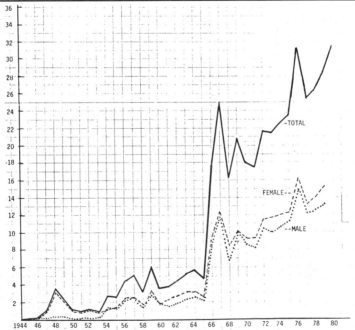

Source: Immigration and Naturalization Service, *Annual Reports* and/or *Statistical Yearbooks*, (Washington, D.C., 1944-1980).

III
Determinants of Immigrant Types

While numbers are one dimension of immigrant influx, characteristics of the immigrants are another. Basically, the characteristics of immigrants are determined in large part by the causes of migration or the migratory forces, whether these causes be structural, behavioral or political factors. Using the Chinese immigrant experience as a model (*See*, Table 3-1), it is evident that at certain periods in history certain types of migrants predominate.

The Chinese migrant labor movement of the Gold Rush period is already well known. The economic forces at work were the lure of gold in California, the labor needs of a developing West, population pressure in China and the unrest caused by war and civil strife in the homeland during the mid-nineteenth century. Since laborers were needed, it was laborers who responded. Naturally, these were young men in their prime—men who could withstand the rigors of hard work and adjustment to a new way of life.

FROM MALES TO FEMALES

A different type of immigrant did not emerge among the Chinese until the late 1940s and the early 1950s. For a period of eight years, from 1947 to 1953, almost 90 percent of the Chinese immigrants admitted to the United States were females—mainly wives or brides of earlier immigrants now able to enter because of the Repeal Act of 1943 and the War Brides Act of 1946. The former act repealed the entire body of exclusion acts against the Chinese and permitted reunification of immediate family members. The latter allowed men who had served in the Armed Forces of the United States during World War II to bring their foreign born wives into the country outside of quota restrictions. The infusion of females into the Chinese community brought about a drastic change in its makeup and structure from one of a group of unattached males to a more stable society of families.

TABLE 3-1

Migratory Forces and Immigrant Types

Period Beginning	Migratory Forces	Type of Migrant	Demographic Characteristics
1848	Lure of gold in California Labor needs of developing West Population pressure in China War and civil strife in China	Laborers	Primarily men. Lower socio- econ. classes
1943	Repeal of Chinese exclusion acts War Brides Act	Wives and children	Primarily women. Lower and middle classes.
1946	Civil war in China, 1946-49 Communist take-over, 1949 U.S. refugee acts	Students Refugees	Primarily men. Intelligentsia. Officials.
1965	Political flight fr. communism U.S. Immigration Act of 1965	Professionals Educated Skilled	Primarily adults, Upper-mid. class.
	Relative preference, non-quota for immediate families	Nuclear family members	Both sexes, all ages/classes.
	Relative preference	Kinship/ family members	Both sexes, all ages/classes.
1979	Ouster of ethnic Chinese fr. Vietnam U.S. Refugee Act of 1980	Refugees fr. Vietnam	Both sexes. Many children, business & professional people.

INTELLIGENTSIA AND OFFICIALS

The 1950s also saw a different socioeconomic group—the intelligentsia—join the ranks of the Chinese in the United States. They were relatively few in numbers, but they added diversity to the former laboring class. Many were students sent to this country for higher education immediately after World War II, so they could help in the reconstruction of their country when they returned home. Mao Zedong's victory over the Nationalist government in 1949 left these students stranded in the United States. Their support from China was cut off. At the same time, the United States forbade their return to China on the grounds that these students had knowledge and skills that might be used against the United States, especially with the outbreak of the Korean War in 1950.

The students, about 2,000 of them and primarily young men, became involuntary immigrants, forced to seek a livelihood in this country as a result of the revolution, war and international politics (Lee, 1960: 103-112).

These same conditions forced other Chinese to flee China and seek refuge in the United States. Many were former officials and people associated with the Nationalist government which had fled to Taiwan. Some were granted political asylum, while others were permitted to enter or remain in this country under a number of Refugee Relief Acts enacted in 1953, 1957 and 1959 (Kung, 1962: 118-120).

The stranded students and political refugees were of the educated or monied classes. As such, they injected into the former laboring class Chinese population a new socioeconomic tier. The Immigration Act of 1965 further increased the ranks of the professionals and educated by granting them occupational preference. The Sixties was the decade when brains replaced brawn in the immigration selection process.

KINFOLK

As noted previously, the family reunification preference system of American immigration laws continues to network family members. Eighty percent of the quota is allocated to relatives. Table 3-2 shows that the fifth preference category, reserved for brothers and sisters of U.S. citizens, has been increasing substantially over the years. In 1983, it was nearly two-thirds of all relative preference immigrants admitted. In other words, Chinese immigration has now entered the phase where the kinship structure of the population is broadening its base, not only vertically but also horizontally to include brothers and sisters, who may also be aunts and uncles to other members of the family. The figures in Table 3-2 also show that second preference immigrants make up one-third of the relative preference Chinese admitted.

REFUGEES

The latest wave of Chinese newcomers to the United States actually has a dual or multiple identity. These are the ethnic Chinese ousted from Vietnam since 1979. In fact, many of those who fled the country immediately after the fall of Saigon in 1975 were also of ethnic Chinese origin, but the largest exodus occurred during the summer of 1979, and they continue to come.

TABLE 3-2

Chinese Immigrant Admitted to the United States
by Relative Preference Categories
1968 to 1983

		Relative	Preference		Categories
	Total Relat. Pref.	1st Pref.	2nd Pref.	4th Pref.	5th Pref.
1968	4,950	130	2,110	882	1,828
1969	10,341	159	2,647	1,681	5,854
1970	5,538	101	2,130	706	2,601
1971	6,539	70	2,789	847	2,833
1972	7,012	75	3,374	592	2,971
1973	8,505	75	3,613	647	4,170
1974	10,707	79	4,749	523	5,356
1975	12,029	118	5,009	743	6,159
1976	15,647	104	5,543	1,084	8,916
1976 qtr.	4,142	20	1,423	211	2,488
1977	15,904	69	5,273	814	9,748
1978	14,848	111	6,017	938	7,782
1979	15,696	391	7,225	2,351	5,729
1980	14,937	327	8,002	1,890	4,718
1981	15,808	392	8,795	1,743	4,878
1982	24,195	319	9,561	4,688	9,627
1983	30,907	279	10,686	6,532	19,871

Note: Total does not include non-quota relatives.

Source: Immigration and Naturalization Service, *Annual Reports* or *Statistical Yearbooks*, 1968 to 1983.

Chinese presence in Vietnam was noted as early as the second century B.C., but the largest influx occurred between the period 1860 to 1930. By 1970, the Chinese population in Vietnam was estimated to be 1.5 million out of a total population of 39 million. Most of these people clung to their Chinese nationality, and during the French occupation served as middlemen between the indigenous citizens and the French colonists. As such, they were primarily businessmen and traders or, in Communist terminology, capitalists. As relations between China and Vietnam worsened after the fall of Saigon and after the departure of American troops, the ethnic Chinese in Vietnam were caught in the middle. Labeled foreigners, capitalists, and eventually enemies after China invaded Vietnam in February 1979, the ethnic Chinese were forced to leave the country but not without payment extorted for their departure. After paying between $1,000 and $3,000 in gold for the "privilege" of leaving, many boarded flimsy boats with no destination in mind. They put out to sea with hopes that they could seek a new life in another land (National Indo-Chinese Clearing House, 1981). Thus, they were labeled "boat people".

From 60 to 90 percent of these expellees or refugees from Vietnam were of Chinese ethnic origin. Hanoi viewed the expulsion as a means of ridding itself of unwanted people, but these hapless souls found no welcome in the neighboring countries of Malaysia, Indonesia, Japan or Thailand. Thailand simply pushed the refugees back into Vietnam at gunpoint. Malaysian Deputy Prime Minister Mahathir bin Mohammad declared that his government would load its 75,000 Vietnamese boat people into boats and push them out to sea, and would fire on any newcomers (Kamm, 1979). Japanese ships steered 200 miles off course to avoid the seas traversed by boat people (Stokes, 1979).

When the plight of these people drifting on the high seas came to President Carter's attention, he ordered the Seventh Fleet in the Pacific to pick up the boat people and take them to nearby receiving centers for processing and resettlement in other countries with the United States promising to take 168,000 a year — more than all the rest of the countries of the world combined (*Newsweek*, 1979:37). Later, at the Geneva Conference convened by sixty-five nations to curtail refugee exodus, Vice President Walter Mondale pledged that the United States would take 14,000 refugees a month for an indefinite period. The pledge was enacted into law by the Refugee Act of 1980. Up to March, 1981, 450,000 refugees from Vietnam had been admitted to the United States, many of whom viewed themselves as ethnic Chinese.

These ethnic Chinese refugees were generally better educated and more sophisticated than other refugee groups. Women and chidren as well as men were among the uprooted. Young and old alike numbered in their ranks, but the refugees were heavily weighted toward the young. Nearly 50 percent were under the age of 18, thus increasing the ranks of children (Montero, 1979:627). Unlike the earlier immigrants, their flight, according to Kunz (1973) study of general immigration patterns, was of the acute rather than the anticipatory type. Anticipatory migrants are those who plan for their departure. Acute refugee movements are caused by massive political and military upheaval. These refugees fled en masse with the emphasis on escape. Since the experiences of these refugees are so dissimilar to the former Chinese immigrants, and since they are marginal to the established Chinese communities with their dual identities, they pose a special set of queries and problems distinct and separate from the Chinese immigrants who came before.

BASIC CHANGES IN TYPES OF IMMIGRANTS

Looking back at the historical pattern of Chinese immigration to this country, one sees that certain levers set into motion the sending or receiving of a specific type of immigrant with distinctive demographic characteristics. Particularly within the last three to four decades, the Chinese population has undergone basic structural changes caused by the types of immigrants coming here. First, the sex composition underwent change. Then the class composition was altered, and subsequently the kinship base was broadened, with age composition undergoing drastic transformation.

The implications of these changes are substantial. Women brought stability, and with their presence, family life replaced the haphazard ways of single male existence. Home became the United States instead of the ancestral place in China where wives and children and parents used to wait for their menfolk's return. Women bore children who formed a native-born second generation. Roots spread into American soil slowly transforming the Chinese identity into a mixed American one. Money formerly sent out of the country to support families in China was now spent here feeding the American economy and vitalizing the Chinese American communities.

Just as the Chinese population of the past was a unisex society, so it was a uniclass society consisting of lower strata laborers, domestic workers and service workers. Racist barriers, combined with the indignities of the Chinese exclusion laws, acted to keep the Chinese at the lower rungs of the economic ladder. What respectable merchant, what person with skills and education, what cultivated man or woman would subject himself or herself to an uncertain length of detention on Angel's Island or Ellis Island to be treated like a criminal without having committed a crime or to suffer the indignities or oppression and discrimination by coming to this country? Only those who had little to lose risked the venture, so immigration was confined to the poorer classes who used it as a temporary means of building up a small monetary base. As soon as this sum was accumulated, they departed, leaving only the losers to continue their quest.

The framers of the 1965 immigration law must have sensed the defects of the former restrictions and gave special priority to those with capital, skills and education in the third and sixth preferences. The flight of refugees and the elite from political instability in China also contributed to a more varied class composition in the immigration waves since 1950. Former government officials, intellectuals, the well-to-do, and large contingents of the middle class now vied to enter the United States. The middle and upper classes presently form an increasingly large proportion of the Chinese population in this country. The stereotype image of the Chinese used to be coolie, domestic, laborer, laundryman. It is slowly changing to that of engineer, computer scientist, mathematician, restaurateur.

Age composition is the third major change in demographic characteristics of the Chinese immigrants. Whereas immigration used to be for able-bodied adult males who could withstand the rigors and risks and who only intended to go abroad temporarily, the age spread now covers the youngest of infants to octogenarians. Table 3-3 shows the number of Chinese immigrant children or youths, age 19 and under, admitted to the United States from 1950 to 1983. In the decade of the Fifties, the number of Chinese children entering the United States was insignificant, from less than 200 per year to less than 2,000 at the end of the ten-year period. The decade of the Sixties showed a tremendous jump in numbers to as high as 8,007 in 1967. The Seventies saw a drop from former years in the number of immigrant Chinese children, but the numbers seem to have stabilized at around 6,000. The Eighties show a substantial increase.

BIRTH RATE

With the huge influx of women and the enlargement of the population base, expectation was that children would be born, thus giving rise to a growing native-born second generation. This expectation has not been borne out to the extent that one would normally presume. Up to 1973, the total number of Chinese births never exceeded 8,000 per year for the entire United States (Department of Health, Education and Welfare).

For New York City specifically, the metropolis that boasts the largest Chinese population in the country, very few babies were born to Chinese mothers (See,, Table 3-4).

TABLE 3-3

Chinese Immigrant Children or Youths Admitted to the United States Age 19 and Under, 1950-1983

Year	Number	Year	Number	Year	Number
1950	199	1960	943	1970	5,051
1951	160	1961	1,064	1971	4,254
1952	152	1962	1,111	1972	5,691
1953	195	1963	1,312	1973	5,548
1954	507	1964	1,406	1974	6,030
1955	537	1965	1,282	1975	6,208
1956	1,310	1966	6,476	1976	8,850[a]
1957	1,273	1967	8,007	1977	6,682
1958	551	1968	4,941	1978	6,474
1959	1,854	1969	7,189	1979	7,031
				1980	7,893
				1981	7,219
				1982	10,211
				1983	13,330

Note: [a] Change in fiscal year from June 30th to September 30th. Three months added to 1976.

Source: Immigration and Naturalization Service, *Annual Reports* or *Statistical Yearbooks*.

TABLE 3-4
New York City Resident Births to Chinese Mothers

Year	Number	Year	Number
1970	1,490	1978	1,629
1971	1,423	1979	1,635
1972	1,332	1980	1,630
1973	1,354	1981	1,751
1974	1,345	1982	1,980
1975	1,576	1983	2,268
1976	1,596	1984	2,506
1977	1,526	1985	2,888

Source: Birth Files, New York City, Department of Health.

At the same time that the number of births were declining, the Chinese population of New York City was increasing. For the five boroughs, the population was 138,000, thus a crude birth rate of 11.8, which is lower than the total New York City birth rate of 13.4 or the U.S. birth rate of 15.9. The phenomenon of declining births was to be expected. According to the theory of demographic transition, declining births inevitably accompany industrialization and urbanization. Consequently, the number of native-born Chinese children will remain small, while immigrant children will make up the bulk. Hence the focus on Chinese immigrant children is especially pertinent and appropriate, because in spite of the low birth rate, the number of Chinese children has risen dramatically over the past few decades. Table 3-5 shows Chinese children and youth, age 19 and under, by decades, 1940 to 1980. The data are taken from the decennial censuses. They show that within the span of 40 years, the number of Chinese children has increased more than tenfold.

The usual train of thought is that children are part of immigrant families, and whatever happens to their parents applies to the offsprings as well. There is a great deal of truth to this reasoning, but in the United States, especially in the highly urbanized areas, children lead lives that are almost compartmentalized and apart from adult lives. A disquieting trend seems to be that family lives

TABLE 3-5
Chinese Children and Youth, Age 19 and Under
By Decades, 1940-1980

Age Group	1940	1950	1960	1970	1980
Under 5	4,375	13,628	27,734	35,813	57,062
5 - 9	5,464	6,543	27,522	39,159	55,310
10 - 14	6,569	7,129	22,638	39,955	57,461
15 - 19	7,318	8,377	11,800	43,607	67,327
Total	23,726	35,677	89,694	158,534	237,160

Source: Decades 1940 and 1950 from Rose Hum Lee, *The Chinese in the United States of America*, (Hong Kong: Hong Kong University Press, 1960), p. 43. Decades 1960 to 1980 from U.S. Census.

are no longer lives intertwined but parallel tracks separate from one another. As this separation becomes more pronounced, it becomes increasingly important to examine what is happening to the children.

Children are dependents—someone must nurture and care for them; others must educate them. Their personalities and characters are impressionable. Their futures may be shakened or shaped by their first encounters in this country. They are confused by different standards and customs, and they need someone to turn to in case of trouble. They need guidance and direction. Children were once a rarity in the Chinese communities here, now these communities must accommodate many children arriving in rapid succession. A community without children had no need for schools, playgrounds, ball parks, day care centers, Boy Scouts, etc. These facilities cannot be set up in a hurry, if indeed they can be provided at all. Children are not miniature grown-ups. Their lives are circumscribed by their families, their school and their immediate neighborhood. Their development is still in the formative stages. If mid-course corrections must be made, there is still time for intervention and improvement. The process of adjustment of immigrant children must be viewed in a separate light from the adult experience, and that is precisely the purpose of this study.

IV
The Community

Immigration is like a surgical process. The immigrant is physically pulled up by the roots and transplanted onto foreign soil. It is not only the physical severance from one's country, community, neighborhood, home, relatives, culture and friends; the immigrant is also cut off from all that is familiar and dear to live in a foreign land. The immigrant is cut loose from the buoy that anchored him and made him feel secure.

Human beings need the security of the familiar not just to absorb the culture shock of transplantation, but also as a springboard to launch them toward a new life. The question is whether this launch can be as successful without the cushion of the familiar.

Fortunately for Chinese immigrants who relocate in New York City, there are ethnic communities that aid these newcomers in their transition. In what ways have these ethnic communities met the needs of the growing numbers coming in, and in what ways have they failed? Satellite Chinatowns are spinning off from the main Chinatown. Are these innovative moves or regressive measures that retard acculturation? The ethnic communities are the neighborhoods in which the Chinese immigrant children live. They are the primary social environment, hence their impact is especially strong.

The concept of community encompasses a common way of life and a common identity. "For Max Weber, the communal relationship is based upon a sense of solidarity resulting from the emotional and traditional attachments of the participants. It is not enough to share common characteristics or a common situation; even racial distinctions do not in any way imply a communal relationship. People may react to their shared situation in the same way, they may also have a common feeling about it without it leading to the creation of community. 'It is only when this feeling leads to mutual orientation of their behavior toward each other

34   Chinese Immigrant Children in New York City

that communal relationship arises among them'" (1970:43). "People begin to feel that they belong together when they acquire a consciousness of kind. Such social bonds are characterized by emotional cohesion and continuity in time" (Kramer, 1970:39).

New York's Chinatown is a community in every sense of the term. It has an history that goes back to 1870 when Wo Kee opened his general store at 8 Mott Street (Lee, 1965:125). The store was a magnet for the handful of lonely Chinese laundrymen who gathered there on Sundays to pick up their mail from home, to exchange pleasantries and small talk, to relieve the loneliness of their solitary existence, and to wager a few bets behind the store. Grocery stores for Chinese foods and supplies sprang up alongside Wo Kee, and restaurants opened to serve the men a decent meal once a week. It was not until the 1890s that Caucasians discovered the Chinese restaurants and began to patronize them.

COMMUNITY BOUNDARIES

The Chinese curio shops, groceries and restaurants spilled over into Pell and Doyer Streets. These short, winding, narrow cobblestone streets are still the heart of Chinatown today, but the boundaries of the contiguous Chinese community of the Lower East Side have been extended. Map 1 shows the enlarged Chinatown of the early 1970s. The northern boundary is Delancey Street, the southern boundary is the Brooklyn Bridge, the eastern boundary is Essex Street, and the western boundary is Lafayette Street. The shaded area shows the core area of approximately nine blocks.

In the early 1960s the community looked as if it was heading for decline. Calvin Lee predicted its demise as the old people died off and the young refused to live there (Lee,1965:143). Changes in the American immigration laws quickly reversed the decline. As more and more immigrants arrived, they headed toward Chinatown causing a tremendous demand for housing. Chinatown became larger and larger. If we define Chinatown as a contiguous community with large concentrations of Chinese population, even the boundaries on the map are already outdated. The expanded borders are 14th Street to the north, Broadway to the west, Columbia Street to the east, and Beekman Street to the south.

MAP 1

Chinatown, New York

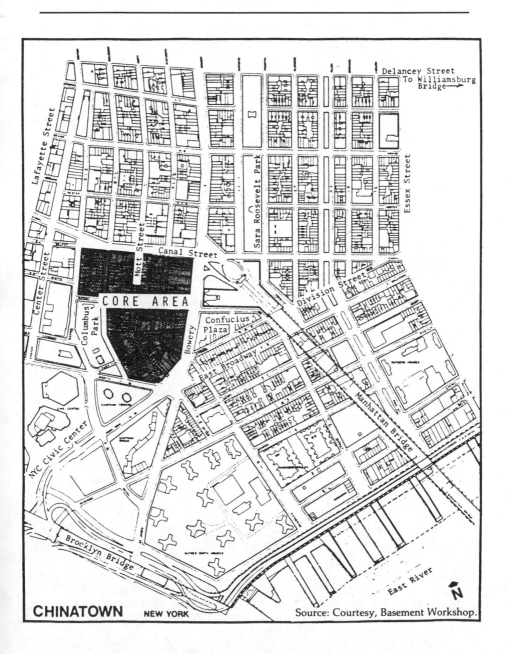

HOUSING STOCK

Most of the housing in lower Manhattan is of ancient vintage. In his survey, C.N. Yung (1969: 196) found that thirty-five percent of the buildings in the core area were built before 1900 and ninety percent before 1935. New construction has been sparse. In the 1950s, when Chinatown was still confined to the nine-block area, there were plans by the New York City Housing Authority to demolish the old buildings and rebuild a modern, well-laid-out Chinatown in stages. The plans were scuttled when a community delegation protested to the Housing Authority any contemplated changes to their community. Those who had businesses and real estate in the area did not want their vested interests disturbed, even if it meant a newer, more attractive and cleaner neighborhood in the long run.

The housing stock of the Lower East Side where the Chinese are moving is already celebrated as a slum area serving wave after wave of new immigrants to these shores. There were the Irish, the Italians and the Jews, and now the Chinese and Puerto Ricans. Most of the buildings are five- to six-story walk-ups. Rents are controlled; the dollar amount is small, but the condition of the housing is deplorable. Landlords have found that it does not pay to fix the roof, or paint the hallways, or provide better lighting, or fix the plumbing. As a result the buildings are generally in advanced stages of disrepair.[1] Nevertheless, for the new immigrants living in or near Chinatown, it means that sense of security of being with one's own kind, so they compete fiercely for these rundown tenements. To take advantage of this demand, many circumvent the rent control laws by means of a convention called "key money"—money paid in advance to either the landlord or the former tenant for the privlege of renting that apartment. Sums ranging from a few hundred to two thousand dollars are not uncommon, and it is money paid in advance. This makes the rents no longer cheap.

Low cost urban renewal projects such as the Alfred Smith Houses, Knickerbocker Village, Rutger Houses, Allen Street House, Gouveneer Gardens, and Seward Park Houses have been

---

[1] The condition of some of these tenements will be described in detail in the discussion of our home visits. See also, New York City Planning Commission, "Chinatown Street Revitalization" (1976) for a detailed and extensive study of Chinatown housing and land use.

put up on the outer fringes of Chinatown. These government sponsored, urban renewal projects, built during the 1950s and 1960s, are rent controlled and occupied largely by Jewish and Italian people who had prior claim to the housing. The low rentals make them much too attractive for the occupants to move, so few Chinese families can get into any of these projects.

Middle income housing projects like Chatham Green, Chatham Towers, and the Southbridge Towers near Beekman Street south of the Brooklyn Bridge have many Chinese tenants. The newest housing to arise in the heart of Chinatown is the forty-four story Confucius Plaza, built in 1976, primarily over the air space of the Manhattan Bridge. The project combines commercial, educational, and residential functions. On the ground level are a 1,200 pupil elementary school, stores, offices and a playground. The upper stories are devoted to 750 moderate income cooperative apartments and most of the occupants are Chinese. The impact of this project on the Chinatown community has been enormous. It has revitalized the Bowery and Division Street, brought many middle income Chinese families back to the neighborhood, and upgraded the entire locality leading to private renovation of buildings nearby. Confucius Plaza is an excellent example of the domino effect of upgrading urban areas.

Shown within the map of Chinatown to the lower left is the Municipal Civic Center where City Hall, the Municipal Building, the court houses and governmental agencies are situated. Chinatown stands on prime urban real estate. However, because of its rundown buildings, the tax base is low, yet abandonment of buildings and tax arrears are minimal. In fact, recent prices for sale of Chinatown property match and even exceed that of midtown Manhattan (New York Planning Commission, 1976:22).

RECREATIONAL AREAS

As a community for growing children, however, Chinatown lacks space, recreational facilities, playgrounds and safe streets. The only playgrounds are those connected with the public schools. The only actual park is Columbus Park, an area the size of one city block and heavily used by the children and elderly as the major open-space recreational facility. Another neighborhood park, Sara Roosevelt Memorial Park, is no more than an elongated center mall of a busy city street. Ball-playing would be hazardous for children who might try to retrieve balls in the street.

Traffic is very heavy. Canal Street is a thoroughfare for traffic to and from Brooklyn and Queens via the Manhattan Bridge and to and from New Jersey via the Holland Tunnel. An hourly vehicle count shows between 1,600 and 1,800 cars and trucks pass on Canal Street at an hour when children are going home from school (five hundred cars per hour is considered high volume traffic). Chatham Square is another nightmare to navigate—ten streets converge into a hub and the volume of vehicular traffic is high. Such traffic conditions are certainly not safe for children playing in the streets.

ETHNIC MAKE-UP

Chinatown and its surrounding environs contain a diverse mixture of peoples. The white ethnics are the Jews and the Italians, but both Little Italy and the Jewish stronghold in the Lower East Side have been infused with large numbers of Chinese and Puerto Ricans. Chinatown is rapidly growing. According to the dress rehearsal census of lower Manhattan taken in September 1978 (the latest available data), Chinese make up 30 percent of the total population south of Houston Street. As such, they are the largest minority group in the area. Puerto Ricans follow with 20 percent, and other Hispanics are 8 percent. Whites of non-Hispanic origin only make up 16 percent, and blacks total 8 percent (U.S. Census Bureau, 1978).

The number of Chinese children, 19 years and under, enumerated for the 1978 census in lower Manhattan was 10,776, of which 5,588 were males and 5,188 females. For Puerto Ricans in the same age group, there were 9,609; for whites, there were 9,386; and for blacks 3,066 (U.S. Census Bureau, 1978). These figures are not comparable, however, because Puerto Ricans may have been counted twice, either as blacks or as whites, and the two racial groups may have included some Puerto Ricans. At any rate, immigrant Chinese children coming into the community find themselves among many faces like their own. Dealing with other racial groups, however, will be a new experience, one they have never encountered before in the homeland, but since Chinese children in this community are in the majority their transition from a Chinese setting into an interethnic one is less drastic.

The ethnic census of one of the neighborhood high schools is another yardstick by which one may gauge how the ethnic composition of this region has changed over time (*See,* Table 4-1). From

TABLE 4-1

Chinatown High School Student Population By Ethnic Group

Ethnic Group	1965	1970	1975	1979
White	40%	23%	10%	8%
Black	21	23	19	17
Asian	8	14	21	25
Puerto Rican	27	38	45	
Other Hispanic	4	2	5	50

Note: Other Hispanics include Caribbean and Latin Americans.

Source: New York City, Board of Education, "Student Ethnic Survey".

1965 to 1979, the white student enrollment dropped from 40 percent to 8 percent, the Asian enrollment rose from 8 percent to 25 percent and Hispanic enrollment increased from 31 percent to 50 percent.

Of course, the ethnic make-up of a school's enrollment may not be an accurate representation of the population of the area. White ethnics in the area are generally the elderly who have no children enrolled in school, whereas Puerto Ricans and other Hispanics have many children. Nevertheless, these figures give us some clues as to the various groups living alongside the Chinese.

Lower Manhattan is an area of lower to middle income working people. The Chinese and Puerto Ricans represent the newest wave of immigrants, and they may be classified as poor. The elderly from the former waves of immigration live on pensions or social security checks. They are also poor, except that they are settled. The working people are mainly civil servants in the government, service workers, clericals and laborers.

ECONOMY

In many ways the Chinese community has generated its own jobs. To meet the needs of these recent immigrants, sales in furnishings, appliances, housewares and clothing are brisk, and demand for services is great. Tourism is big business in Chinatown. Sightseers by the busloads descend upon the community and dash through the curio shops buying souvenirs to take home as mementos. Chinese groceries cater to a clientele that ranges from as far away as Connecticut or New Jersey. That weekly or biweekly trip into Chinatown seems to be a must for Chinese Americans who cannot find the necessary cooking ingredients at the local supermarket. The restaurants are another magnet. Culinary delights from all regions of China are now served in the more than 350 restaurants in and around Chinatown. Nor is Chinatown without its industries. The garment industry is the biggest, and the whirr of sewing machines can be heard coming from hundreds of commercial lofts. According to Local 23-25 of the International Ladies Garment Workers' Union, there were about 350 to 500 garment contractors in Chinatown who employed about 20,000 workers in 1983. It is said that about 70 percent of the garments sewn in New York City are sewn by Chinese seamstresses. The garment industry, only a toddling infant a few years ago, has become one of the economic pillars of the community providing the newly arrived immigrants with ready jobs and the community with a strong economic base. It was fortuitous that Chinatown met the needs of New York City's number one industry at a time when the industry was poised to move south in search of cheaper labor. The influx of Chinese immigrant women provided a large pool of low-cost, reliable labor. Entrepreneurial Chinese were willing to take up the middleman's position by providing contracting services. And they took advantage of the large numbers of lofts in and around Chinatown, vacated by departing manufacturers, to set up shop. The garment industry in Chinatown generates a $125,000,000 annual payroll in 1983. Half of the money is spent in the Chinatown communities. Six out of ten households in Chinatown depend upon the garment industry for a livelihood (I.L.G.W.U., 1983:5).

In some respects, immigrant families are fortunate in that they can find employment readily and easily—especially mothers in the garment factories. On the other hand, children are deprived of their mothers' presence in the home at a crucial time in their lives. In most instances, a working mother is a sharp change for the children. This problem will be examined at greater length in the chapter on the role of the family in the adjustment of the immigrant child.

ORGANIZATION AND STRUCTURE

The Chinese Consolidated Benevolent Association (CCBA) has traditionally been the governing body of New York's Chinatown.

It is an apex group consisting of representatives of sixty organizations in Chinatown, including the family and district associations, the guilds, the *tongs*, the Chamber of Commerce and the Nationalist Party. A small inner circle actually controls the organization and dictates its policies even though its chairman is elected by the member organizations for a two-year term. Members of the inner circle are the Ning Yang Association representing the majority of Chinese Americans from the district of Toishan, the Ling Sing Association representing all non-Toishanese, the two tongs, and the Nationalist Party. The latter three have the most power because they control the financial resources and hold the political clout.

The CCBA enjoyed a time-honored role among the Chinese in the United States when the population was small, consisting primarily of male adults of the laboring class. But times have changed. The decisions and policies made by the CCBA reflect the interests and concerns of a group of old-timers who have vested economic interests in Chinatown, who are closely aligned with Nationalist China, and who are committed to the status quo. The huge influx of newcomers had a different set of concerns and needs for their resettlement and their numbers have overwhelmed the ability of the traditional organizations (family and district associations) to handle the problem.

To cope with the tremendous need for social services by the newcomers in the 1960s, a group of dedicated Chinese American professionals such as lawyers, social workers, doctors and teachers formed an organization called the Chinatown Planning Council (CPC) to deal with the problems. Instead of relying upon the entrenched leaders in the community to provide funds, they wrote proposals and applied to foundations or the government for funding. They were fairly successful in this: the CPC now operates seven day-care centers, youth services such as Project Reach, programs for the elderly, employment referral services, adult education classes in English, immigrant services, and research projects. It has made a large contribution to meeting the social service needs of the community. Although the CPC is governed by a board of directors made up of people invited to sit on the board, and its day-to-day administration is in the hands of a career staff of social workers, it has continually competed with the CCBA for recognition and for funding.

The CCBA feels that the CPC is intruding on its domain and

resents the agency's presence and successes. On the other hand, the CPC continues to snipe at the CCBA, undercuts its functions, and undermines its prestige. For all its successes, however, the CPC is not a governing nor a representative body. For its continued operation it is dependent upon outside funding which is tenuous from year to year, and it does not have the history and tradition of the CCBA. The CCBA, for its part, is hampered by heavy reliance upon the tongs and the Nationalist Party for its financial support.

The CCBA operates the Chinese language school, which enrolls three to four thousand Chinese pupils who attend classes every day after American school. The CCBA is the recipient of government funds for summer youth employment, and it holds English language classes for adults. At one time the CCBA scorned government grants for fear that its influence would be undermined, but it has now learned to apply for these monies to enlarge upon its social services.

The city, state and federal governments continue to recognize the CCBA as the authority for the community. The rivalry between the CCBA and the CPC agencies is keen and sometimes both are the losers in their bids for funding and resource allocations.

The CPC is not the only social service agency serving Chinatown. Similar agencies, although on a smaller scale, have cropped up, such as Chinese Immigrant Social Services, Chinatown Manpower Project, New York Chinatown Senior Citizen Center, The Golden Age Club, Chinatown Health Clinic, Chinese Development Council and Chinese Scholars Service Corps. (*See*, Figure III). These agencies are a new phenomenon on the Chinatown scene, having taken over many of the social and welfare services formerly performed by the family and district associations. Reflecting upon the changes that have taken place in the organizational structure of Chinatown, it is hypothesized that as time, social environment and receptivity toward the Chinese change, the agencies, the institutions, and the means the Chinese employ to establish themselves in this country undergo changes as well. It is further hypothesized that an evolutionary process is taking place involving not only the structure of the community and the network systems that help the immigrant find support and aid, but that the medium of exchange is different in each of the evolutionary processes. If the immigrant is culturally and spatially removed from his source of help and support in adjusting to a new land, he will either suffer an increased feeling of isolation and helplessness or he must be provided with some kind of conduit to lead him to the sources of help—in other words, a culturally familiar network link.

The network links and evolutionary processes can be best explained in graphic form as diagramed in Figure III From the extreme right side of Figure III, the immigrant crosses the wavy lines of the Pacific Ocean and comes to the United States. The strongest impetus toward his migration invariably is family ties. Friendship is a possibility, but a weak one, hence the broken lines. Friends also remain outside the first stage network system.

The three vertical boxes represent three stages in time—the past, the present and the future. In the past, when the immigrant arrived in the United States, he usually contacted his blood relatives or immediate family members. Traditionally, the Chinese concept for family differs from the Western concept. From the Chinese perspective, family is the kinship group which includes uncles, aunts, cousins, grandfather, grandmother, etc. on the father's side. In a larger context, "family" denotes anyone with the same surname, and there are only 435 surnames for the more than one billion Chinese throughout the world. Some surnames such as Wong, Chin, Lee and Moy are very common. It is believed that all Wongs, for example, descended from the same ancestors, thus the incest taboo applies to persons with the same surname. In cities where many Wongs or Lees or Moys resided, family surname associations sprang into existence. Therefore, even if the new immigrant did not have an immediate nuclear family to re-establish his social network link, he could plug into his family association for all his needs. His kinsmen would help him find a job, give him food and shelter, provide emotional support, and lend a hand if needed, and this help extended to the immigrant's entire social and economic spheres. It was a Wong's duty and obligation to help another Wong, and it was his right to expect such help from his kinsmen. No payment was involved, and there was no squaring of debts. If one Wong was not available, another was. The family associations maintained headquarters in Chinatown, and there were no set hours.

The circles within the first-stage box in Figure III show the variations and combinations of organizations that the new immigrant would contact. Even if he had no surname family ties, he could

FIGURE III
Structural Changes in Re-establishing Social and Economic Network Ties for the Chinese Immigrant to the United States

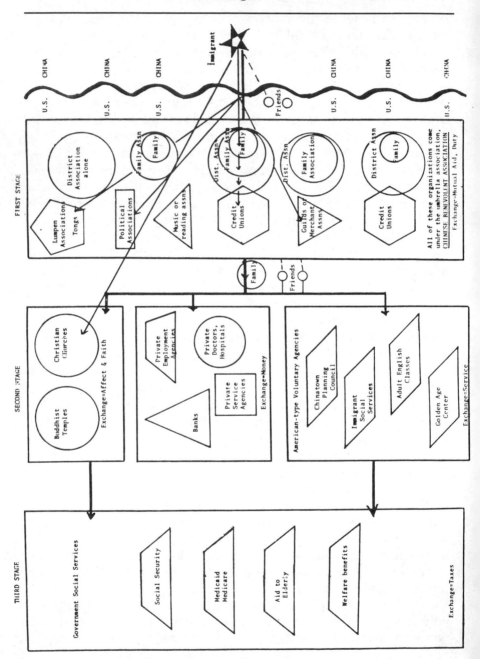

fall back on district associations, which were based upon hometown ties rather than kinship ones. The district association usually provided him with essentially the same social and welfare
services as the family association, except that hometown ties were
never as strong as kinship ones.

Auxiliary to the family and district associations were organizations that catered to special needs. The district associations invariably operated simple credit unions for the members to save or
borrow money. Guilds and merchants' associations served those
with commercial and artisan interests. The political associations
such as the *Kuomingtang* or Nationalist Party drew adherents to
their ideology, and the tongs controlled the vice trades of gambling, prostitution and opium.

In most cities, all of these institutions came under the umbrella
of the Chinese Consolidated Benevolent Association. The CCBA
mediated between its member organizations and served as
spokesman in any dealings with the larger society. In this type of
network and organizational hierarchy, the exchange was mutual
aid and duty. In this way, the new immigrant established ties in a
culturally familiar way within his own ethnic group in the foreign
land. He did not reach out into the larger American society. In
fact, contacts outside his own group were few and far between.
The reasons for this were both historical and cultural.

By 1882, the Chinese made up a sizable proportion of the population on the West Coast. They were a highly visible racial group
and noticeably employed at a time when whites were not. They
had replicated a facsimile society to which they confined themselves, so there was little interaction with the host society. These
factors, along with a number of other reasons, made them ideal
scapegoats for the economic ills of the late nineteenth century.
Beginning in 1882, a series of anti-Chinese exclusion acts which
forbade Chinese from entering the country were passed by Congress. Those who were here could remain, but hatred and hostility against them were pronounced, sometimes leading to mob
riots. Discrimination and persecution were institutionalized in the
form of laws that said they could not own real estate, they could
not intermarry, they could not testify in court, they could not become citizens no matter how long they had been in the country,
they could not vote, etc. This drove the Chinese closer, for they
had little or no recourse to any support outside their own community. Their network was therefore reinforced and confined primarily to the first box in stage one as depicted in Figure III.

In essence, the Chinese immigrants built their ties upon their family-based culture, but their network was also circumscribed by the hostile larger society. Such networks were perpetuated because Chinese immigration remained small, and also because the nuclear family—or rather women and children—was missing. Deprived of their wives and children, the men naturally sought closer ties to one another within the family association structure.

INCREASED IMMIGRATION

As cited earlier, immigration laws were liberalized in 1965. The Chinese, who had been so severely restricted for admission, immediately made use of this liberalized quota, and immigration dramatically increased. The immigration links were still tied mainly to the family. However, individuals with specific qualifications could now apply to come to this country on their own. Nevertheless, they still required someone in this country to sponsor them, assure them of employment and support, and vouchsafe that they would not become public charges. Links with someone in the United States had to be established, and they had to be strong links to offer such guarantees.

SOCIAL CHANGE

The 1960s were a period of rising ethnic consciousness and improved social climate for civil rights. Concurrent with the liberalized immigration laws, opportunities opened up outside the ghettos for Chinese people. For example, the Chinese found credit available to them from private banks. They could utilize private hospitals and look for employment beyond the borders of Chinatown. By and large, the new immigrant waves still came through family links, but they no long entered into a closed community. As more and more immigrants arrived, the facilities and capabilities of the former institutions were overwhelmed. The characteristics and compositions of the new immigrants were changing as well. Immigrants were not just single adult males but women and children, young and old, educated and skilled, as well as illiterate and dependent. Families immigrated as units, and family association headquarters could not accommodate them.

The Chinese communities may now be said to be in the second stage of the evolutionary process of re-establishing network ties in the new land. As mentioned previously, the close family links are still present and the friendship link is greater. Beyond the family, the immigrant now has other options, of which the primary one is the private sector (located in the middle of Figure III). With money, the immigrant can buy the services he needs. However, he must have knowledge of where to go for services and how to tap into them. He must also allocate financial resources to pay for the services. The exchange is impersonal and commercial. Nevertheless, the private sector is the most important link in the immigrant's daily life.

RELIGIOUS ORGANIZATIONS

Christian churches have always played an important role in the Chinese communities in the United States, and they have always rendered vital services to the new immigrants. Oftentimes, an immigrant comes through the church link rather than the family link because he is sponsored by the church, hence the direct line linking the Christian churches with the immigrant in China in Figure III. The churches served the Chinese community in the hopes of converting new adherents to the faith, and the Chinese accepted the services with affection and gratitude. There was no exchange of money. The immigrant went to the church for English language classes, for social events, to seek the pastor's aid in getting medical or other forms of help, and he did not have to pay, except for the offering placed in the Sunday collection plates.

Buddhist temples are a fairly recent institution in the Chinese communities. Most of them are still store-front operations where statues of the Buddhist gods have been installed and where the faithful go to burn incense and pray. Buddhism does not have priests who minister to the congregation and who provide social services as such. There is, however, a social aspect of belonging and being with others of the same faith.

AMERICAN-TYPE VOLUNTARY ASSOCIATIONS

What has sprung up in response to the changing social climate and the huge influx of immigrants is the American-type voluntary associations exemplified by the Chinatown Planning Council, the Immigrant Social Services, the Golden Age Center and similar organizations in New York's Chinatown. The organizations listed in the bottom box of the second stage in Figure III are but examples. These organizations are of recent vintage. The huge increase

in Chinese immigration brought about problems that were overwhelming the associations' ability to handle them. The larger society, saddled with the myth that the Chinese always took care of
their own, ignored the situation. Each day new immigrants arrived who needed help in getting settled, in finding jobs, in trying
to learn a new language, in caring for their children while at work,
in learning about the American way of doing things, in finding
out where places are and how to get there. As mentioned previously, the immigrants often arrived as family units, and the ability
of the immediate kinship family to help a group rather than an
individual was limited.

Sensitive and concerned about the problems multiplying in the
community, a group of American born Chinese professionals
sought to find a means of dealing with them. They appealed to
the elders in the Chinese Consolidated Benevolent Association,
but found them inept and unresponsive. Having been brought up
in the United States, the young professionals sought Amercian
solutions to their problems. They wrote proposals to the governmental agencies and private foundations for funding with which
to set up social service agencies staffed by professionals and paid
personnel. In many ways, these agencies have been dealing with
the most pressing problems facing the newly arrived immigrant.
They maintain English language classes, day-care centers, employment referral services, health clinics, old-age centers, recreational programs for youth, housing referral service, etc. All of
these services are vitally needed and utilized, and the services are
free, so that the exchange is a one-way street without some re-
compense to the agency to enable it to continue to provide service. The agencies are staffed and paid for by grants. There is no
membership or grassroots base in the community, so there is little
loyalty and identification with the programs. Until recently the
expense of providing service was borne almost entirely by the
government and philanthropic sources.[2] Those familiar with how
government funding and private grants operate realize that funding is uncertain from year to year, and a three-year time limit is
the maximum for social programs. The agency director must then
look elsewhere for funds to keep the program going. Such uncertainties are not conducive to a feeling of permanency or security,
and the realities are that the sources of funding may soon run dry.

[2] With government funding serverely cut back in the 1980s fund-raising projects in
the community have been rather successful in maintaining on-going programs.

Then the entire structure of social service programs will come tumbling down, catapulting the entire task into the third stage — government social services.

In many respects, the third stage has already been entered. Oftentimes the voluntary agencies merely act as intermediaries for services from the government. They help the elderly fill out forms for Medicare or social security benefits. They refer the sick and indigent to the free health clinics. They help the families enter their children in school or place them, if needed, in institutional care. They show the poor how to apply for food stamps. The agencies are able to better serve the community in that they are staffed with bilingual personnel who speak the language and understand the customs of their clients. Thus, they provide a very essential link to the third stage process.

GOVERNMENT SOCIAL SERVICES

In many respects, the means of meeting social and economic needs of the Chinese community is following along the lines of the American one. Without question, the satisfaction of social and economic needs of the average American is now primarily the private sector, and the role of the family has declined. The role of the church is shrinking as well. Not only is church membership declining, the way churches deal with their parishioners is also changing. More and more they, too, are referring those who come to them for help to private professionals or to government agencies rather than provide the counseling or service themselves.

The exchange for services provided by the government is taxes, paid by all. Certainly, if the Chinese community pay taxes, it is entitled to its share of the services. Unfortunately, the newly arrived immigrants, trying to re-establish contact in this country, do not understand how the American system works. They do not know what services are available or how to avail themselves of them. The common feeling is that government services are dole, and the Chinese are yet reluctant to accept help from such a source. The realities of the situation may soon be that no other sources will be available to those in need except through government social services, and if the immigrant is spatially and culturally removed from these institutions, he may have little or no access to help at all.

Is it possible to go back to the first stage and re-activate the family associations and ethnic organizations? That may be going against the tide, as the trend in the United States is more toward individualism and less toward family orientation. And if options are open to the Chinese in the larger society, the immigrant will inexorably be drawn away from community organizations because they do not fit the exigencies of American life. The voluntary agencies that are serving the immigrants in Chinatown today are performing a vital service. Perhaps they can be restructured so that they will put down roots in the community and start raising private funds, or they can be given permanent funding from governmental sources based on satisfactory performance. Certainly the services rendered in this manner cannot be less efficient or less effective than if they were taken over and assumed by the more remote, impersonal and unfamiliar government agencies.

MEETING THE NEEDS OF CHILDREN

In a community that had few children previously, it was natural that most organizations catered to the needs of adults who were predominantly men. Now that the community is more evenly distributed in terms of age and gender, the needs of all groups must be taken into consideration. The most important concession to the presence of children and the fact of working mothers is the day-care center. Many of these have been established, but more are needed. Recreational facilities are sorely lacking, but no attention has been paid to this problem at all. Youth gangs have terrorized the community, and the community has been helpless. These issues will be explored more fully in later chapters.

FACTIONALISM

There are commonalities that bind the Chinese community together, but there are differences that divide as well. The splits are along the lines of older versus new immigrants; American born versus foreign born; Cantonese born versus Mandarin speaking; the Nationalist or pro-Taiwan faction versus the pro-Communist faction; the vested interests versus the working class; the Chinese Consolidated Benevolent Association versus the Chinatown Planning Council; and the conservative reactionaries versus the radical activists.

The earlier immigrants had a headstart and are now comfortably ensconced in business and positions of influence and status in the community. In numbers they are the minority, but they call the tune while the newcomers must dance to it. The corps of newcomers is increasing so rapidly that it may dislodge the old timers in due time.

In times past, American born Chinese would move out of Chinatown as soon as possible, but ethnic consciousness and ethnic pride have altered that movement somewhat. Some young American born Chinese are moving back to the community, and they want to make it a better place. They wish to replace the traditional Chinese ways with the more democratic American ways, and they have little use for the elders who do not accept change readily. The young American borns are impatient. Most do not speak Chinese. They feel that the traditional Chinatown organizations are not responsive to the needs of the young or the newcomer. Yet, their concerns do not dovetail with those of the newcomers. While they want to oust the elders and step into positions of authority, they have neither the resources nor the cunning to play Chinatown politics, so invariably they are cut down to size, outsmarted, or ousted.

The struggle between the young and the elders has been going on since the 1960s. At first, the frustrations of the young ran high, but as of this writing many of the younger Chinese, now in their late twenties and thirties, have managed to get into positions of responsibility and are effecting rapid changes.

The majority of the Chinese in New York's Chinatown speak the dialects of Toishan or Canton. Speakers of these two dialects can understand one another, but not the Mandarin dialect. The Mandarin-speaking person is regarded by Cantonese and Toishanese as an outsider. Recently, cleavages along the lines of dialect have multiplied as people from Shanghai, Fukien, Zhongshan, Hakka and other places arrive in the community. Those who are educated will speak a common dialect akin to the Mandarin. In many instances though, the only means of communication is English. Fortunately, the written language is the same, so newspapers are printed in a script common to all Chinese. But distrust and non-acceptance of the Mandarin-speaking person in Chinatown is widespread. Doing business in the community is more difficult for the Mandarin speaker because he does not have the fraternal or family association ties that help the Cantonese.

CHINESE POLITICS

The most divisive issue in the Chinese community exists between the opposing camps of the pro-Nationalist or pro-Chiang faction of Taiwan and the pro-Mainland China faction. The pro-Mainlanders are not necessarily pro-communist in sympathies, although many are, but they are more realistic than the pro-Nationalists and want to identify with a government that is growing in international prestige and stature. The pro-Nationalists are die-hard anti-communists and loyal supporters of the late Chiang Kai-shek and now his son, Chiang Ching Kuo. The overseas Chinese have traditionally supported the Nationalist party since its founding by Dr. Sun Yat Sen when he overthrew the Manchu Dynasty. When the Nationalists fled to Taiwan in 1949, they came to rely heavily upon the Chinese in the United States to retain their position in the eyes of the United States government. And reciprocally, the Chinese in the United States looked to the Nationalists as their identification with a non-communist government, particularly during the Korean War period, for to do otherwise would have drawn upon them the hostility of the American people. Many Chinese during that period wore buttons that proclaimed "I am Nationalist Chinese".

The stream of refugees that left China during the Fifties and Sixties continued to be strongly anti-communist; these were the people whose property had been confiscated and who were persecuted during the struggles of the "anti" campaigns and the Cultural Revolution. The local villagers and cadres saw the overseas Chinese families as the propertied class, but they did not realize what sufferings these Chinese abroad had to endure to be able to accumulate their savings to buy their land. The overseas Chinese families were treated as rich landlords and made the objects of attack and abuse. If the families were able to escape to Hong Kong and eventually to the United States, they joined the ranks of those who were vehemently anti-communist.

The younger students who had studied in the Hong Kong and Mainland Chinese schools had been exposed to the more progressive ideology of the Chinese communists. They came imbued with attitudes different from those of their parents, and they gravitated toward the left and identified with communist China. The turbulent period of the late 1960s and early 1970s brought the American-born youth back into Chinatown to rally against the Vietnam War, which they saw as a racist war against Asians.

It was during this time that emotions revolving around Chinese politics ran deepest. In Chinatown, the Nationalist faction retained absolute control. Merely to label someone as a "Communist" or "Leftist" was to smear his name, affect his business and cause him to lose many friends and contacts. As a result, the circumspect Chinese tried to steer clear of Chinese politics regardless of their own personal convictions.

Richard Nixon's 1973 trip to China legitimized the pro-Mainland sentiments among the Chinese in the United States. They felt that if the President of the United States could reach out in a gesture of friendship with China, then it was not anti-American or subversive for them to do so. On December 15, 1978, in a surprise nationwide broadcast to the American people, President Jimmy Carter announced United States recognition of the People's Republic of China. The step ended thirty years of isolation and alienation of a nation that contains one-fourth of the world's population. Since Premier Deng Xiaoping visited the United States in January 1979, Chinese goods have been found everywhere in Chinatown stores in great variety and great abundance. Chinese Americans are rushing to visit their homeland, and even the staunchest Nationalist supporters have moderated their stance. The political schism remains, but it is hoped that with improved international relations between the two countries, the Chinese in the United States will no longer feel schizophrenic about their ethnic loyalties.

SATELLITE CHINATOWNS

Figure IV is a representation of three types of Chinese communities. The one at the top to the extreme left is typical of former Chinatowns that were isolated and insulated. They existed within American society but were not part of it. Most of the members worked outside of the community, but their private lives took place almost exclusively within the Chinese community.

The center configuration represents Chinatown in New York City today. It is a well-defined community with boundaries and structure, but it is being penetrated from all sides by the government, American values and institutions, the media, tourists, and friends and Chinese residing outside the community. The family and school are within the community, but all are impacted by outside forces and influences. Yet the community remains a viable entity.

Satellite Chinatowns, represented by the third configuration, are new formations where Chinese prefer to live in proximity to one another. The communities are ill-defined, but they do have a

FIGURE IV
Evolutionary Stages of Chinese Communities

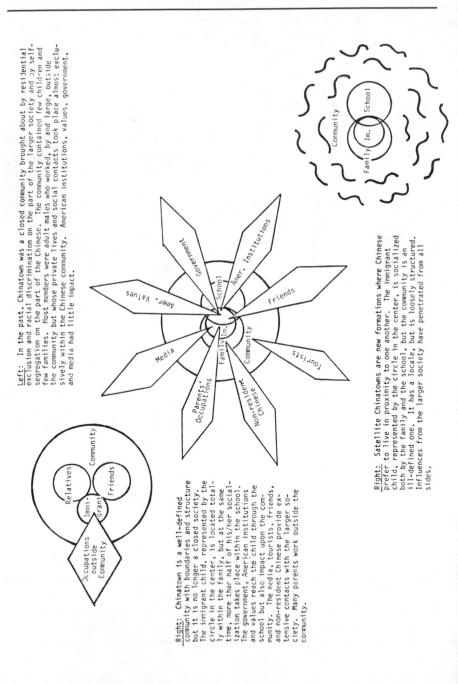

Left: In the past, Chinatown was a closed community brought about by residential exclusion and racial discrimination on the part of the larger society and by self-segregation on the part of the Chinese. The community contained few children and few families. Most members were adult males who worked, by and large, outside the community but whose private lives and social contacts took place almost exclusively within the Chinese community. American institutions, values, government, and media had little impact.

Right: Chinatown is a well-defined community with boundaries and structure but it is no longer a closed society. The immigrant child, represented by the circle in the center, is located totally within the family, but at the same time, more than half of his/her socialization takes place within the school. The government, American institutions and values reach the child through the school but also impact upon the community. The media, tourists, friends, and non-resident Chinese provide extensive contacts with the larger society. Many parents work outside the community.

Right: Satellite Chinatowns are new formations where Chinese prefer to live in proximity to one another. The immigrant child, represented by the circle in the center, is socialized both by the family and the school, but the community is an ill-defined one. It has a locale, but is loosely structured. Influences from the larger society have penetrated from all sides.

locale. There is little structure or organization, and the communities are characterized by a loose sense of common identity and common culture. There are several pockets of high Chinese concentration in the New York metropolitan area. One of these is in upper Manhattan near Columbia University. Two others are in Brooklyn near Prospect Park and in the Bay Ridge area. Two more are found in the borough of Queens.

One of these Queens communities, indicated in Map 2 as the shaded area, is paired with New York's Chinatown for this study because it has the second highest concentration of Chinese population in the city. This book is a study of Chinatown and the satellite community to see if place of residence has any effect on the adjustment of immigrant children. The core area of the satellite is called Elmhurst, but the Chinese have also spread to Jackson Heights and Rego Park. These so-called towns in the county of Queens have no distinct boundaries—they blend into one another to form a continuous expanse. Flushing, the second satellite community in Queens, about four or five miles to the east, is also rapidly gaining in Chinese population, but is comprised of diverse groups of Asian peoples from Japan, Korea, India and Vietnam as well as China (*See*, Map 3). It has thus been labeled, perhaps more accurately, Asian Town.

Elmhurst is reached by subway from Manhattan on the IRT line. Forty-five minutes would be sufficient to ride into Manhattan's Chinatown and much less time is needed to get to midtown. Jackson Heights is one long stretch of high-rise apartment houses. Elmhurst is a neighborhood of one-, two- and three-family homes. Rego Park, along the Long Island Expressway, has some private homes, but apartment houses predominate. The population of this region is extremely dense. It is a bedroom community where most of the inhabitants go into Manhattan during the day and come back to sleep at night.

HOME OWNERSHIP

The Chinese began moving into Elmhurst around the late 1960s. According to Howard Tom, one of the first residents to move into the neighborhood, only three or four Chinese families were around at that time. Row upon row of new two- and three-family brick homes had been built and put up for sale. The first few Chinese families spread the word to their families and friends,

MAP 2
Satellite Chinatown in Queens County, New York

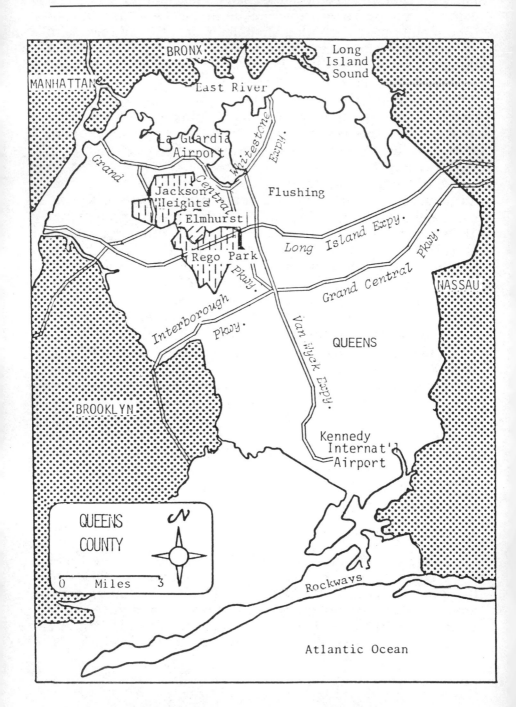

MAP 3
Asian Town in Flushing, New York

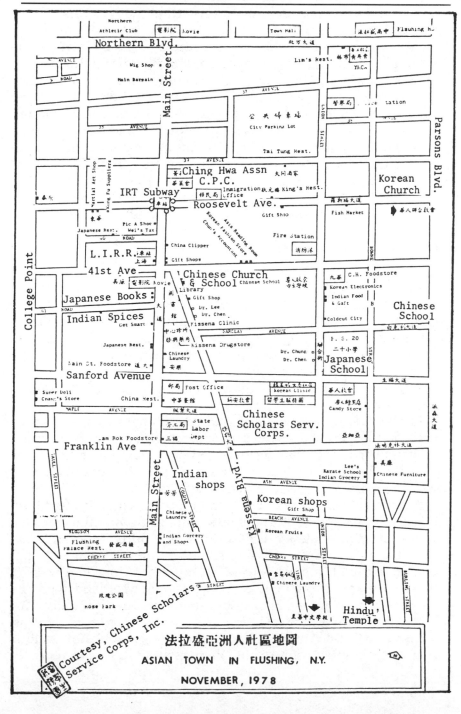

法拉盛亞洲人社區地圖

ASIAN TOWN IN FLUSHING, N.Y.

NOVEMBER, 1978

and the houses were snapped up quickly by other Chinese. The price of houses at that time was about $50,000 for an attached row house with a six-room apartment on each of the two upper floors and a three-room unit and garage on the ground floor. Many owners would rent out the top and bottom units and live on the second level practically rent free in a brand new brick house.

The idea appealed to the thrifty Chinese. Not only were they indulging their intense wish to own a private house, they were also living rent-free and accumulating items deductible from their income tax. In many instances they were collecting more rent than they were paying in mortgage payments and maintenance. Moreover, they were only a one-fare subway ride from Chinatown. These very same houses have quadrupled in value within the last three decades. As more and more Chinese moved into the neighborhood, others followed suit in a snowball effect. This is a distinctive feature of Chinese mobility—whether in residence or in jobs, they tend to move in groups.

ETHNIC COMPOSITION

In the overflow from Manhattan's Chinatown, the borough of Queens has been the recipient of the most Chinese. In 1960, the census counted only 4,585 Chinese residents. By 1970, the number had tripled and in 1980 it tripled again to 39,135 making a ninefold increase in twenty years' time. In 1970, only one census tract in Queens held more than 300 Chinese. By 1980, 23 tracts had this distinction.

The boundaries of the Queens satellite Chinatown are not clear-cut, and the census does not give separate figures for the Chinese in neighborhoods. One way to get an approximation of the Chinese population is to aggregate census tracts, but the tracts as well as the numbers have increased substantially.

We can fall back on the neighborhood high school student population figures for some guidelines, but again, attention is called to the fact that white ethnics have fewer children in school than the other groups (See, Table 4-2). Although the white student population declined from 62 percent to 26 percent from 1971 to 1979, the area is still a predominantly white neighborhood with the largest increase among Hispanics other than Puerto Ricans. Hispanics as defined here include person originating from the Caribbean and Latin America. The Asians in this tabulation include increasing numbers of Koreans, Vietnamese and East Indians.

TABLE 4-2

High School in Satellite Chinese Community Student Population
By Ethnic Group

	1971	1976	1979
Whites	62%	38%	26%
Blacks	9	16	12
Asians	3	10	16
Puerto Ricans	2	5	
Other Hispanics	23	32	45

Source: High School Ethnic Survey

Although the neighborhood contains a high concentration of Chinese they are by no means the dominant group. In fact, the area is quite cosmopolitan except for an area of about four to five blocks, within which most of the houses are Chinese-occupied.

The Elmhurst-Jackson Heights-Rego Park community is primarily a residential neighborhood for the large numbers of Chinese who live there. The only telltale signs of its Chinese population are the few groceries that sell Chinese foodstuff along Broadway and the many Chinese faces near the subway station. There is no distinctive architecture. There is no social structure, nor are there any institutions to give the community cohesion. Certainly there are no tourists nor large numbers of outsiders who visit for purposes of recreation or education. Two Christian churches with Chinese congregations of 200 to 300 are well established in the neighborhood, but act more as a social rather than religious magnet. They do, however, draw Chinese worshipers from other parts of Queens County. There are no social service agencies in the Elmhurst community although some have sprung up in Flushing.

Being a community of mostly private homes and family dwellings, the environs are more appropriate to rearing children than is the urban setting of Chinatown. There are front and backyards in the homes, and most of the streets are lined with trees and shrubs. Although people are stacked on top of one another in the high-rise apartment houses, the feeling of congestion is not as intense as that in Manhattan's Chinatown. And, of course, the traffic volume is much lower, and playing in the streets and on the sidewalks is safe for the children.

Our research shows that the Elmhurst residents fall into three main categories: American-born Chinese, the old timers who have the financial resources and courage to move away from Chinatown, and newcomers with higher educational and socioeconomic backgrounds than those who settled in Chinatown. These newcomers tend not to be Cantonese. They come mostly from Taiwan and speak Mandarin with some basic knowledge of English. They are better off financially than those heading for Chinatown, having migrated with some money. Home ownership requires a large initial down payment, and rentals in the high-rise apartments are more expensive than are those in Chinatown. It is important to keep in mind the higher socioeconomic background of the satellite community residents in comparative analysis of the data.

CONCLUSION

The communities chosen for our study have been described in detail as regards racial mix, physical environs and conditions, the economy, community organizations, and the interpersonal factors that separate or bind a people together. These facts and details are necessary for the proper understanding of the processes by which recent immigrants relate to the community and interact with one another. For example, the fact that the Chinese are the dominant ethnic group in numbers in Chinatown means that the minority experience is modulated, but the presence of other racial groups is still a new factor with which to contend. Even in the satellite community, there is comfort in numbers when the children go out to play in the streets or when they go to school. They are not thrust into the midst of totally strange faces all at once.

It is obvious that the physical environs of Manhattan's Chinatown are not very desirable for the rearing of children. The housing is crowded and dilapidated, the recreational facilities are minimal, and the traffic is dangerous. Yet, the presence of much that is familiar in an ethnic community makes the transition from the homeland to the United States a more gradual one. Satellite Chinatowns may be the answer to better housing and surroundings while at the same time providing the sense of comfort and security that comes with being among one's own kind. In effect, the satellites are an example of adaptation and social change.

The availability of social services for the new immigrants in Chinatown is a tremendous help to the newcomer. Again, we see how the new ways of mutual aid are grafted onto the old. The dependence upon family and kin and the social structure of kinship organizations are slowly shifting toward voluntary agencies and bought services. Even these can now be seen as a transitional phase toward greater government assumption of social services.

The most important service rendered by the Chinatown community is the strong economic base it has created in its businesses and industries, thus generating employment for the newly arrived immigrants. It has capitalized on its renown cuisine, so that more than 350 restaurants provide jobs for many thousands. The exoticism and cultural distinctiveness of the Far East found in the midst of New York draw tourists by the busloads, and the gift shops thrive on the tourism. The garment industry—a hand-me-down from former immigrant groups—was taken over by the Chinese and now is the economic backbone of the community. Without these jobs, the Chinese immigrants might indeed experience severe financial problems and greater adjustment trauma.

Chinatown residents, including the children, cannot help but feel the pull between the political factions, the differences between the American born and the foreign born, the gap between the Cantonese speaking and the Mandarin speaking, and the power play between the Chinese Consolidated Benevolent Association and the Chinatown Planning Council. Such conflicts are divisive and stressful, but according to Coser (1956), they may be a constructive working out of differences leading in the long run to change for the better. From this researcher's point of view, the differences are a healthy indicator that the residents care enough to work toward solutions of problems in their community. The history of ethnic communities in the United States is usually one of decline and demise resulting from the residents moving out rather than their staying and resolving the problems. The satellite Chinatowns may be seen as a change in locale, as a vent for the overflow of population, or as a parceling out of the functions normally performed by the parent Chinatown.

It is difficult to separate the children from their families in assessing the transitional functions of ethnic communities. Children must reside where their parents decide, and the parents need what Milton Gordon calls a "decompression chamber in which newcomers, at their own pace, could make a more workable adjustment to American society" (1964: 105-106). However, the decompression chambers are no longer airtight. They are penetrated from all sides and from every direction. These outside influences impact more heavily upon the children than upon the adults. At first, the children may be cushioned against the culture shock, but in time, they will experience the conflicts that come from straddling two cultures.

V
The School – Enrollment and Profiles

Of the three dominant spheres circumscribing the Chinese immigrant child's life—community, school and family—the school is by far the most pervasive and important. Compulsory education laws decree that the child spend at least six hours in school each day, and if meals and after school activities are taken into account, the hours are even longer. Generally, the community affects the child indirectly, while the role of the family—the Chinese immigrant family at least—is diminishing. The school remains the primary socializing institution, for it immediately takes the immigrant child under its wings to educate, mold and shape that child at all entry levels from kindergarten through high school.

This chapter ascertains the size of the group under study, and looks at the school set-up and environment to properly assess the backdrop against which the immigrant children learn. The following chapters will focus on the processes or the actual experiences of the children as they try to adapt to a new language, new cultural values, a bicultural identity, a multi-racial social milieu, and strange faces simultaneously. To meet these special needs, the schools have devised programs such as bilingual education which will be analyzed to see if they help or hinder immigrant children in their adaptation as well as in their learning. Finally, the school records are examined to ascertain if there are any symptoms of maladjustment. The indicators of their school performance shall be attendance, grades, conduct, dropout rate, graduation rate, and college admission rate. As noted previously, the field work in the collection of these data was done over a two and a half year period from 1976 to 1979.

DEMOGRAPHIC DATA

Ascertaining the size of the group under study was a laborious task. At the time of the fieldwork and research, the 1980 census

TABLE 5-1

Asian Children Enrolled in New York City Schools, 1970-1979

	1970	1971	1972	1973	1974	1975	1976	1977	1978	1979
Manhattan	7,828	8,155	8,361	8,594	8,622	8,812	9,407	9,332	9,150	9,740
Elementary	4,419	4,552	4,489	4,496	4,462	4,371	4,743	4,658	4,588	4,532
JHS/Interm.	1,755	1,785	1,889	1,923	1,875	1,968	2,068	2,034	1,845	1,838
Academic Hi	1,460	1,597	1,768	1,917	1,944	2,109	2,138	1,997	2,031	2,506
Voc/Spec. Sch.	194	221	225	258	341	364	458	643	686	864
Bronx	1,615	1,821	1,999	2,076	2,026	1,802	2,239	2,431	2,673	3,035
Elementary	922	1,038	1,140	1,177	1,157	973	1,180	1,217	1,397	1,445
JHS/Interm.	307	346	414	421	380	339	369	426	456	501
Academic Hi	374	424	431	463	468	472	675	755	776	1,041
Voc/Spec. Sch.	12	13	14	15	21	18	15	33	44	48
Brooklyn	3,430	3,767	4,202	4,587	5,019	5,367	5,703	6,651	6,727	7,515
Elementary	1,725	1,825	1,932	2,102	2,256	2,362	2,552	3,016	3,056	3,305
JHS/Interm.	634	664	805	880	921	965	990	1,283	1,138	1,271
Academic Hi	913	1,120	1,328	1,474	1,652	1,751	1,951	2,138	2,248	2,642
Voc/Spec. Sch.	158	158	137	131	190	289	210	214	285	297
Queens	4,351	4,829	5,485	6,311	7,067	7,715	9,709	11,169	12,919	15,026
Elementary	2,717	2,982	3,326	3,732	4,130	4,408	5,713	6,635	7,750	8,581
JHS/Interm.	800	850	1,054	1,234	1,504	1,609	1,993	2,176	2,459	2,962

TABLE 5-1 (Continued)
Asian Children Enrolled in New York City Schools, 1970-1979

	1970	1971	1972	1973	1974	1975	1976	1977	1978	1979
Academic Hi	754	889	985	1,196	1,268	1,516	1,820	2,099	2,415	3,130
Voc/Spec. Sch.	80	108	120	149	165	182	183	259	295	353
Staten Island										
Elementary	245	321	360	464	518	581	766	825	908	1,023
JHS/Interm.	162	218	240	314	325	390	497	524	530	549
Academic Hi	32	53	56	85	92	103	127	145	193	186
Voc/Spec. Sch.	49	49	59	60	83	70	114	144	171	204
	2	1	5	5	18	18	28	12	14	84
City Wide Total	17,491	18,931	20,452	22,067	23,252	24,277	27,824	30,408	32,377	36,339

had not yet taken place, and demographic data for the Chinese from the 1970 census was woefully outdated. No intercensal data on the Chinese were available. The *Current Population Survey* has only recently included Asians in its sample—but not Chinese separately—and the numbers are too few to provide any degree of reliability. Even after the 1980 census had been taken, the figures were not tabulated and published until 1983. When figures are not provided, one must try to piece together information along some rational lines. This was attempted by utilizing the ethnic student censuses taken annually by the New York City Board of Education, a centralized agency that administers the city's network of public schools. The number of Asian or Oriental [1] students was obtained by culling the figures from each report. The problem remained of identifying only the Chinese students since Asian and Chinese are not synonymous.

Some guidelines were applicable. Based upon the 1970 census figures, five out of every six Asians in New York City were Chinese. However, by 1980, the numerical dominance was reduced to a little better than one half (U.S.Census Bureau, 1980). The other problem was how to delineate the foreign born from the native born using school enrollment figures. Of course, this could not be done, but one can surmise from the very low birth rate among the Chinese in New York City that immigrant children would far exceed the native born. These inferences can only serve as general guidelines in the absence of more reliable data, and readers are cautioned to distinguished between the terms "Chinese" and "Asian" when data are presented.

Table 5-1 shows Asian children enrolled in New York City schools for the five boroughs and by school level or type of school for a ten year period from 1970 to 1979. In addition to showing the number of Asian children enrolled and revealing the spectacular increase that has come about, the data reveal a population distribution pattern as well as school-age cohorts. By 1976, the borough of Queens had outstripped Manhattan in the number of Asian students, and by 1979 Queens had pulled far ahead. The Asian student population in Manhattan seems to be leveling off; there was only a 24 percent increase over a ten year period whereas Brooklyn's Asian student population more than doubled and

---

[1] There was no consistency in the use of "Oriental" or "Asians" by the schools and the Board of Education. These terms seemed to be used interchangeably.

Queens' Asian student population more than tripled. Every borough increased its Asian student population substantially. This means that Asian families are moving away from the central core of the city and that Asians are as much dispersed as they are concentrated.

Using grade level as an indication of age cohort, one finds an inversion in numbers between junior high and high school. High school students outnumbered junior high students by a substantial margin, and this inversion was apparent by the mid 1970s. The birth rate among the Chinese has been declining, but the inversion of the junior high and high school student enrollment is without plausible explanation.

STUDENT POPULATION DISTRIBUTION

In the absence of census data at the time of the research, detailed breakdowns of Asian student enrollment by school district were worked out. Map 4 shows the school districts in New York City. These figures proved to be an excellent indicator of population distribution at the time. However, now there are census tract data.

The 1980 census for New York City gives the number of school-age Chinese children for the five boroughs:

TABLE 5-2
School-Age Chinese Children By Borough, New York City, 1980

Age	N.Y.C.	Bronx	Brooklyn	Manhattan	Queens	S.I.
5 - 9	8,263	322	1,878	3,197	2,714	152
10 - 14	9,002	390	2,076	3,534	2,850	152
15 - 19	10,610	522	2,639	4,043	3,272	134
Total	27,875	1,234	6,593	10,774	8,836	438

Source: U.S. Census Bureau, New York State, 1980 (PC) 1-B34.

School enrollment, as enumerated by the census, very closely approximates the 27,875 Chinese children ages 5 to 19 in New York City. This means that almost all the children and youth within this

MAP 4
School Districts, New York City

age span are attending school, which can be read as a very positive sign for the group. Compare this with the Irish attitude toward the public school as quoted by Diane Ravitch in her book *The Great School Wars: New York City, 1805–1973.*

> To ward off inducements to assimilate as Protestant attempts to destroy the Church, the clergy discouraged their followers from using the schools of the Public School Society. Of about 12,000 Catholic children in the late 1830s, only a few hundred were enrolled in the public schools.

The early Italian immigrants also shunned the public schools. To quote Glazer and Moynihan in their book *Beyond the Melting Pot*(1963: 184,199):

> Do not make your child better than you are, runs a South Italian proverb. Schools, then, were not thought of as a route to opportunity or economic success. There was instead suspicion by closely knit families that the schools would pull their children away from the traditional way of life and displace traditional values; the schools' assimilationism was seen as a potential threat to the continuity of the family and community.

Cultural attitudes toward education, therefore, are a vital factor in the attendance of immigrant children in schools. If the parents have negative feelings toward schools, it is expected that the children will not place a high value on learning. In writing about the Puerto Ricans in New York, Elena Padilla (1968: 210-211) wrote:

> A large number of children of migrants quit school as soon as they can get working papers or as soon as they have passed the required age for compulsory schooling. This is usually what happens with those in the neighborhood when they turn sixteen. While numerous factors enter into making a decision to leave school, beatings by teachers and attacks on the part of other students push many out of school and into job hunting. Others are pressured by their parents to leave school and go to work to help the rest of the family.

Thus, parental pressure and values exert strong bearing upon the Puerto Rican chidren's continuance in school. In this respect, Jewish values are similar to those of the Chinese. Again, to quote Diane Ravitch (1974: 179-180):

> The Jews had their tradition of education...One reporter inspected an Allen Street school which was 90 percent Jewish and recorded that the "impression one gets on leaving this building after having visited all the classrooms is that he has been in a tomb", yet this "wretched ramshackled structure" was so much in demand that children were turned away for lack of accommodations. Far from protesting school conditions, Jewish parents rose up in anger only when their children were not admitted because of overcrowding.

SCHOOL PROFILES

Some of the very same schools that taught the Irish, Italian and Jewish immigrant children of yesteryear are teaching the Chinese and Puerto Rican children of today. Needless to say, the buildings are antiquated, and school plant and environment can affect the learning atomosphere. Even in the face of drastically declining enrollment in New York public schools, those in neighborhoods with expanding Asian populations have experienced enrollment far in excess of the school's capacity.

The schools were the easiest place to start the research. This was where large numbers of Chinese immigrant children could be found, and this was where they spent a large part of their day. As mentioned previously, schools representing elementary, junior high, and high school levels were selected, and one at each level was chosen from the two communities—Chinatown and the Queens satellite Chinatown—for a total of six schools. For obvious reasons, the schools selected had large but not overwhelmingly large Chinese enrollments. Consequently, schools closer to the core of Chinatown were not chosen. In accordance with a condition imposed by the Board of Education, none of the schools is identified by name or number. For background purposes, a profile of each school is presented below.

Chinatown Elementary School

The Chinatown elementary school is housed in a building sixty years old. It has seen many pupils from other ethnic groups sitting at its desks in years gone by. The school fronts directly on the street, and the so-called playground measures about thirty feet square. School capacity is 1,100, but enrollment exceeds that number. Although most schools in New York City have seen a decline in enrollment in recent years, those receiving Asian or Caribbean immigrants are exceptions to that trend. In this school, the Chinese made up about three-fourths of the school population at the time of the study. The remaining ethnic breakdown was about 4 percent blacks, 14 percent Puerto Ricans and other Hispanics, and 7 to 8 percent whites. [2] In School District 2, the area in which this school is located, white families tend to send their children to private schools (New York City Planning Commission, 1974).

Of the Chinese speaking children in the school, about one-third were fluent in English, one-third were hesitant, and one-third spoke English poorly. The reading scores of the total student population were somewhat below grade level and the math scores were on grade level. Daily attendance was above 92 percent (New York City Board of Education, 1973-1974).

In spite of the preponderance of Chinese children in the student body, only six teachers of the fifty or so were of Chinese extraction. However, the principal (a non-Chinese) and his staff were very much a part of the Chinese community. The principal, in particular, attended most Chinese functions. Teachers in all the Chinatown schools regarded their assignment as a "plum". A Chinatown position is, as one teacher phrased it, "Teacher's Heaven", the reason being is that the children are well-behaved and discipline is not much of a problem.

Satellite Community Elementary School

The satellite community elementary school was built about fifty years ago. A new wing was added in 1966, giving the school as a whole a more modern appearance. School enrollment at the time of the study was also about 1,100, the same as that of the paired school in Chinatown. Again, enrollment exceeded capacity, and daily attendance was over 90 percent. Of the Chinese speaking

[2] "White" in ethnic enumerations generally refers to non-Hispanic whites.

students, 62 percent spoke fluent English, 26 percent spoke hesitantly, and 12 percent spoke poorly. Both reading and math scores
of the total student population were on or slightly above grade
level (New York City Board of Education, 1973-1974).

In 1976, Asian students made up 20 percent of the student enrollment, blacks about 15 percent, Puerto Ricans 9 percent, other
Hispanics 22 percent, and whites 34 percent. The population
within this school district was heavily Catholic; 46 percent of the
whites living there sent their children to parochial schools (New
York City Board of Education, 1973-1974). The white population
of this elementary school fell from 57 percent in 1972 to 34 percent
in 1976, while the minority population increased. At that time, the
school was "ethnically balanced", although Asian students were
substantial in number, they did not form the majority as they did
in its Chinatown counterpart. No teacher of Chinese descent was
on the staff of the school at the time of the study.

Chinatown Junior High School

The Chinatown junior high was built about the turn of the century, again pointing to the much more antiquated facilities of the
school buildings in and around Chinatown. Enrollment outstripped capacity to such a degree that an old school building eight
blocks away was called back into service as an annex to house the
seventh graders. The total enrollment in both school buildings
was 1,600 with the Chinese accounting for 1,100 of that number.

At the time of the study, the ethnic composition of this junior
high was 70 percent Asian, 5 percent black, 18 percent Puerto
Rican, 5 percent other Hispanic and 3 percent white. Since the
Chinese were in the majority, the school became the focal point
for many Chinese teenage activities.

While the study focused on seventh graders, the fact that the
entire seventh grade was physically separated from the rest of the
school by eight blocks made the findings less than representative
and reflective of what was happening to students thirteen to fourteen years of age.

Of the Chinese speaking students, 70 percent were rated fluent
in English, 24 percent hesitant and only 6 percent poor (New York
City Board of Education, 1973-1974). These figures are open to
question since the reading scores for that same year were 1 1/2 to
2 1/2 grades below average and the math scores were only slightly
below grade level. Attendance at this Chinatown junior high was

above 90 percent. In general, schools with a large Chinese student population have a higher attendance record. At the time of the study, there were seven teachers of Chinese descent on the annex staff. The two previous years had seen a drastic citywide cutback in school personnel due to budget problems, and since the Chinese teachers were among the last hired, they were the first to go.

Satellite Community Junior High School

The paired junior high school in Queens saw its Asian student population rise from 3 percent in 1971 to 12 percent in 1976. Its black and Puerto Rican enrollment remained steady at 12 percent and 3 percent respectively, but its other Hispanic groups rose from 20 to 27 percent. The proportion of white students declined from 64 percent in 1971 to 46 percent in 1976, but it was still a predominantly white school.

The school was built more than fifty years ago, making it at least twenty years newer than its Chinatown counterpart. The Queens junior high is located in the midst of a neighborhood of small, one-family homes of lower middle-class working people. The school yard is quite large, and during lunch hour and recess the children have ample opportunity to run, play and work off their excess energy.

The capacity of the school is 1,600, but in 1976 actual enrollment exceeded 2,000. Attendance was 88 percent, slightly lower than for the Chinatown school. Asian students numbered 248 in 1976, but Asian groups other than Chinese—namely Koreans, Japanese and some East Indians—made up 40 percent of the total. Chinese students numbered approximately 150, more than half of whom were American-born. This left approximately 70 foreign-born Chinese who were recent immigrants. The ethnic variety and preponderance of American born schoolmates of the Chinese immigrant students at this school provide a different social setting from that of the Chinatown junior high, where an overwhelming number were Chinese immigrants.

The proficiency rating in English of the Chinese speaking students showed that 62 percent were fluent, 19 percent were hesitant and the remaining 19 percent poor. Reading and math scores were on grade level (New York City Board of Education, 1973-1974). Again, the English fluency ratings are questionable; they were lower than those for the Chinatown junior high school even though a greater number of students in the satellite community school were American born.

Chinatown High School

The high school serving most of the Chinese students is on the outer fringes of Chinatown and is located in the heart of a community rapidly changing from Jewish to Chinese and Puerto Rican. The latter ethnic group made up about 45 percent of the student enrollment. Whites were only 10 percent, a drastic drop from 40 percent ten years before. Blacks remained at a steady 20 percent, while Asians increased from 8 percent in 1965 to 22 percent in 1976. Approximately 900 Chinese students attended this high school in 1976, although the figures declined significantly for the first time in 1977, perhaps indicating a trend toward a move away from Chinatown.

Student capacity at this high school was 2,500, but its 1976 enrollment was 3,800. A number of annexes handled some of the overflow, but all of the Chinese students in the bilingual program were housed in the main building. The attendance rate for the entire school was low—65 percent at the time of our study—and the dropout rate was disproportionately high at 45 percent. Of the Chinese speaking students, about 45 percent spoke English fluently, 41 percent spoke hesitantly, and 13 percent spoke poorly.

Considering the age (it was built in the 1930s) and location of the school, its physical condition was good. There was little evidence of vandalism. There is, however, no schoolyard for recreation, and eight security guards patrolled the grounds continually.

Satellite Community High School

The satellite community high school selected for this study was also overcrowded, to the extent that it had to have two end-to-end sessions per day. School capacity was 3,600, but enrollment exceeded 5,200. The first session started at 7:30 a.m. and ended at 11:30 a.m.; the second session started at noon and ended at 4:00 p.m. There was no lunch period. The percentage of white students had been steadily shrinking from 62 percent in 1971 to 38 percent in 1976, while the Asian percentage rose from 3 percent to 10 percent over the same period (*See*, Table 4-2). Blacks comprised 16 percent of the total, Puerto Ricans 5 percent, other Hispanics 32 percent, and Orientals 10 percent in 1976. The school was built in 1922, but modernized in 1954. It was well-maintained and employed five security guards. The attendance rate exceeded 80 percent and the dropout rate was less than 25 percent, which is quite an improvement over the Chinatown high school rate. Of the Chinese speaking students, 80 percent were fluent in English, 19 percent were hesitant, and 3 percent poor.

CONCLUSION

In the absence of reliable statistics on the Chinese in New York City at the time of this study, a method was devised whereby an approximation of the group under study could be obtained. This method was to use ethnic breakdown from school enrollment in the city public schools. The data showed that Asian student enrollment doubled over the ten year period from 1970 to 1979. Chinese students made up three-fourths of this number. By following the school enrollment pattern by school district, one could discern a fairly reliable picture of the settlement pattern of the Chinese in New York City. Although the data was made obsolete when census data became available, it was still a fairly accurate way of ascertaining ethnic population distribution during inter-censal years.

The schools selected for this study mirror the neighborhoods in which the students live. All of the schools showed declining white populations and increasing Asian and Hispanic populations, the two newest waves of immigrants. All of the schools are antiquated and overcrowded. In spite of similarities in the school profiles, schools in Manhattan differ from those in Queens primarily in ethnic makeup and in the ratio of foreign born to American-born Chinese; the Manhattan schools had a larger proportion of foreign born Chinese immigrant children. The reason for pairing and using schools in two boroughs was to ascertain if there were any significant differences in performance and behavior of the students from different neighborhoods—one a predominantly ethnic enclave, the other an ethnically mixed suburban area.

VI
School Performance

The most convenient and reasonable index to use in evaluating the adjustment or maladjustment of the subjects—Chinese immigrant children—is school performance. The school is the arena where the children spend most of their waking hours and where their performance is evaluated and graded at set intervals. Detailed records are kept, and the record keeping procedures are fairly standardized to permit comparative analysis and consistent conclusions. To gauge how the immigrant children were adapting to their new environment, the research relied primarily upon school performance as measured by conduct, respect for the teacher, academic achievement or grades, attendance rate, drop-out rate, after-school activities, and after-school work.

CONDUCT AND RESPECT FOR TEACHER

During my fieldwork at the Chinatown junior high school, a tall, blonde, male teacher introduced himself to me one day. "I must tell you how happy I am to be teaching at this school", he remarked. "My transfer to this school has revived my interest in teaching. I was just about to throw in the towel."

"Where did you teach before?", I inquired. He mentioned a school in an upper middle-class, predominantly white neighborhood. Involuntarily, my face registered surprise.

"Yes", he reiterated, "discipline there was a constant hassle. A Chinatown appointment is a teacher's heaven."

Another teacher, a nineteen-year veteran of the New York City schools, said, "The Chinese children are fantastic. The parents have done their homework. They have dignity, sportsmanship, respect for the teacher, and they fear any loss of face. I taught fifteen years elsewhere before coming here, but I really didn't teach at all. It was enough just to keep discipline and get through the day. It was very discouraging."

At the Queens junior high and high school, I heard the same sort of remarks. At the office of the Dean of Boys at the Queens junior high, an endless stream of students flowed in and out, but rarely was a Chinese student sent there for discipline.

This positive image of the Chinese student may be a stereotype, but it is, nonetheless, an advantage. Both teachers and administrators were favorably disposed toward Chinese pupils. The teachers expected Chinese students to perform well, and psychological tests have shown that high teacher expectations generally result in high student performance (Rosenthal and Jacobson, 1968: 19-23).

Positive student-teacher interaction is built upon the traditional respect accorded the scholar and teacher in Chinese culture. Children try to please teachers, who are looked upon as authority figures second only to parents. The role of the teacher is an exalted one. Parents, as well as children, look up to the teacher in his or her role as dispenser of knowledge and molder of character. No doubt this respect results in a better teaching climate.

The awe and respect for teachers, however, have their side-effects. Students tend to accept without question what teachers say. This tendency is due in part to the Chinese system of education in which learning is largely by rote, and in part because students do not feel it is proper to challenge teachers. The inability of students to express themselves well in English is yet another factor, but the cultural influence—respect for the teacher—is the stronger factor.

Many teachers are happy about how well-behaved Chinese children are, but at the same time are critical of the reluctance of these children to speak up in class.

Coming from an educational system that does not invite the open expression of student opinions, the children need time before they learn that it is acceptable and even expected of them to speak up. Meanwhile, their marks may be downgraded because of lack of participation in class.

In classroom observations, it was noted that nonparticipation was much more noticable in high school classes than in the lower grades. In the elementary grades, the Chinese children were quite animated and waved their hands impatiently, waiting to be recognized by the teachers. Even at the seventh grade level, students were not inhibited in answering questions put to them by the teacher. They would answer when called upon, but did not volunteer.

Respect for the teacher as a revered authority is so ingrained it was difficult for the immigrant children to countenance the misbehavior of some of their non-Chinese classmates toward the teachers. It was bewildering and disgusting to them that some children walked around the classroom while the teacher was talking, threw things across the room, made funny noises, erased what the teacher had put on the blackboard, and generally behaved in a disruptive manner. When asked what they didn't like about school, a common reply was along the lines of: "Some bad classmates are always making disturbances so that we can't learn very well in class".

ACADEMIC ACHIEVEMENT

Elementary Level

In general, elementary schools would not grade new immigrant children until a comfortable period of time had lapsed. Nevertheless, comments from the teachers revealed that the academic record of Chinese immigrant children in the lower grades was maintained at a fairly high level despite their difficulty with the language. Several factors may account for this. The warm and supportive teacher-pupil relationship is one factor. Another is that Chinese students come from an educational system that is competitive to the utmost. Both in Hong Kong and Taiwan, school is a grinding if not grueling ordeal, yet school is the number one ranking priority in the lives of parents who want their children to be upwardly mobile.

Until recently, free schooling was available to all Hong Kong children only to the sixth grade. Within the last few years, this has been extended through junior high. The nine grade limit exists also in Taiwan. At every grade level, the student must pass examinations to be promoted or retained in school. Some schools will allow a student who has failed to repeat the grade, but others will simply drop him. At the end of the sixth grade, the student must pass the Secondary School Entrance Examination. Failure to pass the examination means he cannot get into choice schools such as government subsidized public schools where tuition is cheaper than in nonsubsidized schools and the high reputation of the school is maintained by selecting only the best students. To help the students survive the rigorous elimination system, teachers cram a great deal of subject matter into their courses. They assign a heavy homework load, and the exams are very difficult. In a sense, the exams are a weeding out process; there are simply not enough schools to accommodate everyone who wants to attend.

If the student cannot keep up with the work in school, he tries to catch up at home. Parents try to help with homework, but if they cannot they will make every effort to hire a tutor. The student may go to school from 8:45 a.m. to 4:00 p.m. Monday through Friday and a half day on Saturday. He may spend the good portion of the remaining day doing homework or being tutored. Thus, the Chinese immigrant child is accustomed to a rigorous school program.

When he comes to New York City, he may think school is easy. Homework can be done in half an hour to two hours at the most. Since he is habituated to exerting himself, he will spend the extra time memorizing math theorems or spelling words or rereading the assignment. The Chinese student is outstandingly diligent, and the results show up as academic achievement.

A number of third, fifth and seventh grade students in the study mentioned that school was too easy; they were eager to learn more, and they indicated that they would not mind having more advanced work or being asked to do a little more homework. When asked if they preferred the demanding and competitive atomosphere of Hong Kong or Taiwan, however, not one spoke in favor of it. Even college students who had succeeded in the system, had been admitted to choice schools, and had gone to more prestigious institutions for higher learning condemned the system as "man-eating". Parents would prod their children and if a child did not pass the examinations, would consider that a disgrace to the family name and a dashing of their hopes for the child's future. The pressures on the children were so great that suicides were fairly common among those who failed their examinations. Small wonder that the immigrant children found the workload in America light; they remarked that, in contrast, promotion was almost routine, that one did not have to fight to stay in school, that one's parents did not have to sacrifice and work hard to pay the tuition, and that the family name and honor were easier to uphold. Overwhelmingly, the students were grateful for the chance to obtain their education free.

Junior High Level

At the two junior highs that were studied, the immigrant children took the same subjects as the rest of the student body. The curriculum included English, math, science, physical education, and industrial arts or home economics, and science lab. Usually social studies was deferred to allow class time for English as a Second Language (ESL) classes. Study of a foreign language was also postponed until the immigrant child was more proficient in English. In spite of the language disadvantage, teachers were pleased by what the children actually achieved.

While individual student records were confidential, the Queens junior high provided a sheet listing the grades, attendance and length of stay of all seventh grade students (without names) who were Chinese immigrants. The list is reproduced in Table 6-1, which gives a complete picture of the seventh grade Chinese immigrant children for this school.

A similar list for the Chinatown junior high school was not available. Only a few recent arrivals to this school were selected for interviews; their marks are tabulated in Table 6-2. Chinese in the orientation class were the newest arrivals. Each progressed at his own pace in the ESL classes, and when each felt comfortable enough to move on, he entered the orientation/transition classes and later the transition class. None of the students listed in Table 6-2 had been in the United States for more than two years. The academic record of these students as a group is noteworthy. It indicates individual differences in accomplishment rather than a pattern of difficulty with the school work. The majority of the children interviewed said that they did not understand much of what the teacher was saying, but they did not think the school work was difficult.

High School

Initially only the tenth grade students were to be used as subjects for this research, but the setup of the Chinatown high school made it possible to include the eleventh and twelfth grade students as well because their records were located in the same bilingual program office. It would have been more difficult to separate the tenth grade students from the entire group of recent immigrant Chinese youths than to include them. In addition, the larger group afforded a broader sample upon which to base the findings.

A jump from the seventh grade to the tenth grade or above revealed wide differences in the grades and achievements of the immigrant youths. The ages of the students ranged from fifteen to over twenty years. In New York, the students are placed in a

TABLE 6-1

Marks of Foreign-Born Chinese Seventh Graders
Satellite Community Junior High, 1977

Student	Years in U.S.	Engl.	Soc. St.	Math.	Sci.	Lang.	Read Score	Math Score
1	1	ESL	85	—	—	50	—	—
2	2	60	75	75	85	—	—	—
3	3	85	91	90	90	95	6.7	—
4	3	90	92	92	85	92	7.7	—
5	3	70	75	95	80	—	6.4	5.3
6	3	75	75	90	80	60	—	—
7	4	85	85	99	80	75	6.8	—
8	4	85	75	90	90	91	8.2	—
9	4	80	85	93	70	90	5.7	—
10	4	85	85	80	80	85	8.7	8.5
11	4	90	98	98	96	92	6.7	6.2
12	5	60	80	90	80	75	—	—
13	5	90	90	98	99	—	9.0	9.5
14	6	75	80	80	80	60	7.8	5.4
15	7	75	75	85	85	75	7.1	—
16	7	80	80	90	80	65	—	—
17	8	65	85	93	75	70	6.2	7.0
18	8	85	80	90	90	80	9.0	—
19	8	90	75	80	—	95	10.5	8.5
20	8	90	85	85	85	90	10.0	7.5
21	10	90	85	85	85	90	9.0	8.2
22	na	85	85	90	80	85	—	—
23	na	80	80	80	80	55	—	—
24	na	98	98	85	98	65	—	—

Note: Foreign-born Chinese students in the satellite junior high have been in this country much longer than those in the Chinatown junior high.

Source: Satellite junior high school.

TABLE 6-2

Marks of Recent Immigrant Chinese Children in the Seventh Grade Chinatown Junior High School, 1976

Class Level Student No.	English	Math	Subjects Soc. Stud.	Science	ESL
Orientation					
1	90	98	a	85	90
2	75	85	a	80	75
3	75	70	a	70	70
4	75	55	a	65	65
5	85	80	a	75	85
6	75	65	a	65	70
7	70	55	a	70	70
Orientation/Transition					
1	85	85	90	95	
2	85	90	90	95	
3	90	93	90	95	
4	65	75	80	65	
5	65	75	80	65	
Transition					
1	65	50	65	65	
2	75	90	85	85	
3	85	90	85	85	
4	85	85	85	85	

Note: None of the above students had been in the United States for more than two years.

a Social Studies omitted until students had time to learn some English.

Source: Students selected for interviews.

homeroom class by chronological age, not by the number of years of schooling they have had. In Hong Kong and Taiwan, children do not necessarily start the first grade at six years of age. A child may start the first grade at ten years of age, so that by sixteen he will have completed only the sixth grade. Yet, if he comes to this country, he will be put in the tenth grade with other sixteen year olds. Table 6-3 shows the level of education of the sample before they immigrated. They were all in the tenth, eleventh and twelfth grades at the time of the survey.

TABLE 6-3

Former Grade Level of Chinese Immigrant Students
in Chinatown High School Bilingual Program

Former Grade	Number	Percent
Lower than 6th Grade	25	9
6th Grade	28	10
7th Grade	15	6
8th Grade	40	15
9th Grade	48	18
10th Grade	56	21
11th Grade	37	14
12th Grade	18	7
Total	267	100

Source: Student Survey Questionnaire, 1978.

The above table reveals that 58 percent of the students were placed in classes beyond their former school level attainment. Consequently, these students had to contend with more advanced work as well as the entire spectrum of language difficulties and cultural adjustment.

Inasmuch as student grades from the official records were confidential, indirect means were used to obtain some indication of academic achievement. The easier way was to ask the students themselves. These interviews, with graduating seniors, were brief and were only conducted with a few who consented to talk. Therefore, the interpretation of the data must take these factors into consideration. Brief case histories of fourteen students are presented below.

CASE STUDIES

Case 1: Male. Born in 1957. Arrived September 1975 from Hong Kong. First year tenth grade, failed three subjects, eleventh grade average: 88; twelfth grade average : 87.5. Graduated 1978. Accepted at New York Community College to study hotel management. Worked twenty hours per week in garment factory hanging dresses.

Case 2: Male. Born 1960. Arrived September 1975 from Hong Kong. Brother to Case 1. Average grade—tenth grade: 85; eleventh grade: 86.7; twelfth grade: 92. Accepted at State University of New York, Stony Brook, to study computer science. Worked twenty-four hours per week delivering food orders.

Case 3: Female. Born 1959. Arrived 1975 from Hong Kong. First year multiple failures. Attended Manpower Training classes for clericals in 1976. Returned to high school; graduated 1978 with 79.5 average. Worked twenty-five hours per week in garment factory.

Case 4: Female. Born 1958. Arrived 1977. Failed American history, Spanish, hygiene. Transferred to secretarial school.

Case 5: Female. Born 1959. Arrived 1974 from Hong Kong. Average first year 71; second year: 73. Accepted at community college to study data processing. Worked thirty hours per week in sewing factory.

Case 6: Male. Born 1957. Arrived 1975 from Mainland China. Four semester averages; 94,92,92,87. Graduated with honors. Accepted at State University of New York, Stony Brook, to study computer science. Worked twenty hours per week as cashier.

Case 7: Male. Born 1959. Arrived 1975. Four semester averages: 91,90,80,84. Perfect attendance. Accepted at State University of New York, Buffalo, to study electronics. Worked twenty hours per week in supermarket.

Case 8: Male. Born 1957. Arrived 1974 from Hong Kong. Four semester averages: 85,90,80,80. Accepted at Staten Island Community College to study data processing. Worked twenty-five hours per week pressing clothes.

Case 9: Female. Born 1960. Arrived 1975 from Hong Kong. First year grades: World History-D; Biology-D; Health Education-Unsatisfactory. Subsequent year averages: 91,89,85. Perfect attendance. Accepted at New York State College at Binghamton.

Case 10: Female. Born 1957. Arrived 1975 from Mainland China. Averages: 78.4, 92.9. Accepted at State University of New York, Stony Brook, in math program.

Case 11: Male. Born 1957. Arrived in 1975. In 1976 multiple failures, many absences. Worked thirty-six hours per week in laundry. Dropped out and went to work for airline.

Case 12: Male. Born 1958. Arrived 1976 from Hong Kong. Averages: 67,83,81. Accepted at Brooklyn College to study computer science. Worked in restaurants on weekends.

Case 13: Male. Born 1957. Arrived 1975 from Burma. First year failed many subjects. Twelfth grade average: 73. Accepted at City College of New York to study science.

Case 14: Male. Born 1959. Arrived 1974 from Taiwan. Ill health. Failed health education and social studies. Averages: 84,81,80.

The above fourteen cases were about one-fifth of the 1978 graduates in the Chinatown high school bilingual program, but the fact that they were about to graduate biases the picture considerably. Note that many of the students were twenty to twenty-one years old at the time, an age somewhat older than the average high school graduate. Most indicated that their first year was difficult; failures were common that year, but it seems that in subsequent years grades picked up enough for the students to pass and, for most, eventually to graduate.

The school records of these graduating immigrant youths is fair to excellent considering the multiple handicaps under which they operated. To get some sense of how the other Chinese students in the bilingual programs of the two high schools were faring with their school work, the children were asked "Are you satisfied with your school work?". Three-fifths of those replying said yes; two-fifths said no (See, Table 13-3). As reasons for the favorable response, many checked that the teachers were nice, they were grateful for a free education, and they felt they were learning a great deal. Unfavorable comments were fewer, the leading ones being poor English skills and lack of order in the classroom. Considering that 117 of the 270 high school students surveyed had been in this country for less than a year, and another 77 for less than two years, it is noteworthy that they had learned enough to be able to do their written assignments, work at outside jobs for many hours, and still pass their courses with decent grades.

WORK AFTER SCHOOL

The one fact that stands out in the case studies of the Chinese immigrant students is their heavy work load. Most of the students interviewed had jobs that required more than twenty hours of their time per week. It was not only high school students who had jobs, but the junior high students as well. Even some grade school students, especially from the Chinatown school, went to the garment factories after school to help their mothers hang up garments, turn belts, or prepare garments for sewing.

Because all their waking hours are so fully occupied with school and work, most immigrant youths do not have time to get into trouble. They have a real sense of the work world and the dead-end jobs in which they see their parents toiling day after day. They may realize that education is the key to a better job and a better life, so their motivation is sufficiently high to do well in school.

In a sense they are fortunate that the community provides jobs like the ones the students hold in the garment factories, grocery stores, and restaurants. By working in these ethnic enterprises, the young immigrants are still surrounded by a familiar environment where the Chinese language is spoken, where the value of hard work is quite evident, and where social control is extremely strong under the watchful eyes of parents or relatives. Most of these young people are not only earning spending money for themselves, they are contributing to the family purse as well. In this way, the sense of family duty and obligation is instilled.

ATTENDANCE RATES

As previously noted, at all of the schools with high percentages of Chinese student enrollment, the attendance rates were exceptionally high. For instance, for the school year 1976 to 1977, the attendance rate at the Chinatown elementary school was 93 percent. At the satellite Chinese community elementary school it was 91 percent. For the junior highs, the rates were 91 percent and 89 percent respectively. For the high schools, it was 77 percent and

84 percent respectively (New York City Board of Education, 1978). Contrast these rates with the citywide one of 82 percent. The citywide average masks the lower rates in the high schools, which may run as low as 58 percent.

Graduates

A follow-up of graduates of the Chinese bilingual program in the Chinatown high school from 1975 to 1978 was done by the guidance counselor, and her findings are given in Table 6-4. Note the threefold increase in graduates over the course of three years. This may be due in large part to the implementation of the bilingual program in 1976. Note also that over 90 percent of the graduates in the last two years went on to college!

TABLE 6-4
Future Plans of Chinatowns High School's Chinese Bilingual Program Graduates, 1975-1978

Future Plans	1975-1976	1976-1977	1977-1978
Work	3	1	0
College:			
2 Year	1	27	23
4 Year	8	37	46
Manpower Training Institute	5	5	2
Military Service	0	0	3
No Information	8	1	1
Total	25	71	75

Source: High school bilingual program guidance counselor.

An attempt was made to find data on the number of college-bound students in the bilingual education program at the satellite community high school, but comparable data were unavailable. No figures by ethnic group were kept by the college office counselor. The bilingual program had been established a mere two years previously, and there was no bilingual guidance counselor. According to the director of the bilingual program at the satellite community high school, none of her students were ready for graduation; all were still in the tenth or eleventh grades. To get a general idea of where Chinese graduates from this high school were heading, this researcher combed the 1979 graduating class roster for Chinese-sounding names. Of the 84 graduates, 70 planned to go to four year colleges and 14 planned to go to two year colleges. In other words, 100 percent were heading for colleges. However, there was no way of telling how many of these students were immigrants and how many were born in America.

DROPOUTS OR DISCHARGES

What about those who did not graduate? How many dropped by the wayside? What happened to them? Why did they leave school? Again, the researcher turned to the same Chinatown guidance counselor who had kept excellent records of her discharges. [1] These are tabulated in Table 6-5. Note the dramatic drop in the total numbers of students who were discharged from the bilingual program at the Chinatown high school, from 122 in 1976 to 77 in 1977 and to 32 in 1978. Each year, the numbers were approximately halved. One can surmise from the large percentage who went on to college and the dramatic increase in graduates that the bilingual program did encourage immigrant children to finish their high school education and perhaps aim higher.

An attempt was made to find data on the number of discharged students in the bilingual program at the satellite community high school, but comparable data were unavailable. No figures by ethnic group were kept by the attendance office, but this researcher tried to construct a profile by utilizing the discharge records to tabulate those with Chinese-sounding names. Consequently, the figures for discharged students included American born Chinese as well as foreign born immigrants. Table 6-6 gives a breakdown of the discharges by reason for the three years 1976 to 1979.

Many students from the satellite community school moved out of New York City to such faraway places as California, Texas, and Illinois. This phenomenon was not true in the Chinatown high school; transfers to schools in other parts of the city were more common there. The dropout rate was greater in the satellite community high school. It could not be determined why except that the bilingual program at this school was not established until the 1977-1978 school year, and the staff did not include a bilingual

---

[1] Not all discharges are dropouts as can be seen from Tables 6-5 and 6-6. Some are transfers, and some move away.

TABLE 6-5

Discharged Chinese Students from the Bilingual Program at Chinatown High School, 1975-1978

Reason for Leaving School	1975-1976	1976-1977	1977-1978
Transferred to another school [a]	42	31	8
Working at a job	22	6	5
Returned to Hong Kong/Taiwan	1	1	2
Transferred to Manpower Training Inst.	7	4	4
Marriage	1	0	0
Already completed H.S. in HK/TW/China	1	2	2
Illness or death in family	0	1	0
Personal or mental health problem [b]	1	7	0
Moved away (no follow-up)	10	3	2
Gangs [c]	5	1	3
Financial hardship	8	1	1
No reason given	24	20	5
Total Discharged	122	77	32

Notes: [a] To nearby alternative school or other schools in the city.

[b] Most personal problems involved difficulty getting along with parents.

[c] Suspended because of gang activity.

Source: High school bilingual program counselor.

guidance counselor. The lack of both could have been responsible for the higher dropout rate.

CRITICAL REMARKS

Lest this report card sound too rosy, there were some reservations and critical remarks made by students and teachers. One very profound comment, made by a young girl, was puzzling at first, but it persists as an enigma. When asked if students enjoyed the more permissive atmosphere of schools, many did not know how to handle their newfound freedom. The girl's reply was, "Too much freedom is no freedom". She went on to explain her seem-

TABLE 6-6

Discharged Students with Chinese Surnames from Satellite Community High School, 1976-1979

Reason for Leaving School	1976-1977	1977-1978	1978-1979
Transferred to another school	10	8	11
Working at job	0	1	0
Moved out of New York City	18	5	17
Returned to Taiwan/Hong Kong	1	5	2
Equivalency diploma	1	4	1
Died	0	0	1
Home instruction	1	0	0
Dropout, 17 years +	17	9	15
No reason given	2	1	6
Total Discharged	50	33	52

Note: Includes American-born as well as immigrant students.

Source: High school attendance office.

ingly contradictory statement by saying, "We are constantly asked to make decisions. Where would you like to go? What do you want to do? What do you think? I don't know what to do. It is so hard to make decisions. I'm not used to it. I even find it painful, so I end up doing nothing."

If teachers were to recognize that Chinese immigrant children do come from a school situation and home environment that is more structured, less egalitarian, and more authoritative than that of their fellow students, they might be better able to help Chinese students make choices and explore options. It would also be helpful if the classroom environment were more structured until the immigrant became accustomed to a more relaxed atmosphere.

TEACHER CRITICISMS

The warm, supportive attitude of the teachers is oftentimes counterbalanced by their critical attitude toward the cultural traits of the children or the behavior of the children's parents. Examples of the criticisms heard from teachers are:

1.The children act like little adults.

2.The children do not fight back even when they are abused.

3.The mothers are overprotective. They bring their children to school and pick them up. At lunchtime, many mothers even bring food to school and feed their children.

4.The parents do not allow their children to go anywhere after school. They must go straight home or to the factories where the mothers work.

5.The children work too many hours in the factories or in the stores. They come to school very tired.

6.The parents do not keep their children at home even when they are sick. If the school wants to send the sick child home, the child prefers to stay in school because there is no one home.

7.If a Chinese child gets sick, the parents do not take him to a Western doctor. They cook up an herbal brew for the child or they rub him with some Chinese ointment. They also pinch him on the neck until he is red and blue because they believe this relieves. his fever and cures him. Some teachers used to think that the child was being abused.

8.The Chinese parents must learn to be less autocratic and less absolute in their authority over the children. This is America, not China!

9.The parents discourage their children from playing or interacting with children of other ethnic groups. They are very clannish.

To respond to these remarks the following chapter deals with specific instances of bicultural conflict, which cause misunderstanding and sometimes create difficulty for the children.

SUMMARY OF FINDINGS

By and large, a positive interaction exists between teachers and Chinese pupils in the schools visited and studied. A cultural carryover of respect for the teacher and a high value placed upon education are important contributing factors. Chinese children pose less of a behavioral problem than others in the student body, thus meriting further teacher favor. The attendance rates for schools with large Chinese enrollment were high.

The academic achievements of Chinese immigrant children were good in spite of a language barrier because they are accustomed to a more rigorous standard in the Hong Kong and Taiwan schools. According to the teachers, the first year was the most difficult.

Many of the children—even some in the elementary schools—worked after school. In the Chinatown high school, 20 percent of the students surveyed worked twenty-five hours per week or more. In the satellite high school, the percentage was 17 (*See*, Table 9-1).

Of the graduates from the Chinatown high school bilingual program, over 90 percent went to college. College was almost a certain sequel for the graduates of both high schools.

Discharges from the Chinatown high school bilingual program dropped drastically from 122 in 1976 to 32 in 1978. Some of these were transfers. True dropouts were few. Discharges from the satellite community high school revealed that many were moving away from New York City.

Teacher criticisms included student passivity, a non-questioning attitude, discomfort in dealing with a relatively loosely structured classroom atmosphere, parental overprotectiveness and methods of treating the sick child, and a tendency to stick with their own ethnic group.

THEORETICAL IMPLICATIONS

Reference Group Theory

In their study of the American soldier, Samuel A. Stouffer *et al.* (1949) developed the concept of relative deprivation. They found that men in the army, essentially living under the same conditions and undergoing the same experiences, viewed their situations with varying attitudes and perceptions. For example, the actually more deprived group of soldiers seemed little more critical than the less deprived. Black soldiers stationed in the South felt less deprived when they compared themselves against black civilians in the South, but they felt more deprived when they compared themselves with black civilians in the North. In short, the sense of satisfaction or dissatisfaction was a function of expectations and achievements relative to others in the same situation. W.I. Thomas (1930-1931) called it "definition of the situation".

Stouffer *et al.* were eliciting patterns of response to a basically deprivational situation—compulsory military service. The concept of relative deprivation was utilized to account for feelings of dissatisfaction, but the more significant aspect of the concept is its stress upon social and psychological experience as relative. The practice of comparing one's own situation with a reference person or group can also result in satisfaction, and in the case of the Chinese immigrant children, the obverse of relative deprivation would be viewing oneself in a position of relative advantage.

In most instances, these children came from a less desirable environment than the one in which they found themselves in New York City. The population congestion in Hong Kong or Mainland China was certainly worse than found in New York. Housing was more crowded. Material goods were less plentiful. Education was not easily obtained. The political situation was unstable in both Hong Kong and Taiwan, and if they came from Mainland China, the feeling of relief from political oppression was even greater. Coming to the United States was viewed as a golden opportunity, and to quote Jay Sommer (1981), "Free public education is the legendary gold that paves the streets of America".

Viewed against the reference group from which they came, therefore, the children and their parents considered themselves fortunate to be in the United States, and they strove to make the best of their opportunity. Measured against the lower standards and demands of American public schools, the Chinese children did not find their schoolwork overwhelming in spite of the language handicap. Their perception of the situation was one of relative advantage and satisfaction. In fact, Hurh and Kim (1980) described the initial stage soon after arrival as one of euphoria and excitement, having finally made it safely to the country they had aspired to settle in and in being reunited with family, friends and relatives. In their study of Korean immigrants in America, Hurh and Kim drew a hypothetical model of six adaptive stages resembling a J-curve.

The six stages are: excitement; exigency; resolution; optimum; identification crisis; and marginality acceptance. After the initial excitement, the exigency stage sets in. The stage is characterized by "disjuncture between one's high expectations and one's perception of limited ability and opportunity leading to a condition of cognitive ambivalence and exigency". As time goes on, the immigrant resolves to make the best of it (stage 3), leading to limited success (optimum stage), but usually this phase is accompanied by a shifting of the immigrants' reference group from his own ethnic group to that of the dominant white group. The immigrants would now compare their life conditions to that of white Americans, not to their pre-emigration status nor to their fellow immigrants. Thus the identification crisis stage follows in which the immigrants begin to discover the immutable race barrier which blocks their way toward structural assimilation over which they have no control. The last stage is the acceptance of one's marginality. This study of the Chinese immigrant children dealt primarily with recent arrivals, so the euphoria and excitement stage predominated to lend an aura of successful entry into American life. If Hurh and Kim's model holds, however, the successive stages of their transition will lead to ups and downs in their psychological outlook, which will come at a later date.

Cultural Insulation

For the sake of gaining access to large numbers of Chinese immigrant children, the fieldwork for this study was targeted at schools in two communities with large numbers of Chinese students. As a result the foreignness of American ways and the sense of being a minority group member was not as acute as being the lone member in a sea of alien faces. The newly arrived immigrants were cushioned and surrounded by others like themselves. One could speak Chinese and still be understood by someone. One could follow the same customs of the old country and not be ridiculed. There were white faces and black faces and Hispanic faces to contend with, and this was a new situation, but there were enough yellow faces around to be reassuring. The ethnic communities were decompression chambers, which made the process of adaptation a more comfortable one. As pointed out previously in this chapter, the students' contacts outside of the school, family and community were very limited. Even though these children and youths had migrated from the Far East to the United States, they were still culturally insulated by their concentration in ethnic communities.

Symbolic Interactionism

As George Herbert Mead (1934) postulated, each person adjusts his perceptions and actions to the expectations of "generalized others". In the school, the most "significant other" is the teacher, and the position of the teacher is further enhanced by the exalted respect accorded the scholar in Chinese tradition. Since the students are very deferential toward teachers, are less boisterous and better behaved in the classroom, are diligent in their studies, and are more easily controlled, the teachers react by being more favorably diposed toward the Chinese students and by expecting better academic performance from them. In response, the students try to live up to the expectations of the teachers and bask in the teachers' favor. The reciprocal positive impressions that teachers and students have of each other bolster the students' spirits and help them in their adjustment.

Presently, the schools and American society are more appreciative of cultural diversity. Instead of trying immediately to divest the newly arrived immigrant of his cultural heritage, some attempts are made to bridge the gap gradually, and programs such as ESL or bilingual education have been instituted, whereas formerly new immigrants were expected to "sink or swim". The more receptive social climate that now exists undoubtedly makes life for the new immigrant less difficult, and the results show up in less trauma and fewer problems.

VII
Bilingual Education

What steps are being taken by the schools to help children who have just been set down on American soil and who speak a language other than English? How are they being received and aided? Our contention is that the process is as important as the goals, and it is not enough merely to relate the techniques or strategies, but to look closely at how they are implemented empirically and to see what results actually flow from good intentions to help. This chapter looks at how the school tries to help the non-English speaking child overcome the language barrier.

LEARNING THE LANGUAGE

Imagine for a moment that you have lost your power of speech and that it will take a great deal of effort on your part to regain it. At the same time, in order to survive and carry on your daily activities, you must communicate. Sign language, body language, and pantomime will work to a degree, but how can you tell someone in sign language that George Washington was the first president of the United States? If you can imagine this perhaps you can feel for the immigrant child who has to deal not only with the total adjustment of being uprooted and transplanted in a new country, but also with the sudden loss of almost all his ability to communicate.

Luckily, the immigrant child has a recourse; compulsory education laws decree that he must go to school, so he oftens finds himself sitting in a classroom within a few days of his arrival. The school's first task is to teach the child English as quickly as possible so he can join his peers in the regular classes. The school's task is no less difficult than that of the immigrant child.

In this country children are placed in a class according to chronological age. A child starts school at age five or six, and promotion is generally routine. He completes elementary school at twelve, junior high at fifteen and high school at eighteen. Age and grade level are fairly well synchronized.

The immigrant child may not fit into this mold. He may have started school late or repeated a grade or two because he failed his exams or otherwise was unable to measure up. Yet, when he comes to this country he is generally placed in a grade corresponding to his age.

If he attends a school where he is an isolated Chinese immigrant, he is expected to keep up with his class work. He may get no special help in English, although a sympathetic teacher may ask a classmate to look after him a bit, or she may be somewhat more lenient in grading him or may keep him after class for extra help. The options open to the teacher are few. Lesson plans and course schedules make no allowance for the child who does not speak English. His failure or success is obscured by his nonparticipation in class. According to a number of students interviewed, they felt as if they were in a semi-daze for the first year.

In schools where immigrant children attend in greater numbers, their difficulty with the language is immediately apparent because the problem is aggregated. One child can be overlooked, but a larger number cannot. There seem to be three approaches to dealing with the problem: "sink or swim", English as a second language (ESL), and bilingual education.

SINK OR SWIM

The philosophy behind this approach is self-explanatory: put the child in his chronological age class and he will be forced to learn. For those in the younger age groups, this method, although frightening at first, can work. It works better on the younger child because his mind is flexible and receptive to the learning of languages, and the vocabulary and subject content of his lessons are not as advanced. For the teenager, this approach is questionable.

Proponents of the sink or swim approach maintain that this is what most immigrants did in the past and they managed. [1] What they forget to mention is the number who could not swim and who sank to the bottom, out of sight and out of mind.

[1] In fact, Ling Chi Wang (1976) documented in his article, "How San Francisco School Administrators Block Bilingual Education", that in 1974 in San Francisco, of Chinese speaking children, 1,138 were getting ESL, 193 were getting bilingual education and 1,000 were getting no help at all.

ENGLISH AS A SECOND LANGUAGE (ESL)

Many schools adopt this approach. The immigrant child is placed in his chronological age class, but special attention is given to teaching him "survival English"—the phrases necessary to meet his basic needs. The amount of ESL that a child gets depends upon the resources of the school district and the importance that the school administrators attach to it. In some schools, immigrant children may take ESL only once or twice a week, whereas in other schools ESL is part of the daily curriculum. In the former one, a teacher visits a number of schools, and the students are pulled out of their regular subject classes on the days that the ESL teacher comes. The drawbacks to this system are obvious: the children miss their regular subject classes, and neither the ESL nor subject classes are consistent.

Often Chinese children are placed in ESL classes with many Spanish speaking students. Most ESL teachers are Spanish speaking and some are monolingual. The teachers say that principles of teaching ESL are the same for any foreign language pupil and it is not important for the teacher to know the pupil's primary language. This premise can be challenged.

In ESL classes, instruction in the formal structure and grammar of the English language is subordinate to fulfilling the need for the immigrant child to communicate orally. Some of the basic phrases and vocabulary necessary in our day-to-day activities are taken for granted, and we do not realize how confusing they may be to someone unfamiliar with the nuances of American expression.

In the six schools studied, each teacher taught ESL differently and each chose his or her curriculum materials according to personal preference (*See,* Table 7-1). Thus, there was no uniformity. Some used pictures cut out of magazines as visual aids, others used first and second grade basal readers, while still others took advantage of specialized ESL curriculum materials such as the *Lado English Series,* the Scott Foresman *English Around the World Series,* and the Addison-Wesley *New Horizons in English Series.* One teacher used the silent method: she spoke as little as possible and used props to substitute for certain questions and words. In this way, the teacher would not use class time repeating questions or instructions. For instance, holding a long red plastic rod would mean, "What is Pedro wearing?" A yellow rod might stand for,

"You used the wrong tense". A green rod might mean, "Repeat the sentence". Of course, the association of the props with words would have to be established first and could be changed with each new lesson. This was a novel way of forcing the student to do most of the talking.

TABLE 7-1

Language Programs for Chinese Immigrant Students

School	Program
Chinatown Elementary School	Three bilingual classes combining 1st & 2nd, 3rd & 4th, 5th & 6th grades. Classes taught in both English and Chinese.
Satellite Community Elementary School	Three hours of ESL pull-out weekly (two 1½-hour sessions). No bilingual program. Buddy system of tutoring by fifth graders about 15 to 20 minutes in the morning. Tutors meet with English teacher once each week to report on progress.
Chinatown Junior High School	Twelve hours of intensive ESL weekly. New arrivals first placed placed in an orientation class, from which they progress to Orientation/Transition, and on to Transition class before they are placed in regular classes. Each class is progressively more advanced. Bilingual approach[1] used. Lessons taught in English. Bilingual teacher may answer in Chinese or students may ask questions in Chinese. Class may be assisted by bilingual paraprofessional. Chinese offered as a foreign language.
Satellite Community Junior High School	Five hours ESL pull-out weekly; no bilingual education program.
Chinatown High School	Well-organized bilingual/bicultural program in its third year of operation. Bilingual classes in history, math, and science; bilingual approach[1] for other subjects. Students take 12 hours ESL weekly for four semesters before going on to fulfill graduation requirements for English. Chinese offered as a foreign language.
Satellite Community High School	Bilingual program in its second year using bilingual approach.[1] Chinese dialect used is Mandarin rather than Cantonese. Ten hours of ESL weekly the first year, five the second year. Chinese offered as a foreign language.

Note: [1] Bilingual approach means class taught primarily in English, but explanation or interpretation may be given in Chinese by teacher or bilingual paraprofessional.

Source: Personal observation and on-site research.

BILINGUAL EDUCATION

It is easy to confuse ESL with bilingual education—the schools themselves sometimes are not clear about the distinction. ESL is the teaching of functional English to persons who are already conversant in another language. Bilingual education means using two languages as the medium of instruction in subject areas where course content may be lost on a person who does not have command of the second language. For example, a Chinese teenager, sixteen years of age, is put into the tenth grade when he arrives from Hong Kong. He simply cannot make up ten years of English to deal adequately with his courses in history, economics, science, math, hygiene and social studies. Perhaps he is taking ESL, which teaches simple phrases of speech, but this does not enable him to do his reading and writing assignments. The possible outcomes are that he will fall behind, or that he will become discouraged and give up. The rationale behind bilingual education is to provide instruction in both Chinese and English to allow such a student to learn history, social studies, math and so forth with assistance given in his native tongue.

This concept was recognized by the *Lau v. Nichols* decision handed down by the Supreme Court in 1974, which stated:

> ...There is no equality in treatment merely by providing students with the same facilities, textbooks, teachers and curriculum; for students who do not understand English are effectively foreclosed from any meaningful education.

Even before the decision was handed down, Congress had already authorized appropriations for bilingual education under the Elementary and Secondary Education Act, Title VII (also known as the Bilingual Education Act) as early as 1968. In the act's first five years of operation, federally funded bilingual programs representing twenty-four languages serviced 180,000 children in forty-one states.

Some states have their own laws mandating bilingual/bicultural education, and the U.S. Congress has mandated that a five-year plan be drawn up to expand bilingual education services. In New York City, there is no mandate, but there is a consent decree between the Board of Education and Aspira whereby the Board agreed to work with Puerto Rican groups to implement bilingual programs. At the end of 1977, 537 of the city's 931 schools offered Spanish bilingual programs to a total of 61,190 students (Williams, 1977).

By 1985, these figures had been reduced to 338 schools that offered bilingual education to 43,600 students, of which 2,959 were Chinese (New York City Board of Education, Office of Bilingual Education).

Because no agreement was worked out with any Chinese organization, bilingual programs for the Chinese are few and of recent origin. They are largely supported by state and federal funds, and only in isolated instances are they part of the school budget. It is not an integral part of the curriculum, but is looked upon as a frill to be dispensed with as soon as federal and state funds cease. Were it not for the fact that proposals were submitted and grants approved from Title VII, federal sources, and Chapter 720 state funds, there would be no Chinese bilingual program at all.

The first bilingual program for Chinese speaking students was initiated in the Chinatown district three years prior to this study's field work. Expansion came about solely because a number of dedicated and concerned Chinese American teachers wrote proposals, solicited funds, and worked unceasingly to establish the programs. Even then, the number of students serviced and the personnel hired for the programs were minimal. Bilingual paraprofessionals are the largest group of personnel employed for these programs (See, Table 7-2). They assist the teacher in the classroom and carry the load of translating, interpreting, and tutoring, yet they have no professional status.

In New York City schools, federal funds cannot be used to pay classroom teachers. Consequently, even if the coordinators were able to obtain federal funds and to employ bilingual teachers who speak Chinese and English, the funds could not be used to pay these teachers—the most important component of a bilingual education program. Such funds can be used only for resource teachers, those who develop curriculum materials.

Evaluation of Bilingual Education

A number of evaluative studies that were published in 1977 were highly critical of bilingual education. These include the Rand Report, the American Institute for Research Report and the Department of Health, Education and Welfare (HEW) Report (U.S. Department of Health, Education and Welfare, 1977); (*See also, New York Times*, 1978). All three compared limited English speaking children enrolled in Hispanic bilingual programs that had been in operation for at least four years with children in regular classes who were of the same socioeconomic background. The major findings were:

1. In English reading and vocabulary, the bilingual education (BE) students' performance was poorer than that of students in the regular classes.
2. In Spanish reading and vocabulary, however, the BE students performed better than those in regular classes.
3. In math, the BE students scored higher than expected.

TABLE 7-2
Chinese Bilingual Programs in New York City
1977-1978

Participating School Level	No. of Schools	No. of Students	Personnel		Source of Funds
Elementary K-6	11	682	Coordinators	2	Titles, I, VII
and			Classroom teachers	19	Chapter 720
Junior High 7-9	4	236	Resource teachers	4	Units 12, 13
			Paraprofessionals	31	
			Guidance counsellor	3	
High Schools 9-12	3	667	Coordinator	1	Titles I, VII
			P/T Classroom		Chapter 720
			teachers	22	Tax Levies
			F/T Resource teacher	2	
			Area specialists	3	
			Guidance counsellor	1	
			Paraprofessionals	14	
Auxiliary Center	1	50	Teacher	1	Title VII
			Paraprofessionals	2	
Total	19	1,585			

Source: New York City Board of Education, Office of Bilingual Education.

4. Costs per BE student averaged $400 more than for regular students.

5. Two-thirds of the students enrolled in the bilingual education program were not limited English speaking, and once in a program, students tended to remain. Only 15 percent transferred to regular classes even after they could function well enough in English.

However, the findings from these three studies are not applicable to the Chinese bilingual education programs in New York City. No Chinese bilingual education program was included in any of the studies mentioned. None of the Chinese programs had been in existence long enough to be included. This researcher's study and evaluation of the bilingual education programs for Chinese immigrant children is based on teacher comments, parents' attitudes, student response, and observations and assessments.

TEACHER'S COMMENTS

New York City had just been through a financial crisis when this study was conducted, and the schools had been hit hard. In 1975, 6,000 teachers were laid off, and new hiring was out of the question except for those teachers trained in bilingual education. Teachers with a bilingual background were given priority over those with seniority, and this set off a fight for job security that unleashed its full wrath upon bilingual education.

New York City's population has been declining and changing in composition. As seen in Tables 4-1 and 4-2, the blacks, Hispanics, and Asian population is increasing while whites flee to the suburbs or send their children to private schools. In 1975, school enrollment was down due to the lower birthrate, so teaching jobs were scarce. Some teachers who did not have a second language facility felt that their jobs were threatened; they masked this fear by attacking bilingual education itself. Under these circumstances, teachers' attitudes were colored by economic and political considerations. If they accepted bilingual education, they might have been jeopardizing their own jobs.

Teaching in two languages takes highly developed skills. One must be fluent in both languages and in subject content as well. The teacher must be sensitive to the student who has just been uprooted and, be aware of possible conflicts in cultural values as well. Meeting the first criterion is difficult enough. In many instances, a person is fluent in one language and functional in another. For example, if the teacher is fluent in Chinese, but speaks with an accent in English, students will not learn the standard spoken English. If the teacher is fluent in English and speaks Chinese but is not well versed in the written language, she may find it difficult to get lessons across when it comes to the translation. To be conversant in two languages with facility and be able to teach biology or economics or any other subject calls for talents which are in short supply.

Obviously, these demands make it more difficult to teach a bilingual class. Even those who are quite facile in the language must spend extra time looking for the appropriate curriculum materials or creating their own. According to some bilingual teachers, they must also spend a great deal of time preparing lessons and looking up translations of unfamiliar terms. These disadvantages naturally affect the teachers' attitudes toward bilingual education.

One teacher who had taught bilingual classes felt that teaching in both languages was harder on the teacher and easier on the students. Another very conscientious teacher became ill from overwork after two years in the bilingual program. A third chose to go back to her regular classes because she felt that the students tended to rely too much on bilingual education. Another teacher spoke favorably of bilingual education, saying that with it the students can keep up their work during a stressful period of their lives when they have to make so many adjustments. Strong students are further strengthened although they probably would have survived the sink or swim philosophy. The weak ones, however, would fall by the wayside without bilingual education.

There is often a hesitancy on the part of the teachers to make judgments about the bilingual programs in their schools. One former bilingual education teacher, however, had strong criticisms. She felt that "bilingual education slows down the process of learning English, and it draws out the laziness in the student". Her philosophy was that if one wants to succeed, one must strive to learn, "Bilingual education takes away the challenge". Another criticism was that bilingual classes segregate the immigrant children and thus lessen their opportunity to deal with others not like themselves. She also felt that the bilingual program only delayed the students' learning of English until college, at which time the problem may be compounded. This teacher had a number of suggestions for alternatives to bilingual education:

1. Use English as the only medium of teaching in the classroom, but provide Chinese speaking tutors.
2. Provide children with stipends so they do not have to work and can spend more time catching up with their school work.
3. Tutor the recent immigrant arrivals before placing them in classes.
4. Limit bilingual education to the early grades of the American born whose parents feel that the maintenance of their native tongue is important.

It seems unfair to judge the Chinese bilingual programs that have been in existence for only two or three years. In the rush to implement the Supreme Court decision of *Lau v. Nichols*, little time was given to long term planning. At the same time, commitment to bilingual education has been half-hearted. The programs are structured so that they will self-destruct within a short period of time, thereby fulfilling the doomed-to-fail prophecy. For example, in Table 7-2, we see that the largest number of bilingual personnel—almost one-half—were paraprofessionals. There were only twenty-six full-time and twenty-two part-time teachers for 1,585 students. Funds committed to bilingual education come from non-budgeted sources, which are uncertain from year to year. Unless someone takes it upon himself to apply for grants, there will be no money. Restrictions against use of federal funds for the hiring of classroom teachers also hamper the optimum use of bilingual resources. The law and court rulings still require that bilingual education be offered, but implementation varies with school districts. Add to this the political atmosphere and the economic issues of job competition and the result is a situation complicated by factors that do not address the fundamental question of whether bilingual/bicultural education helps immigrant children in their transition.

PARENTS' ATTITUDES

The parents' feelings were ambivalent and sometimes unrealistic. They wanted their children to learn English as quickly as possible, yet they were afraid that the children would lose their command of Chinese and become estranged from them. Their expectations of their children's achievements were much too high. They felt their children must do well in school; their hopes depended upon it. If the children fell behind or did not bring home good grades, the parents were extremely disappointed. They were influenced by the whirl of debate that went on about bilingual education. Those who were ambitious for their children insisted on the sink or swim approach, arguing that the only way their children could get ahead was to devote full attention to mastering the English language. Immigrant parents in New York tended to think that the primary emphasis should be on learning English because their children already knew some Chinese, whereas second generation parents who gave up or had no chance to learn Chinese in their formative years now felt the void in their lives and wanted their children to be exposed to their cultural heritage. Some parents wanted their children in bilingual classes so that they could learn English and Chinese simultaneously. The issue in this case was not one of facilitating the immigrant's entry into the mainstream as quickly as possible, but of maintaining his mother tongue.

STUDENTS' ATTITUDES

All the recent immigrant children interviewed mentioned language as their most formidable problem. They were extremely hesitant or timid about speaking in class. Some were fearful and apprehensive. Strange faces, strange ways, a foreign language they could not understand—all these added up to anxiety and stress during the first year or so after the immigrant child's arrival in this country.

In the survey questionnaire administered to the high school students, one of the questions sought to discover the student's attitudes toward bilingual education—almost all were enrolled in the bilingual programs. The students' opinions were just as ambivalent as their parents'. Table 7-3 shows the answers to the question "What is your opinion about bilingual education? Check all those that apply."

The responses indicate that opinion is divided down the middle. There is very little difference in the responses between the boys and girls and in the favorable and unfavorable opinions. For example, 153 students said bilingual education helped them understand better, yet 125 checked that they would rather be in the

TABLE 7-3
Attitude of High School Bilingual Program Students
Toward Bilingual Education

Attitude	Males (131)	Females (138)	Total (269)
Favorable			
Helps me understand better	80	73	153
Helps me retain Chinese	24	45	69
Like bilingual education	45	50	95
Would quit if no bilingual education	5	8	13
Total			330
Unfavorable			
Rather be in regular classes	61	64	125
Bilingual education for slow learners	38	47	85
Learn English slower	62	56	118
Total			328

Source: Student Survey Questionnaire, 1978.

regular classes. On the other hand, 95 (about one-third) liked bilingual education, yet 85 felt that the bilingual program was for slow learners and 118 said that it impeded their learning of English. Few would quit school if there were no bilingual programs.

There is a strong stigma attached to being in the bilingual classes. Some think such classes are for the slower students, which is not actually the case. On the contrary, if there were no bilingual education program, the immigrant children would be put into slower track classes because they would be unable to keep up at first with the "special progress" or "academic track" students. The worst part of this alternative is that students in the slower track classes often exhibit behavioral problems that are disruptive to classroom learning.

The students interviewed were eager to learn and their motivation was high. Given a little encouragement and some extra help, they could do well. In fact, by the second year, a somewhat miraculous "great leap forward" could be observed. This is confirmed by the students' records and by the teachers interviewed.

Teachers felt that generally one year was about the time it took for the immigrant child to feel that he could cope with his lessons. For those in the Chinatown schools, the period was a little longer. The younger the child, the quicker he adapts. The high school student has more difficulty, and his sense of frustration with the language barrier is more keenly felt.

In New York City, where the emphasis on bilingual education is transitional rather than maintenance, children are not retained in the bilingual or ESL programs if they can move on. There is constant movement in and out of the programs as new immigrants come to the school and the "graduates" move out. Loose guidelines state that students should complete their transition within two years.

LANGUAGE: A CREATIVE AND PSYCHOLOGICAL FORCE

In the haste to gain a tool whereby one can begin to deal with one's new environment, other facets of language that should be taken into account are often lost. According to Dean Marta Sotomayer (1977) of the University of Houston School of Social Work, language has many functions other than that of communication.

> The mental function determines the perception and definition of reality. Language is the intermediary of ideas, which allows people not only to think in that language, but also to think through the vehicle of language itself. Thus, it is a creative force, molding one's thoughts and inevitably influencing behavior...
> Language is also a cohesive force that promotes a sense of belonging and group solidarity. Psychologically language plays an important role in the formation of the self-concept. It is generally agreed that a positive self-perception is crucial to functioning adequately and comfortably in one's surroundings. The sense of belonging, vital to the development of the self-concept, becomes blurred if one's language, cultural patterns, and ethnic experiences are not reflected and supported, but given a negative connotation. (pp.195-203)

In other words, low self-image, lack of motivation, and unsatisfactory performance are often interrelated in a child who is hampered by a language barrier. Repeat failures can only result in loss of confidence and self-esteem. Children with negative self-images are threatened and frightened by new or demanding tasks. They construct defense mechanisms for protection that may prevent them from being receptive to new experiences. They approach learning with fear and anxiety, which reduces their ability to learn.

Over the three year period that the Chinese bilingual program had been in existence in the Chinatown high school at the time of this research, Chinese student discharges dropped from 114 in 1976 to 77 in 1977 to 32 in 1978. According to the dean of boys, a number of teenagers who had joined gangs were induced to return to school with the implementation of bilingual classes. More students were encouraged to complete their high school education with bilingual and counseling help provided. In assessing the value of bilingual education programs, the evaluators should look at these aspects of the language question as well as at pre-test/post-test reading scores.

This researcher found that the guidance counselors hired with bilingual education funds are the most important components in the bilingual programs. These are the people who keep close watch to spot any impending difficulties and deal with them immediately. For example, if a student is marked absent or late, a call is made to the family to find out why. If a student is out for three days, a visit is paid to the home. If the student is encountering problems with his school work, he is called into the counselor's office for a chat to discover the source of the problem and to deal with it immediately. The counselor keeps track of the student's total setting: himself, his family, his job (if any), and his school work. Such supportive service is one of the most valuable aspects of the bilingual program as presently constituted.

SUMMARY

True Chinese bilingual education programs in New York City's public schools were only implemented in 1975. What passed for bilingual education prior to that was English as a Second Language programs in which immigrant children were taken from their regular classes for special sessions in survival English. Much controversy has revolved around the teaching of subject content in two languages. The differences of opinion have been colored by political considerations, economic issues, ethnocentrism, monetary funding, fears of loss of ethnic identity, and concerns about prospects for the future without a strong base in English. These issues have clouded the fundamental one of whether or not bilingual education is an aid to immigrant children in their adjustment to a new life in this country.

The attitude of the parents and the students toward bilingual education is ambivalent. The students recognize that it helps them learn, and they realize that the side benefits of bilingual education are just as important. At the same time, their impatience to learn English as rapidly as possible and the disdain attached to bilingual classes make them hesitant about the program.

The "fringe benefits" of bilingual education must be assessed along with the learning of English and subject content. Among these benefits are higher student retention rate, more graduates, higher self-esteem that comes with the acceptance of one's own ethnicity, and the scaling of the language barrier that may be an impediment to creativity and psychological well-being.

VIII
Bicultural Conflict

The moment a child is born he begins to absorb the culture of his primary group; these ways are so ingrained they become second nature to him. Imagine for a moment how wrenching it must be for an immigrant child who finds his cumulative life experiences completely invalidated and who must learn a whole new set of speech patterns and behaviors when he settles in a new country. The severity of this culture shock is underlined by Teper's (1977:20) definition of culture:

> Culture is called a habit system in which 'truths' that have been perpetuated by a group over centuries have permeated the unconscious. This basic belief system, from which 'rational' conclusions springs, may be so deeply ingrained that it becomes indistinguishable from human perception—the way one sees, feels, believes, knows. It is the continuity of cultural assumptions and patterns that gives order to one's world, reduces an infinite variety of options to a manageable stream of beliefs, gives a person a firm footing in time and space, and binds the lone individual to the communality of a group.

This researcher found that language barrier was the most common problem among immigrant Chinese. Language looms largest because it is the conduit through which people interact with other people. It is the means by which we think, learn and express ourselves. Less obvious is the basis upon which we speak or act or think. If there are bicultural conflicts, these may engender problems and psychological difficulties which may not be immediately apparent but may nevertheless impact on the development of immigrant children.

This chapter highlights some of the cultural conflicts that commonly confront the Chinese child in the home and, particularly, in the schools. Often teachers and parents are not aware of these conflicts and ascribe other meanings or other motives to the child's behavior, frequently in a disapproving fashion. Such censure confuses the child and quite often forces him to choose between what he is taught at home and what is commonly accepted by American society. In his desire to be accepted and to be liked, he may wish to throw off that which is second nature to him. This may cause anguish and pain not only to himself but also to his family. A few specific examples of bicultural conflict are presented below to show how everyday occurrences can result in dilemmas for Chinese immigrant children.

AGGRESSIVENESS

In Chinese culture, the soldier or the man who resorts to violence is at the bottom of the social ladder. The sage or gentleman uses his wits, not his fists, so the Chinese child is taught not to fight. The popular American perception is that the ability to fight is a sign of manhood. Thus, some American fathers will give their sons a few lessons in self-defense at the age of puberty. The Chinese parent teaches his son the exact opposite: Stay out of fights (Sollenger, 1968:17). However, when the Chinese child goes to the school playground, he may become the victim of bullies who call him a "sissy". Some teenagers can be tough and cruel. Yet, if the child chooses to fight and goes home with a black eye and bruises, his parents chastise him. What is he to do? The unresolved conflict about aggressive behavior is a major problem for Chinese American males. They feel that their masculinity has been affected by their childhood upbringing.

In some instances, teachers or monitors are derisive of the Chinese boys. "Why don't the Chinese fight back?" they exclaim. "Why do they stand there and take it?" This derision only shames the Chinese boys, who feel their courage is questioned. This bicultural conflict may be reflected in the self-hatred of some Asian American male activists who condemn the passivity of their forefathers in response to the discrimination and oppression they endured. Ignorant about their cultural heritage, these activists want to disassociate themselves from such "weakness", and they search for historical instances in which Asians put up a brave but costly and oftentimes futile fight to prove their manhood. The outbreak of gang violence may be another manifestation of the Chinese male's efforts to prove that he is "macho". He may be overcompensating for the derision that he has suffered.

SEXUALITY

In American public schools, sexuality is a very strong and pervasive force. Boys and girls begin noticing each other in the junior highs. At the high school level, sexual awareness is very pronounced. School is as much a place for male/female association as it is an institution for learning. Not so for the Chinese. Education is highly valued, and it is serious business. Interest in the opposite sex is highly distracting and, according to some old-fashioned parents, is improper. Dating is an unfamiliar concept and sexual attractiveness is underplayed, not flaunted as it is according to American ways.

This difference in attitudes and customs poses a dilemma for Chinese boys and girls. In school, the white, black or Hispanic girls talk about clothes, makeup and dates. They talk about brassiere size and tampons. The popular girl is the sexy one who dates the most. She is the envy of the other girls.

For the Chinese girl, this openness is extremely embarrassing. Chinese girls used to bind their breasts, not show them off in tight sweaters. Their attitude toward the opposite sex is quite ambivalent. They feel they are missing something very exciting, yet they will shy away and feel uncomfortable if boys show an interest in them.

Most Chinese parents have had no dating experience. Their marriages were, by and large, arranged by their own parents or through matchmakers. Good girls simply did not go out alone with boys, so the parents are suspicious and apprehensive about their daughters dating, and they watch them very carefully. Most Chinese girls are not permitted to date. For the daring girl who tries to go out against her parents' wishes, there will be a price to pay. It is no easier for Chinese boys. The pressure to succeed in school is even greater than for girls, and parental opposition to dating is even more intense. Yet, these children are bombarded by television, advertisements, stories, magazines, and real-life examples of boy-girl attraction. The teenager undergoes puberty and experiences the instinctive urges surging within him or her. In this society they are titillated, whereas in China they are kept under wraps until they are married.

The problem is exacerbated when teachers make fun of Chinese customs and parents. In one instance at one of the Chinatown schools, a young Chinese girl had been forbidden by her parents to walk to school with a young Puerto Rican boy. To make sure that the parents were being obeyed, the grandmother would walk behind the girl as she went to school. Grandma even stayed until her granddaughter went into class, and then she would peer through the window to make sure all was proper before she went home. Naturally, this was embarrassing for the girl, and it must have been noticed by the homeroom teacher. He exploded in anger at the little old lady and made some rather uncomplimentary remarks about this being the United States and Chinese customs should have been left behind in China. This teacher's attitude and remarks could only push the daughter farther from her parents. He should have explained to the girl, or even to the entire class, the cultural values and traditions of her parents, so that the girl could understand how they thought and why they behaved in such a fashion. Putting down the parents and their customs is the worst thing he could have done.

SPORTS

The Chinese attitude about sports is illustrated by an oft-told tale about two Englishmen who were considered somewhat mad. The two lived in Shanghai where they had gone to do business. In the afternoons, they would each take a raquet, go out in the hot sun, and bat a fuzzy ball across the net. As they ran back and forth across the court, sweat would pour down their faces, and they would be exhausted at the end of the game. To the Chinese onlookers standing on the side, this was sheer lunacy. They would shake their heads in disbelief and ask: "Why do these crazy Englishmen work so hard? They can afford to hire coolies to run around and hit the ball for them." The Chinese attitude towards sports has changed considerably, but it still does not assume the importance that it enjoys in American life.

In the traditional Chinese way of thinking, development of the mental faculties is more important than development of the physique. The image of a scholar is one with a sallow face and long fingernails indicating that he spent long hours with his books and did not have to do physical labor. Games that require physical prowess such as football and boxing were not even played in China. *Kung fu* or other disciplines of the martial arts did not call for physical strength as much as concentration, skill, and agility. In the minds of many Chinese, sports are viewed as frivolous play and a waste of time and energy. Add to this the generally smaller physique of the Chinese immigrant student in comparison to his classmates, and we do not find many of them on school teams.

What does this mean to the Chinese immigrant student, especially the boys? On the one hand, they may think that the heavy emphasis upon sports is a displaced value. They may want to participate, but are either too small in stature or unable to devote the practice time necessary to make the school teams. If the "letter men" are the "big wheels", the Chinese student will feel that his kind are just the little guys. But most important of all, an entire dimension of American school life is lost to the Chinese immigrant children.

TATTLING

Should one report a wrongdoing? Should one tell the teacher that a schoolmate is cheating on an exam? Should one report to the school authorities that a fellow student is trying to extort money from him? The American values on this are ambiguous and confusing. For example, in the West Point scandal a few years ago, most of the cadets involved were not cheaters themselves, but they knew about the cheating and did not report it to the authorities. The honor code required that they tell, but the unwritten code among their fellow cadets said that they should not. If they had reported the cheating they would have been socially ostracized.

This bicultural conflict was noted by Denise Kandel and Gerald S. Lesser (1972) in their book *Youth in Two Worlds*, in which their reference groups were Danish and American children. Danish children, like the Chinese, feel duty bound to report a wrongdoing. There is no dichotomy of consequences here. Authorities and peers are consistent in their attitude in this respect, and this consistency helps to maintain social control. The teacher cannot be expected to see everything. Parents cannot be aware of everything their children are doing during the day. If the siblings or schoolmates will help by reporting wrongdoing, the task of teaching the child is shared and made easier for the adults. But when social ostracism stands in the way of enforcing ethnic values, an intense conflict ensues and contributes to the breakdown of social control.

DEMONSTRATION OF AFFECTION

A commonly voiced concern among Chinese children is, "My parents do not love me. They never kiss or hug me. They are so cold, distant, and remote." The children long for human warmth and affection because they see it on the movie and television screens, and they read about it in books and magazines. Because their family experiences are so formal and distant, they come to the conclusion that love is lacking. In China, where such behavior is the norm, children do not question it. But in this country, where expressions of affection are outwardly effusive and commonly exhibited, they feel deprived.

This lack of demonstrative affection extends also to the spouse and friends. To the Chinese, physical intimacy and love are private matters never exhibited in public. Even in handshaking, the traditional Chinese way was to clasp one's own hands in greeting. Kissing and hugging a friend would be most inappropriate, and to kiss one's spouse in public would be considered shameless.

Nevertheless, Chinese children in this country are attracted to the physical expressions of love and affection. While they crave it for themselves, they are often unable to reciprocate or be demonstrative in their relations with their own friends and, later on, their own spouses and children because of their detached emotional upbringing.

In the schools, this contrast in cultures is made all the sharper because of the large numbers of Hispanics in the same schools. In general, Hispanics are very outgoing and are not the least bit inhibited about embracing, holding hands, or kissing even a casual acquaintance. The Chinese children may interpret these gestures of friendliness as overstepping the bounds of propriety, but more often than not they wish they could shed their reserve shells and reach out to others in a more informal manner. On the other hand, the aloofness of Chinese students is often wrongly interpreted as unfriendliness, standoffishness, or as a desire to keep apart. If all the students were made aware of these cultural differences, they would not misread the intentions and behaviors of one another.

EDUCATION

That education is a highly prized cultural value among the Chinese is commonly known, and that Chinese children generally do well scholastically may be due to the hard push parents exert in this direction. None of this means, however, that these children do not experience a bicultural conflict regarding education when they see that the bright student is not always the one who is respected in American schools. Labels such as "bookworm", "egghead", and "teacher's pet" are often applied to intelligent students. When parents urge their children to study hard and get good grades, the children know that the payoff may not be social acceptance by their schoolmates. The rewards are not consistent with values taught at home.

Nevertheless, Chinese immigrant high school students indicated in their survey questionnaire that they prized the opportunity to get an education. In fact, they identified the opportunity to get a free education as one of the most important reasons for their satisfaction with their school work – of 143 students who said that they were satisified with their school work, 135 mentioned this one factor. Education in China, Hong Kong or Taiwan is attained at great personal sacrifice on the part of the parents and by diligence and industry on the part of the student. In this country, school is free through high school; everyone must go to school until sixteen years of age in New York. It is not a matter of students trying to gain admittance by passing rigorous entrance exams, but a matter of authorities trying to keep dropout rates low that characterizes the educational system here. Since education is free and easy to obtain, it is often taken lightly.

New York academic standards are lower than those in Hong Kong or Taiwan, and the school work is easier. As a result, there is less distinction attached to staying in school or graduating. What the Chinese immigrant students prize highly has less value in the larger society, and again newcomers to this country have doubts about the goals for which they are striving.

THRIFT

Approximately eighteen banks are found within the core of New York's Chinatown. When the Manhattan Savings Bank opened a new branch in October 1977 it attracted to its coffers $3 million within a few months' time. Most of the large banks are aware that Chinatown is fertile ground for the accumulation of capital because the Chinese tend to save more of what they earn than most other ethnic groups in America in spite of the fact that their earnings are small. The savings grow because of two major factors. One is the sense of insecurity common to immigrants, who need a cushion for the uncertainties that they acutely feel. The other is the esteem with which thrift is regarded by the Chinese. A person who is frugal is thought of more highly than one who sports material symbols of success.

The value placed upon thrift poses acute bicultural conflict for Chinese immigrant children who see all about them evidence of an economic system that encourages the accumulation and conspicuous consumption of material possessions. A very important segment of the consumer market is the teenage population. The urge to have stylish clothes, stereos, cameras, hi-fi radios, sports equipment, and even cars creates a painful conflict in the child who is enticed by television and other advertising media, but whose parents reserve a large percentage of their meager earnings for saving in the banks.

In school, the girl who gets money to spend on fashionable dresses and the latest rock records often feels more poised and confident than do her less materially fortunate classmates. She is also admired, complimented, and envied. In the Chinese community, on the other hand, a Chinese girl who spends a lot of money on clothes and frivolities would soon be the object of grapevine gossip, stigmatized as a less-than-desirable prospective wife or daughter-in-law, whereas praises would be sung for the more modestly dressed girl who saved her money.

Chinese students sometimes complain about their parents being "money-hungry". They give their children very little spending money. They do not buy fashionable clothing; rather, they buy only servicable garments in which the children are ashamed to be seen. The Chinese home is generally not furnished for comfort or aesthetics, so when Chinese children visit the homes of their non-Chinese friends and compare them with their own living quarters, they feel deprived and ashamed of their family. They certainly do not want to bring their friends home, and teenagers may themselves stay away from home as much as possible, feeling more comfortable with their peers in clubhouses or on the streets. The contrast in spending attitudes between the underdeveloped economy from which many Chinese immigrants have come and the American economy which emphasizes mass and even wasteful consumption is very sharp, and it creates many an unresolved conflict in the immigrant children, who do not realize that cultural differences lay behind it. They may think that their parents value money more than they care for their children, and exhibit this by denying them material possessions that give them pleasure and status in the eyes of their peers.

Credit is another concept foreign to immigrants from the Far East. If one does not have the money, one should not be tempted to buy. Credit is borrowing money, and borrowing should be resorted to only in extreme emergencies. The buy now, pay later idea goes against the Chinese grain. So Chinese families postpone buying until they have saved enough to cover the entire purchase price. This attitude is fairly common even when it comes to the purchase of a home. The Chinese family will scrimp and economize, putting aside a large portion of its income for this goal, denying small pleasures for many, many years until the large sum is accumulated. To the Chinese way of thinking, this singleness of purpose shows character, but to the more hedonistic American mind, this habit of thrift may appear asinine or unnecessary.

DEPENDENCY

In her study "Socialization Patterns among the Chinese in Hawaii", Nancy F. Young (1972) noted the prolonged period of dependency of the children commonly found in the child-rearing practices of the Chinese in Hawaii. She wrote:

> Observations of Chinese families in Hawaii indicate that both immigrant and local parents utilize child-rearing techniques that result in parent-oriented, as opposed to peer-oriented behavior...Chinese parents maximize their control over their children by limiting their experiences with models exhibiting non-sanctioned behavior.

Analyzing and comparing the results of the Chance Independence Training Questionnaire that she administered to six ethnic groups and local (American born Chinese) as well as immigrant Chinese, Young found the mean age of independence training for American born Chinese to be the lowest while that for immigrant Chinese to be the highest (*See*, Table 8-1).

Immigrant mothers exercise constant and strict supervision over their children. They take their children wherever they go, and babysitters are unheard of. They prefer their children to stay home

TABLE 8-1
Mean Age of Independence Training for Selected Ethnic Groups

Ethnic Stock	Mean Age of Independence Training
Local Chinese (American born)	6.78
Jew	6.83
Protestant	6.87
Negro	7.23
Greek	7.67
French-Canadian	7.99
Italian	8.03
Immigrant Chinese	8.85

Source: N.F. Young, 1972.

rather than go out to play with friends. Friends are carefully screened by the mother, and the child is not expected to do things for himself until two years beyond the mean age that a Jewish mother would expect her child to do for himself. On the other hand, American born Chinese parents expect their children to cut the apron strings sooner than any of the other ethnic groups surveyed.

However, there are areas of dependence and independence in which Young found divergence. The immigrant Chinese child is expected to be able to take care of himself at an earlier age, but he is discouraged from socializing with people outside of the family until a much later age.

The extremes exhibited between the American born and immigrant Chinese may be indicative of bicultural conflict that the Chinese in this country feel. As children, they may have felt that their parents were overprotective; this was frequently mentioned by the teachers in this study. Evidence of this was observed in elementary schools in the practice of mothers coming to the school from the garment factories during their own lunch hours to feed their children. Many walked their children to and from school, even at the junior high level, but it was not clear whether the parents were justifiably afraid for their children's safety from the gangs or whether they were being overprotective. Teachers thought the mothers were smothering the children and restricting their freedom of action. By adolescence, the children must have felt the same. They were chafing against parental control over what they presumed to be their own business, while the parents thought they were merely doing their parental duty. Teachers and parents do not agree on this score, thus parental authority is often undermined by a teacher's scoffing attitude.

RESPECT FOR AUTHORITY

The Chinese value of respect for one's elders and for authority is common knowledge and needs no further elaboration here. Already mentioned is that Chinese immigrant children encountering the disrespect accorded teachers and school authorities for the first time in American classrooms become upset and dismayed. In interviews with students, this concern was voiced frequently.

Challenge against established authority has been a notable feature of youth culture over the past two decades. Parents, teachers, the police, the government, the church—all authority figures in the past—have been belittled and even reviled. Violence against teachers is a leading problem in schools across the nation. If students do not have respect for the teacher, neither will they have respect for the knowledge that the teacher tries to impart. The issue is a disturbing one, not only for the immigrant children but for the entire American society as well.

HEROES AND HEROINES

Who are the people that are praised, admired, looked up to, and revered? This varies with cultures, and the values of a society may be deduced from the type of people who are respected and emulated in that culture. In the United States, the most popular figures are movie, television and stage stars, sports figures, politicians, successful authors, inventors, and scientists, probably in that order. Who are the heroes and heroines of China? Using literature as a guide, they are the filial sons or daughters, the sacrificing mother, the loyal minister, the patriot or war hero who saves his country, and revolutionaries who overthrow despotic rulers and set up their own dynasties. Even in modern-day China, the persons honored and emulated are the self-sacrificing workers who put nation above self.

Priests, ministers and rabbis once commanded prestige in this country, but the status of these men of God has declined. In

China, monks or priests have always occupied lowly positions. In contrast to the United States, in China actors were "riff-raff". Women did not act in the theater, so men had to play the female roles. Western influence has brought about changes in the pseudo-Chinese cultures of Hong Kong and Singapore where stage performers and movie stars are now popular and emulated.

As a rule, Chinese heroes and heroines were people of high moral virtues, and they set the standards of conduct for others. In this country, the more sensational the exposé of the private lives of our national leaders or entertainment figures, the more our curiosity is aroused. How movie stars retain their popularity despite the relentless campaigns to expose them is very difficult for someone not brought up in the United States to comprehend. An old adage says, "No man is a hero to his valet". Yet, the very fact that American heroes and heroines survive and thrive on notoriety and self-confession can only mean that the American people secretly admire such behavior. One might say, Chinese heroes are saints; American heroes are sinners.

INDIVIDUALISM

Dr. Francis L.K. Hsu, noted anthropologist, has written extensively about individualism as a prominent characteristic of American life. According to Dr. Hsu (1960, 1972) the basic ingredient of rugged individualism is self-reliance. The individual constantly tells himself and others that he controls his own destiny and that he does not need help from others. The individual-centered person enjoins himself to find means of fulfilling his own desires and ambitions.

Individualism is the driving force behind the competitiveness and creativity that has pushed this nation forward. Loose family ties, superficial human relationships, little community control, and weak traditions have given the individual leeway to strike out on his own without being hindered by sentimentality, convention, and tradition. Self-interest has been a powerful incentive.

In contrast, Dr. Hsu contends, the Chinese are situation-centered. Their way of life encourages the individual to find a satisfactory adjustment with the external environment of men and things. The Chinese individual sees the world in relativistic terms. He is dependent upon others and others are dependent upon him. Like bricks in a wall, one lends support to the other and they all hold up the society as a whole. If even one brick becomes loose, the wall is considerably weakened; interlocked, the wall is strong. The wall is the network of human relations. The individual subordinates his own wishes and ambitions for the common good.

Dr. Kenneth Abbott, in his book *Harmony and Individualism*, also points out that Western ideas of creativity and individualism are not accented in Chinese and must be held within accepted norms. One of the reasons for this is the importance ascribed to maintenance of harmony. Harmony is the key concept in all relationships between god(s) and man and between man and man. It is the highest good.

To the Chinese, the sense of duty and obligation takes precedence over self-gratification (it is not uncommon to find Chinese teenagers handing over their entire paychecks to their parents for family use or for young Chinese males to pursue a course of study chosen for them by their parents rather than one of their own choosing). Responsibility toward distant kin is more keenly felt by the Chinese than by Americans. Honor and glory accrue not only to the individual but to all those who helped him climb the ladder. This sense of being part of something greater than oneself gives the Chinese a feeling of belonging and security in the knowledge that they do not stand alone. On the other hand, individual freedom of action is very much restricted.

The foregoing are but examples of the many areas of bicultural conflicts that confront a newcomer to these shores. In sum, they are:

Chinese children are brought up to refrain from aggressive behavior, whereas the masculine image in this country often stresses the macho type. Chinese males are particularly troubled by this bicultural conflict.

Sexual attractiveness is expressed subtly according to Chinese custom, whereas it is stressed according to American customs. This is an area of special concern for the high school age Chinese American female.

Sports are a consuming pastime for the American people, whereas it takes a backseat to scholastic achievement for the Chinese.

Chinese children feel that they are duty-bound to report wrong-doing; yet tattling is a serious offense in the eyes of their American peers.

Chinese children in this country are attracted by the physical expressions of love and affection customary here, but they are inhibited by their less demonstrative upbringing. At the same time, they may question their parents' love in light of the more overt affection they observe among their peers' parents.

Education and scholastic achievement are not as highly valued in the United States as they are in China.

Thrift is a worthy character trait according to the Chinese way of thinking, whereas conspicuous consumption is favored in the United States. The two ways of thinking are imcompatible and cause conflict for Chinese children.

Immigrant Chinese parents do not encourage early independence in their children. They discourage their children from socializing outside the family until a much later age than do other ethnic groups.

Immigrant Chinese children find it hard to accept the lack of respect for authority—especially toward teachers—among their peers in school.

Chinese heroes and heroines tend to be persons of high moral caliber. American idols tend to be entertainment figures, sports stars, or persons who have achieved tangible success in terms of wealth and material attainment. The more sensational the private lives of these people, the more they attract public attention.

The Chinese try to fit themselves into the scheme of things whereas the American way is based on individualism.

Such better known examples of cultural conflict as respect for elders, modesty and humility, male superiority, and others have been omitted here because they have been dealt with at length elsewhere.

MARGINALITY

There are two divergent trains of thought regarding cultural conflict. Robert E. Park first coined the term "marginal man" for this predicament. Park, in the *International Encyclopedia of the Social Sciences* (1968, vol.4: 427) stressed that "marginal men are—precisely because of their ambiguous position from a cultural, ethnic, linguistic, or sociostructural standpoint—strongly motivated to make creative adjustments in situations of change, and in the course of this adjustment process, to develop innovations in social behavior." However, the evidence is not clear. Marginal individuals are more prone to succumb to anomie and thus become carriers of social disorganization rather than creative change. Everett Stonequist, in his work *The Marginal Man* (1937:3-4,8), brings out the latter veiwpoint. He wrote:

> The marginal personality is most clearly portrayed in those individuals who are unwittingly initiated into two or more historic traditions, languages, political, loyalties, moral codes, or religions. This occurs, for instance, as a result of migration...

> When the standards of two or more social groups come into active contrast or conflict, the individual who is identified with both groups experiences the conflict as an acute personal difficulty or mental tension...

> So the marginal man...is one who is poised in psychological uncertainty between two (or more) social worlds; reflecting in his soul the discords and harmonies, repulsions and attractions of these worlds, one of which is often 'dominant' over the other; within which membership is implicitly if not explicitly based upon birth or ancestry (race or nationality); and where exclusion removes the individual from a system of group relations.

Adults tend to perceive their marginality as a sense of wanting to be accepted members of a group or groups and conversely a sense of exclusion from such groups. Children, on the other hand, perceive of their marginality as a dilemma. They are faced with a situation where courses of action are diametrically opposed or radically different. They do not see the dilemma as rising from cultural differences; they just see it as an impasse. The choices are painful and more often than not immobilizing. Not having the maturity to evaluate or modify their courses of action or to adjust their values, they do nothing; the vacuousness of their indecision or their inability to decide is extremely uncomfortable.

For Chinese immigrant children who live in New York's Chinatown or in the satellite Chinatowns, these conflicts are moderated to a large degree because there are other Chinese children around to mitigate the dilemmas that they encounter. When they are among their own, the Chinese ways are better known and better accepted. The Chinese customs and traditions are not denigrated to the degree that they would be if the immigrant child were the only one to face the conflict on his or her own. Even so, teachers and parents should be made aware of these conflicts to avoid exacerbating the differences and to inculcate in both the Chinese and non-Chinese a healthy respect for cultural differences.

Robert Park's sanguine outlook, however, leads us to expect that discomfort, generated by the conditions of the marginal state, may lead to new forms of adaptive behavior more in tune with the changed environment in a new homeland. To him, marginality is the soil from which creative change sprouts.

IX

After-School Hours

Even at the elementary school level, children hurry off to the garment factories right after school. That is where Mother is, and they go to join her or to report to her for assignment of their daily chores before going home to an empty apartment. Many of the children stay beside Mother's sewing machine doing homework or helping her ready garments for sewing. The bosses do not object to the children being underfoot; they accept the daily presence of children after three o'clock as the normal course of events. After the children finish their homework, and if they do not have work to do, they play with each other among the empty boxes or between the bundles of garments piled high.

ELEMENTARY LEVEL

Children aged ten, eleven or twelve often are given jobs that become steady employment for them, such as putting plastic bags over finished garments, turning belts inside out, cutting threads, or folding finished garments. They are paid a penny or two for each garment hung or for each belt turned. On average days, they earn two to three dollars, which is added to the mother's paycheck.

The hours worked depend upon the season and how long the mother chooses to work. Garment workers are paid on a piece-rate basis so the mother can generally set her own hours. When there is a rush job or a deadline on a shipment, however, the boss asks the women to stay until the job is finished.

Besides working at garment factories children perform other work as well. These include delivering take-out orders for restaurants, peeling onions and shrimp, making won-ton or meat dumplings, filling small containers with soy sauce or mustard, sweeping out stores, or running errands. The variety of jobs are endless, and more often than not they are performed for relatives or parents who own the restaurant or store. One must have some kind of family connection to get a job.

JUNIOR HIGH LEVEL

At the junior high school level, however, parents expect children to contribute to the family income. At the junior high in Chinatown, six children out of the fourteen who were in the seventh grade orientation class (the class for the most recent immigrants) were interviewed. This is what was discovered:

Student 1: Girl. Helps mother in factory until 8:00 p.m. daily. Does not have to, but wants to be close to her mother.
Student 2: Girl. Six members in family. Mother and three older sisters work in garment factory. She helps after school. Father dead.
Student 3: Girl. Does not work but would like to get a job.
Student 4: Girl. Does not work. Father works for American employer as a chef.
Student 5: Girl. Nine members in family. Parents, three older sisters, and grandmother work in garment factory. Younger members go after school. All finish at 5:00 or 6:00 p.m. They go home, cook and eat together.
Student 6: Boy. Five in family. All work at the same factory, including older brother, 17, and younger sister, 10. He is 14.

In a seventh grade class, the teacher asked who held jobs after school. Of the 71 students, 20 worked and 4 went to Chinese school. It seems that the more recent immigrant families are very anxious for their children to work, most likely because of economic necessity brought on by the huge expenses incurred for transportation and relocation.

At the Chinatown junior high school, a number of teachers mentioned that the children were very sleepy in the mornings. At first they thought the children stayed up late watching television, but discovered that they had worked until late at night. One Chinese American teacher commented:

The immigrant Chinese are very conscious of money. Money seems to be the overwhelming goal in their lives. They work very hard and they expect the children to help out. Once a teenager gets the feel of money in his hands, he wants to go to work and he wants to drop out, especially if he is having difficulty with the language and his school work.

Fortunately, the parents want their children to finish school, but at the same time, the children are expected to contribute to the family expenses.

In the satellite community schools, the children are located far from the heavy concentration of garment factories and restaurants found in Chinatown. Work was not readily available for these youngsters. Besides, as previously noted, the suburban immigrants usually have more of a financial cushion and are not as frantic about economic security. Only a few students from the elementary or junior high schools in the satellite community had after-school jobs.

HIGH SCHOOL LEVEL

In the high schools, there were two sources of data regarding the extent of after-school employment. Neither is based on scientific sampling, but both are indicative of the overall situation. One was the records kept by the bilingual program guidance counselor consisting of 435 students in the bilingual program in the Chinatown high school for the year 1976. Over 80 percent of these students indicated that they worked twenty hours or more per week, and 43 percent said that it was necessary for them to contribute to the support of the family. The other source was the survey questionnaire administered in the same school in 1978. These are not exactly the same students, although there may be some overlap. Tabulation of the hours spent by the 270 students surveyed showed that approximately one-half of the Chinatown high school students worked sixteen hours or more and about one-fifth worked twenty-five hours or more per week (See, Table 9-1). On the other hand, about one-third did not work at all. Since groups from these two sources are not identical, the figures are not comparable. In interviews, however, this researcher gained the impression that the students put in a substantial number of hours at jobs. Fewer satellite community high school students worked at regular jobs and not many had household chores either. It was presumed that since the mothers worked, the domestic chores would have been relegated to the children, but this turned out not to be so. Either the mothers shouldered the extra burden or household duties were neglected.

TABLE 9-1

Weekly Hours Spent on Job, Chores, or Television by Chinatown
and Satellite Community High School Students

Hours	C.T.	Job Sat.	Total	C.T.	Chores Sat.	Total	Television
	N=199	N=71	N=270	N=199	N=71	N=270	N=270
0	31%	61%	39%	45%	51%	47%	26%
1-5	5	1	4	22	21	21	14
6-10	6	7	6	16	10	14	22
11-15	11	1	8	9	8	9	24
16-20	16	3	13	3	1	3	11
21-25	12	10	11	3	4	3	3
25+	20	17	19	3	4	3	0

Source: Student Survey Questionnaire, 1978.

ECONOMIC VALUE OF CHILDREN

To many onlookers or well-meaning persons, the long hours worked—even by very young children—in the garment factories or at other jobs smack of child labor or child exploitation. In the United States, children are not expected to contribute to the family purse, and when they are utilized to produce economically, social disapprobation is strong.

In agrarian or other societies, a child's contribution to the family gives him a sense of worth. At an early age, children are given responsibility for household chores. As they grow older, they are expected to participate in the family economic enterprise, which may be on the farm, at a trade, or in the shop. "The evolution of our society from a rural to an urban-based family system, from an extended to nuclear family system, and from a labor intensive to a machine economy has made the children no longer an economic asset", writes Orville Brim (1979:p.2). Thus, "We are, in this nation, moving into an era that may be historically the most precarious for America's children....Marked increases in the cost of raising a child cause individual parents, and the economy generally, to view child-bearing and children-rearing as an economic liability, in competition with other values." The lower economic value of children is clearly reflected in the declining fertility ratio. In 1880, the average number of children per woman of childbearing age was seven (Beels, 1976:9). In the 1980s, the number is less than two (U.S. Bureau of the Census, 1980).

Although the working hours of Chinese children in Chinatown may be long and tiresome, the children do gain by feeling that they are productive and helpful to the family unit. They are kept busy so they do not have time to get into mischief. At the same time, they are not only under the watchful eyes of their mothers but of a host of other women in the factories as well. Their upbringing is diffused and shared by the mother's co-workers. For instance, if a child gets too rambunctious, the ladies might admonish him to stop running around and go help his mother. "Can't you see how hard she is working?" These words instill a sense of duty to the mother and discourage the child from being too rowdy. If a child is balky and disobedient, the disapproval of a score of ladies nearby will lighten the mother's task of child-rearing because she has a support group to back up her authority. Too often, in the nuclear family, the mother is almost alone in her responsibility of child-rearing, and the isolation in itself can become an overwhelming burden.

RECREATION

In the lower grades, the children invariably reported that they had few recreational outlets after school. Their one most important pastime was watching television. The streets certainly were not safe for play. Watching television is not unique to Chinese immigrant children. According to the Neilson reports, preschoolers in the United States watch an average of thirty-three hours of television per week. Six to eleven-year-olds average twenty-nine hours, while teenagers get in from twenty-four to twenty-six hours. Probably because of long hours spent at jobs, Chinese teenagers do not watch much television.

Aside from going to the movies occasionally, watching television, participating in sports, and reading for pleasure, the high school students indicated that they had few other recreational outlets. Very few went to dances, parties, or social events. In fact, the lack of recreation for these young people is striking. Chinese student clubs and organizations at high schools or colleges used to sponsor dances or parties, but since 1971 gang intrusion into social events and dances have all but stopped these activities. If thwarted, gang members would brandish guns, and on a number of occasions "shot up the place". Thus, Chinese American clubs no longer dare to have dances. So there are few opportunities for young people to get together.

The effects of this vacuum can be deleterious to these young people who have little opportunity to acquire the social graces and ease needed to associate and deal with people. As one Chinese American principal put it, "Our youth are becoming 'socially retarded'". This lack of finesse in the social sphere becomes apparent only when these young people go out to work after graduation from high school or college. In a survey of City College of New York graduates conducted by this writer, many of those interviewed mentioned their lack of social graces and contacts as a huge barrier to career advancement.

AFTER-SCHOOL CENTERS

For some of the Chinese children in Chinatown, the school day extends from 8:30 a.m. to 6:00 p.m. In the morning, free breakfast is served to provide the children with enough energy to get through the morning. Hot, nutritious lunches are also served at midday. In January 1979, at the Chinatown elementary school of this study, 809 out of the 847 students were signed up for free breakfast and 795 for free lunch. At the Chinatown junior high school 200 out of a total of 470 students were served free breakfast and 400 were served free lunch.

The principal of the elementary school said, "Some people say that we are surrogate parents in feeding the children two meals out of three, but I don't mind doing these things even if they are not properly within the province of the school. Children used to pass out in the mornings before we served breakfast. I would like to see these services coordinated under the school."

When the three o'clock bell rings, the normal pattern for many American school children is to go home, eat a snack, go out to play or do chores, wash up, eat dinner, do homework, watch television for a while, and go to bed. For the Chinese children there are four main activities: go to the factory where mother is, go to Chinese school, go home and do homework and chores or watch television, or go to an after-school center.

Most of the after-school centers are located right in the schools, utilizing school facilities to look after the children until the parents come for them at 6:00 p.m. The Chinatown Planning Council (CPC) operates the largest after-school programs in seven of the public schools enrolling large numbers of Chinese children. The centers pick up right where schools leave off. As soon as the children come into the center, they are served a nutritious snack consisting of juice or milk, fruit or raw vegetables and cookies or sometimes Chinese pastries.

The children are expected to do their homework while teachers and tutors supervise. After the homework is done, the children can play, do arts and crafts, take part in skits, and have music lessons. In some of the after-school centers, Chinese lessons are offered. The Chinatown Planning Council after-school centers are staffed by professional personnel, and they provide a secure, creative, and healthy experience for the children of working parents. In addition, a family service worker maintains contact with the families to provide referral services for other problems that may arise.

The facilities of the seven CPC after-school centers can accomodate approximately 1,000 children and the waiting lists are long. The fee is based upon a sliding scale; parents pay what they can, but most pay very little. Another 500 children attend after-school centers run by churches and other voluntary organizations. Some are funded and some are not. Those endowed with little money can serve only as baby-sitting agencies. They cannot provide the professional supervision that the other after-school centers can. The 1,500 slots available are a long way from meeting the needs of the applicants for such services. Parents who cannot get their children admitted to the after-school centers must either take them to the factories or restaurants where they work, leave them at home to fend for themselves, or leave the children to look for other after-school diversions with their peers.

DAY CARE

Day-care center facilities for preschoolers are equally scarce. As of 1978, only three centers—the Chinatown Day Care Center, the Hamilton Madison House Day Care, and the Educational Alliance—accommodated about 250 children. In our research in the community, we came across many horror stories of children left alone in apartments. One, a two-year-old girl, was tied up in front of the television everyday. Her mother would come back occasionally to check on her. Another three year old girl took care of herself, spending her time with the television from morning until her sisters came home from school at 3:00 p.m. A ten-year-old boy was discovered by the school principal to be living alone. His father worked in Philadelphia and came to New York once a week to look in on his son.

YOUTH CENTERS

Places where older children can go after school hours are in a constant state of flux. The Community Service Society withdrew from Chinatown in 1976. A Youth Consortium consisting of Project Reach, Project Hing Dai (Big Brother-Little Brother), and Young Life was aborted in 1978 when funding was cut off by the Criminal Justice Coordinating Council of the City of New York. Only Project Reach was retained under the aegis of the Chinatown Planning Council. A new group, Better Chinatown Project, was founded in 1978 and is housed in an old school building. These two organizations still provide services like, tutoring, counseling, recreation, arts and crafts, music and painting, and an opportunity for young people to get together in a supervised, wholesome atmosphere. The Chinese Benevolent Association sponsors basketball tournaments in its gym. However, these few facilities are only skeletal and they are far from filling the need.

PARENTAL CONCERN

For the immigrant parents, it is a new experience to leave their children without adult supervision. In the home country, mothers generally did not work, and if they did, invariably there would be any number of relatives or neighbors around to look after the children. Parents are not the only ones who supervise the children's upbringing. Aunts, uncles, grandparents, and older siblings all exert some influence. To have their child unattended or in someone else's care must be a guilt-laden experience for the parents.

SUMMARY OF FINDINGS

A significant number of immigrant children and youth work after school. These even include children at the elementary school level. The hours are long. Of the high school students surveyed, 32 percent in Chinatown and 27 percent in the satellite community worked twenty hours or more per week. One could look at after-school work in two ways. One is that it is a very heavy load leaving little time for recreation or play. The other is that these young people are initiated early into the real world of work. By contributing to the family purse they gain a sense of responsibility and worth. Luckily, the Chinese community provides the opportunity and the jobs in its garment factories and restaurants. Without the availability of these jobs, there might be large numbers of idle youths with time on their hands. The Chinatown youth centers have been in a constant state of flux, here one day and gone the next depending upon uncertain funding. The facilities are skeletal in relationship to need. A few after-school centers serve approximately 1,500 children in Chinatown. These few slots are a long way from meeting the needs of the applicants for such services.

In Chinatown, opportunities for socializing, for sports, or for cultural appreciation are extremely limited. Life for the immigrant child is the serious business of school and work. The little time left is spent watching television. The streets are unsafe and social activities, like parties and dances, are few. The lack of experience in knowing how to relate to other people in a social setting may result in what one Chinese American principal of a New York City high school labeled "social retardation". To him, symptoms of this malady were already quite apparent.

X

The Deviants—Chinatown Gangs

If there are positive forces that help immigrant children in their transition from one culture to another, there are also negative influences that prey upon the weak and vulnerable. The most pernicious of these are the youth gangs that have terrorized the community.[1] Their wanton shooting and killing, their high-handed extortion, their tactics to coerce other youths to join their ranks, and their total disregard for the safety of innocent bystanders have gripped the community in utter and unspeakable fear.

It is no coincidence that the waxing of the youth gangs has accompanied the phenomenal increase in immigration since 1965. Prior to that time, the lack of juvenile offenders among the Chinese had drawn the attention of social scientists and law enforcement officers. Chinese children had been held up as models of behavior, and Chinatown was always the safest neighborhood in the city. In the past, restaurants and businesses stayed open until 1:00 a.m. Now iron gates and metal shutters clang shut over the storefronts at 9:00 p.m.

How does one explain the phenomenon? As long as youth gangs roam the streets, how can we report that Chinese immigrant children are managing quite well after an initial period of difficulty? The answer is that the two groups are separate and apart. The large majority of Chinese immigrant children are in the schools, are serious and concerned about their future, and are taking the conventional route through hard work and education. The gangs' members are more attracted to the lure of easy money, the excitement of the streets, and the camaraderie of the peer

---

[1] *See*, Lee Sung "Gangs in New York's Chinatown" Department of Asian Studies, City College of New York, 1977. This report gives considerable detail about the gang situation, presenting interviews with the police, community leaders, gang members, social or agency workers, and the press. Thus a multifaceted picture of the gangs was drawn by the people who are daily involved with the gang problem.

group. School work takes a backseat to these enticements, and gang members drop out of school or are truant.

What leads some youths astray while most strive diligently to adjust to their new homeland in an exemplary manner? Is there a characteristic profile of the gang member? Are there underlying currents that have given rise to this surge in violent and disruptive behavior? The reasons are many. First among them is the increase in the number of children in the Chinatown community since the liberalization of the immigration laws. As pointed out previously, Chinese children, once a rarity on the American scene, total more than forty thousand in the New York City school system alone. The Chinese American population, once a predominantly adult male society, is now balanced with women and children.

The lack of juveniles naturally means an absence of juvenile delinquents, but the sudden presence of large numbers of young people can embolden those who held back from antisocial behavior before. It is common knowledge that a loner who may hesitate to step out of bounds or protest his treatment will, when part of a crowd, muster courage from the group and behave in a manner quite contrary to his usual self. There is no doubt that the increase in the number of Chinese teenagers has a direct connection with the upsurge in gang activities.

Gang members in New York's Chinatown are almost exclusively foreign-born immigrants who are having difficulty adjusting to a new way of life in a new country. Disillusioned, they find the easy buck more appealing than the laborious tasks of school and work. They may be coerced into joining a gang against their will or may chose to join because the gang fills a void in their lives. Given a sizable number of vulnerable young people, the tongs quickly seized upon the opportunity to advance their own ends. In large measure, the tongs are responsible for the rising incidence of gang activity.

TONGS

The tongs are secret societies engaged in illicit activities such as extortion for protection, gambling, prostitution and drugs. They have been part of the history of the Chinese in the United States since its earliest days (See, Glick and Hong, 1947; Dillon, 1962; Wilson, 1931). They were the highbinders who imported girls for prostitution. They controlled the opium dens and the gambling parlors. They collected money for protection of legitimate as well as illegitimate businesses.

In the United States the image of the Chinese American has been tarnished repeatedly by the tong wars that erupted periodically until the 1930s. Those conflicts persisted as rival tongs sought exclusive control over certain streets of Chinatown and certain segments of the Chinese population. For their own safety, the Chinese had to pay protection money to either one or the other tong. Gambling houses in particular allocated a percentage of their profits to the tongs; likewise the opium dens and houses of prostitution. Hatchetmen, employed by the tongs, enforced the decrees of the tong leaders, or highbinders, by splitting open the skulls of adversaries with hatchets.

Whenever the interests of competing tongs were at odds, open warfare ensued. These wars became so vicious that American authorities threatened to deport en masse the tong leaders and combatants. This deterred the fighting. Common cause in defending China against Japan during World War II united the Chinese in the United States and led to a lull in tong activity from the 1930s until the 1960s.

In New York, there are two main tongs: the Hip Sing and the On Leong. With the huge influx of new immigrants into Chinatown after 1965, the ground was laid for a comeback of the tongs. Opium was a thing of the past; with the sex ratio becoming more balanced among the Chinese, prostitution was unprofitable; but gambling has continued to flourish. Newcomers, with little outlet for recreation in Chinatown, found excitement and thrills in the bones and cards. Long hours and hard work brought them a few dollars, but gambling offered the prospect of getting rich quick. In New York's Chinatown, $600,000 easily passes over the gambling tables weekly.

To protect this flourishing industry, the tongs needed strong-arm bodies; they needed lookouts for raids; they needed guards; they needed escorts for those with large winnings. But more often, they needed people to collect gambling debts. Hatchetmen were passe, whereas young boys, preferably under the age of sixteen, were well suited to their purposes. They were hot-headed and willing to take chances. If caught, they were largely immune from severe punishment since the laws of the state until 1978 were extremely lenient toward youthful offenders. Eighteen months was the maximum sentence for murder, and when the youth reached sixteen his record was wiped clean. Teenagers could literally commit murder with impunity, and many did.

THE MAJOR GANGS

The tongs do not hire boys individually. They contract with a gang leader for the services of the group. Money is paid to the gang leader, and he apportions it to his followers. Gangs fight over who will be in the employ of the tongs, so in addition to aggression on behalf of the gambling houses, each gang also has to defend itself against a possible takeover by another gang.

Being in with the right gang means getting good money: $200 to $300 a week, an astronomical sum to a teenager who could hope to earn only a few dollars washing dishes, waiting on tables, or making deliveries. Some receive more and some receive less depending upon their rank in the gang hierarchy.

Gangs come and go; some may disband, but new ones crop up. Gangs with names like the White Eagles, Quon Yings, and Ernie's Boys had their heyday in the late sixties. By 1971, the Black Eagles and Flying Dragons were the top gangs. The Eagles worked for On Leong, the Dragons for Hip Sing. On Leong has the more profitable turf of Mott Street. Hip Sing controls Pell Street, Division Street, and the Bowery. A lesser gang, the Ghost Shadows, covered East Broadway, Hester Street, and Eldridge Street. In 1973, the Black Eagles enraged the elders of On Leong by extorting money from the same merchants who were paying for protection and by robbing those whom they were paid to protect. The last straw came when an Eagle poured tea down the brocade jacket of an On Leong elder. On Leong withdrew its support from the Black Eagles and installed the Ghost Shadows in their place. The years 1976-1977 were the pinnacle of these two gangs' reign of terror. By 1979, racked by internal dissension, they seemed to be on the way out.

GANG ACTIVITIES

The level and extent of gang activity are well mirrored in the headlines of the New York press. In the late sixties an occasional article would appear in the papers, but the articles increased in frequency as the seventies wore on, indicating stepped-up activity on the part of the gangs. (*See,* Table 10-1).

TABLE 10-1

Gang-Related Arrests of Chinese in New York City's Fifth Police Precinct, 1955-1978

Year	No.	Year	No.	Year	No.
1955	1	1963	8	1971	47
1956	1	1964	3	1972	58
1957	1	1965	9	1973	112
1958	3	1966	8	1974	160
1959	1	1967	21	1975	85
1960	0	1968	13	1976	135
1961	2	1969	59	1977	74
1962	7	1970	58	1978	68

Note: It was impossible to obtain more up-to-date figures after 1978. The officer who had kept such records retired, and his successor did not continue the collection of such statistics.

Source: New York City Police Department, Fifth Precinct.

Instead of confining themselves to protecting gambling interests, the gangs began systematic extortion of legitimate businesses. Either the business made regular payoffs with protection money or the young hoodlums would tear up the store or restaurant, threaten the owner and his family with bodily harm, sit in the premises so that the regular customers would be scared away, eat in the restaurants or take merchandise and not pay, or as an example to others, shoot the hapless proprietor in cold blood.

Few stores in Chinatown escaped the extortionists. The gang members paced the streets and visited the stores frequently, their usual tactic being to ask for a donation for a "brother in need". Most businessmen paid up quietly without reporting to the police. To report the incident meant retaliation from the gangs; not to report and to pay off continuously meant bleeding to death economically. Without report of the incident, there could be no arrest or prosecution. The situation was nightmarish. The gangs had the merchants by the neck and were strangling them slowly.

To insure their control over certain streets in Chinatown, gangs had to defend their territory against other gangs. The resulting gang warfare was the most terrifying prospect of all. It was not uncommon for one gang to swoop down with guns blazing on members from another gang. Innocent bystanders, caught in the crossfires, often were the victims of such confrontations. The savagery of the gangs was expressed most vehemently when the gangs fought one another. They literally hacked away at each other with cleavers and guns. In one instance, a group of Flying Dragons eating in a restaurant were caught off guard by the entrance of a group of Ghost Shadows. Neither group had guns, so some Ghost Shadows ran into the kitchen, grabbed meat cleavers and tried to chop off the leg of a Flying Dragon. The killings resulting from intra or inter-gang rivalries made up most of the murder statistics for deaths attributed to gang violence.

One of the main functions of New York's Chinatown is as a social gathering place for life's important events: births, deaths, and weddings. Wedding banquets in particular bring friends and relatives from all over the country, and they usually come wearing their jewlery and finery. The gangs soon seized upon these occasions to rob guests of their money and jewels. They would brazenly walk in amidst the festivities, ask the guests to drop their jewels and money into shopping bags, and just as brazenly walk out. This tactic was also employed in movie houses. Gang members were known to walk up and down the aisles collecting watches and wallets from patrons. The movie houses consistently denied such activity for fear that such news would hurt their business. They paid the gangs heavily for protection from other gangs, but this did not insure them immunity from their own "protectors" or from other gang members trying for a take over.

In fact, the gang members became so cocky that they often defied the tong leaders themselves, some of whom complained that they had "gotten on the back of a tiger and did not know how to get off". An abortive attempt was made by the tongs to disassociate themselves from the gangs by hiring a white security agency to guard the gambling houses and provide merchants protection from the gangs. The gangs responded by throwing bombs into the tong headquarters and by applying for jobs as guards in the security agency. Merchants quickly recognized behind the new uniforms the faces of those who used to extort money from them as gang members.

POLICE RESPONSE

The police said that their hands were tied. During the period of this fieldwork, only one policeman of Chinese extraction was on the entire city police force. The few that had been hired in a special recruitment campaign were quickly laid off when New York City's budget crunch occurred. Two men in the Fifth Precinct, which covers the principal streets of Chinatown, were assigned to deal with the gangs. They built up thick folders on gang members and probably knew more about them than the gang members knew about themselves. The two detectives walked among the gangs on the streets and knew them by name and by sight. Yet they made few arrests and obtained fewer convictions.

An attempt was made to ascertain the number of arrests from official sources such as the *Uniform Crime Reports* and the computerized crime statistics of the New York Police Department, but these data were so erroneous that they had to be discarded at once. For example, the *Uniform Crime Reports* stated that there were only five Chinese arrests for homicide and attempted homicide in the entire United States in 1976, whereas the Fifth Police Precinct had twenty-seven arrests alone (*See,* Table 10-2).

TABLE 10-2

**Chinese Youth Arrests by Crime in New York City's
Fifth Police Precinct, 1975-1978**

Crime	1975	1976	1977	1978
Murder & Attempted Murder	1	27	5	1
Possession of Weapons	19	38	7	15
Assaults	21	13	2	11
Extortion	0	12	13	10
Robberies	14	27	32	9
Burglaries	9	1	0	5
Rapes	15	0	0	0
Other	6	17	15	17
Total	85	135	74	68

Source: New York City Police Department, Fifth Department.

Table 10-1 attests to the phenomenal increase in arrests of Chinese youths under age twenty-one from the occasional one or a few a year to the hundreds of arrests in the 1970s, but these arrests were only the tip of the iceberg. They in no way reflected the actual perpetration of criminal acts in New York's Chinatown. The merchants and residents were simply too scared to report the crimes, and if they did they would back down immediately if they had to go to the police station to file a complaint or if they had to testify in court. As mentioned previously, juvenile offenders under sixteen years of age usually were given lenient treatment even if convicted. They would soon be back on the streets to exact their revenge. In essence, the gangs almost had *carte blanche* to do whatever they wanted. Over a period of two years (mid-1975 to mid-1977) only one gang member, a Black Eagle, was sentenced to prison for shooting a Ghost Shadow, and he was convicted only because there were two non-Chinese witnesses to the act (Jacobson, 1977:16).

From January to October 1977, over thirty killings were reported in Chinatown, and there have been many more that were not reported (Rice, 1977), but not one resulted in a conviction. A hired assassin stabbed M.B. Lee, unofficial mayor of Chinatown, in the stomach for trying to get the Chinese people to testify in court; Lee survived the attempt on his life. To salvage their authority and respect in the community, the police and city administration launched an all-out campaign to find the criminal; it resulted in Chik Keung Pang's arrest and conviction in March 1978. The capture of the would-be assassin shows that the police can obtain results if a concerted effort is made. In this instance, the criminal had to be brought to justice because the unofficial mayor was trying to help the police. He also had friends in City Hall. If his would-be assassin escaped punishment, the police and city administrators would look like fools. If the same effort had been made toward the thirty other unsolved killings that year, the gangs may not have gotten so far out of hand.

GANG MEMBERSHIP

Gang membership is not large and it fluctuates drastically. The police believe there are only about 200 to 300 members at the most; 150 or less are hard core. But it takes only an isolated few "Sons of Sam" or "Boston Stranglers" to terrorize an entire city, and New York's Chinatown comprises only a few city blocks. According to a member of the Ghost Shadows, there were about 130 members in his gang in 1977, 50 of them females. The Eagles, both White and Black, had a total of about 115 members in their groups. The White Eagles were older; the Black Eagles were usually their younger brothers. The Flying Dragons had 70 to 80 members, 20 to 30 of them girls.

Gang members are constantly on the lookout for new blood to replenish or bolster their ranks. They hang around the high schools and junior highs looking for likely prospects among teenagers who are having trouble in school. They spot the truants and dropouts. They want the ones who are physically fit, yet easily cowed and misled. Strong-arm tactics are employed to recruit the youths. Sometimes girls are kidnapped and made to do the bidding of gang members. The most terrifying experience of Chinese teenagers is to be confronted by gang recruiters. To show how unsuspecting and naive children can be trapped in the vicious grip of the gangs, one young boy was followed through his ordeal to show how he, the school authorities, his family, the social workers, and the courts handled the problem.

CASE STUDY (PSUEDO-NAME BIP)

I had met thirteen year old Bip in the Chinatown junior high when I inquired if there were some immigrant children who seemed to be having difficulty adjusting. Bip had come to the guidance counselor's attention because of his excessive absences and cuts. She had talked to him on numerous occasions and found that he could hardly read. His record card showed that he was failing in almost every subject, yet she could not believe that Bip was a slow learner or low in intelligence. The counselor had already arranged for Bip to take the communication disorders test at Hunter College, and a social worker was going to take him there.

An appointment was made for Bip to meet me at the counselor's office. The first time he never showed up. He had left school right after lunch. He came for the second appointment, and we had a long, long chat.

Bip's spoken English was good. He enunciated very clearly and had no accent despite the fact that he had been in the country for only three years. Physically, he was big for his age, a little on the plump side, with fair smooth skin. He was very talkative, extremely open, very innocent and naive. One could almost describe him as cherubic.

The Deviants — Chinatown Gangs

TABLE 10-3

Total Arrests of Chinese by Cause in New York City's Fifth Police Precinct, 1975-1978

Month	Gang Related				Gambling				Other				Total			
	1975	1976	1977	1978	1975	1976	1977	1978	1975	1976	1977	1978	1975	1976	1977	1978
Jan.	11	12	4	5	0	0	52	0	4	3	0	7	15	15	56	12
Feb.	17	4	1	7	50	1	0	20	4	9	4	7	71	14	5	34
Mar.	4	2	7	10	15	0	0	4	2	11	10	5	21	13	17	19
Apr.	9	0	14	8	21	49	19	45	9	3	7	7	39	52	40	60
May	11	12	11	8	0	13	31	25	6	8	3	9	17	33	45	42
June	4	12	11	6	0	0	12	10	1	6	5	12	5	18	28	28
July	1	14	3	6	0	0	15	0	2	13	7	3	3	27	25	9
Aug.	10	8	7	1	0	0	31	0	10	6	5	4	20	14	43	5
Sept.	0	10	6	5	0	0	24	15	7	5	7	8	7	25	37	28
Oct.	5	40	3	4	0	0	18	24	5	5	0	3	10	45	21	31
Nov.	12	17	1	6	0	14	5	4	3	1	3	1	15	32	9	11
Dec.	1	4	6	2	0	23	51	1	9	3	5	3	10	30	62	6
Total	85	135	74	68	86	100	258	148	62	73	56	69	233	308	388	285

Note: Most offenses committed by Chinese are for gambling or they are gang-related. It seems that as gambling arrests decrease, gang-related offenses rise.

He was in seventh grade although he had finished only third grade in Hong Kong. He remembered that school work there was very hard for him and that he had been hit by the teacher quite often and sometimes put in a dark room because he did not do his homework. At the junior high, he was taking math, science, social studies, language, art, music, woodshop and typing. He was not interested in math because he had already learned some of it in the Hong Kong school. He liked social studies. In all his subjects, however, he could not read his assignments. Bip repeatedly told me that he found it difficult to read although I found he talked easily and readily. He was getting help in reading from a number of sources. One was the reading lab at the school, to which he had been going for a month. According to Bip, the lab helped him a little, but he had a defeatist attitude and felt that he could not do the work before he even tried. Bip told some fancy stories. He said he and some others stole a "madelo" from an Italian man. When asked what a "madelo" was, he said, "It makes a big bang and can blow this door off". He said he had a gun, but it was broken. He wanted to steal a car because he wanted a car. He once stayed with some gang members from Sunday until Tuesday. Afterwards, his father would not let him go out on weekends, and he felt that he was a prisoner in his home. When asked what he did when he cut out from school, he said he rode his bicycle around the neighborhood, played ball, went around with his friends. Sometimes he worked delivering papers for a store for which he was paid two dollars an hour.

It was alleged that he and a friend had gone to another school and had threatened a child with a knife. Looking at this young boy of thirteen, I could not imagine him hurting anyone. Asked what he wanted to be when he grew up, he said, "A doctor, because a doctor makes alot of money".

"Who are your friends?" I asked. Bip mentioned an older boy in the main building of the Chinatown junior high school and some Hispanic and black boys. He had Chinese friends as well, but they were not his "best friends". One Chinese friend had accompanied Bip to our interview and had sat with us the entire time. The two boys were close, but the other boy was doing quite well in school (90 average), despite the fact that he had been in the United States only two years.

I sought out Bip's homeroom teacher, who confirmed my impression that Bip had a defeatist attitude. "Bip believes he cannot succeed. He becomes frustrated very easily. He's basically quit the American education system. Yet I think he is definitely intelligent." The teacher continued, "This class is made up of language-deficient children. They have been here too long for the ESL class and are too slow for the regular mainstream class. I teach the students both English and social studies. In English, we work phonetically because Chinese phonetics are obviously different from English phonetics. We work with sounding out words, so that hopefully when they leave here in June they will be able to sound out every English word in an attempt to read it. They will not know all the meanings or all the words because their vocabulary is still rudimentary and will have to be built up gradually. Students like Bip, who are deficient, should have another teacher work intensively with them. Bip understands everything that is explained to him, and he answers my questions in English, but when it come to written work he makes a small attempt and then gives up."

Does Bip pay attention in class? Does he misbehave? "Bip seems interested. He pays attention as long as I am verbalizing. If we go to the reading exercises, he will quit and just sit quietly. He is not a discipline problem at all—he is an attendance problem. The first time I heard he was in another school 'shaking down' a kid with a knife I was absolutely shocked. I've been in this school twelve years now, and Bip does not appear to be a typical gang member although there were only two that I know of. One was shot in the movies. One was a runner for the gambling houses. All of a sudden he fell down an elevator shaft one day and was killed. Some people say he was executed."

What was the teacher's assessment of the problem? "Frustration is a key factor. Bip needs some sort of praise, some sort of success. He needs to bolster his ego, so when he tells people he is part of a gang, he feels important; this may be the success factor that Bip craves."

A few days later, I learned that Bip had been absent from school since I last spoke to him and that he was now under court supervision. Bip's father had petitioned the court to make him a PINS (Person In Need of Supervision) case. The father felt that he could no longer handle his son, and he had asked the court to assume responsibility. A social worker and legal advisor had been assigned to Bip, and he had appeared before a juvenile court judge. The case was beginning to assume proportions that I had not imagined. I paid a visit to the social worker, having first called Bip's father to obtain permission for both the social worker and the judge to reveal anything about the case.

The social worker and the legal advisor felt that it was their obligation to protect Bip's legal interests, which they interpreted to mean that Bip was not to be put into a foster home if they could help it. The urgency of Bip's plight demanded other courses of action, but neither the social worker nor the legal advisor had alternatives to offer.

The father was pleading for help. He asked the social worker to find him a private school where he could send Bip to remove him from his present friends and influences, which he thought were leading his son astray. He was willing to pay up to $2,000 per year for tuition and board for a place outside New York City. The social worker had called a number of places, but she told me that the private schools were asking for $5,000. The father could not afford this on his meager salary, so he dropped this prospect. He felt frustrated and disappointed. To send his son back out into the streets or into the school was to put his life in jeopardy. Events were moving too swiftly for the bureaucracy and the family to handle in a leisurely fashion. The father withdrew his son from court supervision and took matters back into his own hands.

Next, I interviewed the Family Court judge who had heard Bip's case. In his eleven years on the bench, the judge mentioned that few Chinese boys had appeared before him, but more were coming to his attention of late. He could not recall the particulars of Bip's case, but after reviewing the records he said that the father had first asked for help and that the court responded by providing a social worker and legal counsel to help Bip work out his problems.

I made an appointment to see the father. I was surprised when he asked me to come at two in the afternoon. I found him living in the heart of Chinatown in a third-floor walk-up apartment, taking care of a newborn infant and a little girl of one and a half. One could barely squeeze into the tiny space called an apartment. We sat at the kitchen table that took up one third of the room. An old gas jet stove, a refrigerator, and a television were the rest of the furnishings. Part of the room had been partitioned to hold a bed that took up the entire floor space. The only way to get into the room was to climb over the bed. This is where the parents slept.

There must have been another bedroom for the three children, but I did not see it. The only space to turn around in was in front of the stove, and it was no bigger than four feet square. There was only one window in the entire apartment, making it very dark and dreary.

The father was a soft-spoken, gentle man judging by the way he fed the baby and handled the little girl. I explained to him that I wanted to know about his son to learn what kind of difficulties immigrant children encounter so we may devise ways to help others like Bip. The father was very understanding and perfectly willing to cooperate with me. He said he had gone through a very trying period with his son, and then told me that Bip had been escorted to the airport by four policemen the night before. The mother had taken him to Hong Kong to live with relatives. She had given birth to the baby just ten days earlier, but Bip's life was in danger and that took precedence. He had been peripherally involved with gangs. He wanted out, but found that the idea was not received with approval by them. He knew who the members were and where they hung out. He knew too much for his own good and, therefore, had to be done away with.

The father was in his forties. He had come to the United States much earlier, but his family did not join him until three years ago. He worked as a cook and his wife worked in the sewing factory on his day off. Most of the time she stayed home to take care of the children.

"Bip didn't like to stay home", said the father. "He always wanted to be out on the streets running around with other boys." I looked around at the cramped living quarters and could well understand why the two rooms held no attraction for a restless teenager. Obviously, family member contacts were close, for the father said he spent whatever time he could talking to Bip, teaching him, urging him to be a good boy. Apparently the father's words fell on deaf ears, and he felt totally helpless to keep his son from bad company and harm. In desperation, he had been willing to turn Bip over to the courts.

I asked him if he had ever heard of special agencies such as the Chinese Family Consultation Center or Project Reach (a pre-delinquent agency) that might have helped him. I also inquired whether he had kinfolk who might have exerted some control over Bip, but the father said he was so ashamed of his son's behavior he did not want anyone in Chinatown to learn about it.[2]

Bip's flirtation with gangs brought about a drastic change in the family. The mother eventually returned to the United States, but her son remained in Hong Kong. In the meantime, the father could not work because he had to care for the younger children. And I knew Bip would be very unhappy because he had told me that he did not like Hong Kong and that he had been very happy when he heard that he was coming to the United States. Besides, I think he had forgotten a great deal of his Chinese; when I spoke to him in Chinese, he told me that he didn't understand Chinese very well anymore. If Bip had to start all over again in Chinese school in Hong Kong, he would have to make another drastic adjustment without his parents beside him. His disillusionment with school and his flirtation with the gangs had cost him very dearly, but at least he did not pay with his life.

The events in Bip's case followed each other swiftly. Altogether it was a matter of weeks from the time I first met Bip to his forced departure from the United States. It is my firm belief that had he not left the country, he would have been another gang casualty. I followed the case in all its ramifications because it is a classic example of how young, naive teenagers are trapped in a vicious cycle from which it seems difficult, if not impossible, to extricate themselves once they go beyond a certain point. Events start out simply enough. A young boy cannot handle his school work because of a reading disability. The first symptoms are cutting classes and truancy. The more exciting world of the streets beckons, and a young boy in his early teens cannot resist. In this instance, Bip was fortunate in that he had loving and concerned parents, but being truant meant that he was a prime target for gang recruitment. He could have become a hardcore gang member, shooting, extorting, killing, and perhaps ending up being killed or incarcerated. Bip only flirted with the gangs, and he did not like what he saw, but the gangs would not let go. Their code was total commitment or death.

What about societal assistance? The school, in its way, did try to help with the reading lab and the special class. Did the courts,

---

[2] Loss of face and feelings of shame are such strongly ingrained Chinese cultural traits that they often obstruct realistic solutions to problems. There is a tendency for the persons involved to try to cover up the problem by not recognizing it or letting anyone know about it. At the same time, persons trying to help are hampered in their efforts by repeated denials that anything is wrong.

the social workers or the legal advisor help Bip or the distraught parents who were beside themselves with worry? The important thing was to remove Bip from the reach of the gang members who were out to get him, but the social worker wanted to keep him at home. She was operating with mistaken notions, and it is my belief that she did not or could not devote too much time to finding a reasonable private school in which to place Bip even for a short period of time. If the father had turned to some of the Chinatown family agencies, they would have understood the urgency of the situation. Agencies like Project Reach were set up to help teenagers stay out of gangs. On their staff are street workers who know the gang members, who know the gang mentality and their traditions, and who are experienced in dealing with situations like these. An agency no longer in existence since they lost their government funding, Project Hing Dai (Big Brother/Little Brother), was set up to work directly with the hardcore gang members. In many instances, they were able to defuse potential gang fights by acting as intermediaries. As effective as such agencies may be, the father did not want other Chinese to know about his son's misconduct. In Bip's case, the police were alert in learning about the contract on his life and gave the parents ample warning. The decision to send Bip back to Hong Kong was a drastic step. Its impact on the family may be shattering. On the other hand, Bip may be considered fortunate in having escaped with his life, but the consequences were overwhelming, considering the small seed from which the problem sprang.

GANG THREAT

The gang threat is a constant cloud hanging over the heads of Chinese youth living in Chinatown. Parents hurry their sons home from school and forbid them to go out to play. Many want desperately to get out of Chinatown. As a former Project Reach director said, "If you live in Chinatown, even an ordinary kid will find it hard not to come in contact with the gangs in one way or another. If you are not a 'jock', you're in a gang. If you are not in a gang, you'd better be protected" (Sung, 1977:10). One simply cannot go to school, mind one's own business, and go home unscathed. Boys get waylaid or beaten up in school, in the schoolyard, on the way to school, in the playgrounds, or on the streets. They are afraid to go to the bathroom. Young teenagers have to be part of a group for protection. This is another reason why boys join, and once in the gang they follow the group; there is no turning back.

CASE STUDY (PSUEDO-NAMES WON AND YIP)

In order to do a parallel study of deviant youths in the satellite Chinatown area for purposes of comparison, inquiries were made about incidences of truancy, misbehavior, gang membership, and other manifestations of maladaption. The teachers were not aware of any cases, but the dean of the satellite community junior high school, who had been at the school for fourteen years, could remember two cases of problem Chinese boys. One was already dead, "executed" gangland style five years earlier. The other was enrolled in the school at the time of this research.

This young boy had a brother, one year younger than he, who was his exact opposite. They had the same parents, lived in the same room, came to the United States at the same time, went to the same school, yet the problem child, whom we shall call Won, was completely different from his brother, whom we shall call Yip.

As the dean pointed out, Won's case was not a serious one, and if he were not of Chinese origin, he wouldn't stand out from the hundreds like him who came into the dean's office regularly. The telltale signs were truancy, cuts, and poor school work. At the time of my interview with Won, he had been in the United States for four years. The family spoke Mandarin rather than Cantonese, and they had migrated from Taiwan. Won had already forgotten most of his Chinese, and he admitted that he was having trouble with English in spite of the fact that he had attended English school in Taiwan before coming to this country. He was not doing well in school.

Won and Yip looked like twins, except that Yip had a lighter complexion. Both were of the same height, same build, and had the same features. Although at thirteen Yip was a year younger than Won, he was in the eighth grade while Won was in the seventh. Won had been put back a year and Yip had skipped a grade. Yip was an excellent student and highly praised by his teachers and his mother. The boys shared a room, but Won expressed a strong dislike for his brother. They did not play together, nor would Won go to his brother for help with his school work. Recreational facilities were no problem in their neighborhood. Both brothers had many friends, but Won chose his friends from another school—a high school in the adjacent town. His best friend was white and older than he. They would go to the beach or fishing or to the movies by bus. Sometimes they would not come home until ten in the evening. Yip's friends, on the other hand, were a grade below him. They were from the same school, but he kept his friends from his former class when he skipped to the eighth grade.

In my interviews with the boys, I detected what I think is a significant factor in the differences in their behavior. When they first arrived in New York, they were put in different classes. Yip said he was utterly lost until another Chinese boy in his class befriended and helped him. Won had no such friend. He began to fall further and further behind in his school work. Won exhibited a strong hostility toward his brother, he may have been jealous of Yip's achievements, and perhaps he was rebelling to get his mother's and teachers' attention.

The parents had been in the United States for six years. They had come first and sent for their children two years later. Both parents were college graduates. Before they emigrated, the father worked as a ship's engineer, and the mother worked for the U.S. Army as an English secretary. Now she worked as a cashier in a New Jersey restaurant. On her day off, she invited me to their home.

The mother was a lovely woman in her late thirties. The family lived in a modern apartment house where the faces of the tenants showed a wide variety of ethnic origins. The three-and-one-half room apartment was clean and well kept. There were two bicycles for the boys in the living room. Rent and utilities at that time, came to about $325 a month.

The mother drove to work six days a week from her home in Queens to the restaurant in New Jersey (more than an hour's drive). She left the house around 10:00 a.m. and came home after midnight. When the boys came home from school, they were to play until dinnertime, when the maternal grandmother, who lived nearby, would come to fix their dinner and stay with them until 10:00 p.m.

The family did not move closer to the mother's place of work because she wanted to be near her own mother, who could look after the boys in the afternoons. Asked why she didn't find work closer to home, she said she could earn more in the restaurant, which was owned by a relative. Yet when calculated by the hour, she was earning less because of the twelve-hour day plus two hours commuting time. In addition, the car was an extra expense. The mother was qualified for a better job since she was a college graduate and could express herself well in English, yet she was timid about seeking employment in a non-Chinese setting.

She and her husband had once owned and operated a restaurant, but it was not a success because they were inexperienced in this line of work. When they had the restaurant, the boys would come home from school and help out. When the business, failed the father went out of town to train as a chef in a niece's restaurant. Neither parent thought about resuming his or her former career so that the family could be reunited. Instead, they sank into restaurant occupations for which they had no experience and no aptitude. They stayed in such occupations because restaurant work is a conventional field for the Chinese. This disinclination to break away from the few traditional occupations is extremely strong and is a barrier to the solution of some of their problems.

Won said he wanted to go back to Taiwan because his father was there. When asked who his hero was, he replied, "My father". Obviously the boy missed his father, however, his father was not in Taiwan. The mother said her husband was in California; the brother said he was in Mississippi. The fact that family members live apart from one another is not uncommon in Chinese American families. It does not mean that the parents are separated or divorced.

Won's mother said she wished her husband was in New York and that she did not have to go to work so she could stay home to take care of her boys. She confessed that she did not know how to handle her son. She scolded him, she hit him, she sent him away to summer camp, but he came back the next day. She threatened to send him back to Taiwan or to a friend in Mississippi who had three boys and was willing to let Won live with them. He refused to go. She appealed to Won's love for her and his grandmother. She did not give him an allowance. He had to ask her for spending money, but somehow he had money to take the bus to the beach or go to the movies. Nothing worked. Won was frequently absent from school, and he came home late. The mother was very concerned about her son, but she felt helpless. "Every time Won is absent from school, the dean at school calls me", she said. "If you misbehave in Taiwan, the school metes out the punishment; it does not keep calling the family. Here, the school cannot do anything with the boy. I can't either."

This type of rebellious attitude by their offspring is very difficult for immigrant parents to handle. It is a new experience for them to be confronted by a disobedient and disrespectful child. By and large, Chinese immigrant children still retain a strong measure of filial piety and respect for the parents. When they first arrive in this country, they are still obedient.

In checking back with the family a year later, I found that the father was still absent from the home and the mother had the same job. Won had been sent to a private boarding school outside of New York City, so I could not ascertain how he was doing. Yip continued to do well in his studies and had gone on to high school.

A COMPARISON: CHINATOWN AND SATELLITE COMMUNITY

Parallels cannot be drawn between Bip, who lived in Chinatown, and Won, who lived in a satellite community. Obviously, Won's parents came from a much higher socioeconomic and educational background; nonetheless, both fathers worked in restaurants. Won's family was Mandarin-speaking; Bip's was Cantonese-speaking. Both boys had best friends who were not Chinese. When Bip fell behind in his school work and became a truant, he quickly became a target recruit for the gangs. Gang affiliation is for keeps, even for those who join in naivete. Bip's parents were neither sophisticated nor well-off enough to find a boarding school for their son. Their only recourse was to send him to relatives in Hong Kong. The consequences of his poor marks and truancy were much greater than those for Won. Won's mother had also thought of sending her son back to Taiwan, but in the end she managed to place him in a private boarding school and to keep him in this country. Obviously she must have had some financial reserves to be able to do so. But what is fascinating is how, as in the case of Won and Yip, two sons from the same womb and same circumstances can react so differently to their common immigrant experience.

GANG PROFILE

In both of the above cases, the young boys were still in school. The hard-core memberships of the gangs are those who have

TABLE 10-4
Characteristics of Chinese Gangs

Personal Characteristics

1. Male (mainly)
2. Age 14-18 (generally)
3. Immigrant from Hong Kong
   (almost without exception)
4. Doing badly in school
5. Truancy, dropout (first signs)
6. Hedonistic values
7. Selfish, me-first attitudes
8. Realize that they are doing wrong

Prime Supporters

1. Gambling establishments or tongs
2. Hired as a gang — money paid to
   gang leaders who parcel out money
   to followers

Activities

1. For tongs: to provide security and act
   as lookout for gambling places, to
   escort winners home, protect
   territory, enforce gambling debts
2. Extortion of business and professional
   and service enterprises in Chinatown — protection money
3. Fighting other gangs who try to move
   into territory
4. Some mugging and burglaries
5. Murder, if ordered to do so
6. Recruit other members
7. Hang out and have fun together

Group Characteristics

1. Very loosely organized
2. Turnover in membership great
3. Life-span of any one gang short
4. Members recruited constantly to
   replenish ranks
5. Most coerced into joining
6. Recruit those 16 years and under
   to take advantage of juvenile laws
7. Low profile, do not invite publicity
8. Attempts made to organize them on national
   or international basis unsuccessful

Attraction in Being a Member

1. Easy money
2. Lack of viable opportunities
3. Cameraderie in being a member of group
4. Excitement

Victims

1. Other gang members (primarily)
2. Other Chinese
3. Those who are an easy target in
   Chinatown
4. Those who are more vulnerable
5. Those who want to leave the gang

given up, and the streets of Chinatown are their training grounds. A more detailed account of their attitudes and exploits is given in my monograph, "Gangs in New York's Chinatown" (1977). An outline of their characteristics is presented in Table 10-4. Differences between Chinatown gangs and other minority gangs are most apparent in the group characteristics. The fact that there is a rapid turnover in membership and that rigorous efforts must be made to coerce others to join means that gang membership is not particularly appealing to the youths.

The life span of gangs is short. Members do not sport a distinctive style of clothing, nor do they wear any emblem or distinguishing identification. They shun publicity. Their victims are other Chinese because they are unfamiliar with and afraid to pick on other ethnic groups. They realize that what they are doing is wrong, so they do have a conscience. Knowing these traits, people trying to deal with the gang problem can devise levers to defuse the explosive situation.

A LULL–HOPEFULLY

By 1978, gang activity in New York's Chinatown seemed to slacken. Five bullets were shot into the leader of the Ghost Shadows the summer before, but he survived the attack. Within the gang's own ranks, members were vying to take over the leadership, and this brought about a three-way split. About a dozen gang members were languishing in jail as a result of a stepped-up police offensive. But most important, the police Morals and Vice Squad was "busting" the gambling joints. Raid after raid kept the gamblers off balance and dried up the money for gang members. The police crackdown did prove one thing—vigorous law enforcement can deter gang activity.

An extraneous factor—unrelated to the Chinatown gang situation—came to impact heavily upon the local scene. Nearby Atlantic City on the New Jersey coast opened up to legalized gambling in the late 1970s. To entice patrons to their tables, the casinos provide virtually free buses that leave from Chinatown on a regular schedule. For a bus ticket costing about $6, the rider gets round-trip transportation, a roll of quarters worth $10, free lunch, and sometimes a free show. A trip to Atlantic City is an outing, entertainment, and gambling all combined and within the law. As a result, local gambling establishments are losing customers, so they do not need and cannot support as many gang members. With the source of revenues decreasing, gang activity has abated appreciably.

COMMUNITY REACTION TO GANGS

The community reaction is one of intense fear. Families move out of the neighborhood if at all possible, or they send their sons to live with relatives in other cities. They pay extortion and do not report the incidences to the police because they are afraid of reprisal. If their own sons are involved, they try to cover up because of loss of face. The anomaly of it all is that the Chinatown elders are also tong members.

LARGER SOCIETY AND POLICE RESPONSE

The police complain that the community and gang victims will not cooperate in reporting crime, in coming forth to be witnesses or to be plaintiffs, so they say their hands are tied. There have been very few apprehensions and even fewer convictions. Juvenile justice is very lenient. Little effort is made to help immigrant youths resist gang recruitment. My recommendation to the schools is that they should have gang-prevention drills just as they have fire-prevention drills. Twelve or thirteen-year-old boys are petrified when first confronted with gang recruiters. They should be told where to go for help and given protection and support so they will not be drawn into the gangs under duress. Unfortunately, the larger societal attitude is that the Chinese are only killing other Chinese, so there is little cause for alarm. Witness the cessation of funding from the Criminal Justice Coordinating Council of the City of New York to three out of four youth programs in Chinatown in 1978.

THEORIES OF CRIME

In looking at the most flagrant example of deviant behavior—the gangs—to manifest itself among Chinese immigrant youth, one is drawn into relating this manifestation with theories of crime. These run the gamut of the biological to the social, and to the economic and psychological. Christians believe that man is born cloaked in sin. Some geneticists would have us believe that hereditary genes are responsible for criminal inclinations. Psychological theories such as internal conflicts and psychopathic behavior are plausible, but only individually applicable. Crime has always been strongly associated with poverty, so that economism has it adherents.

Sociologists have their theories too. Emile Durkheim spoke of the normality of crime and found it functional as a vehicle for innovation (Coser and Rosenberg, 1969: 570). By normality, he meant the generality of such phenomena in society, but crime itself is abhorred by all societies and sanctioned by few. When criminal behavior becomes widespread, society may become aroused to correct the underlying conditions, so crime can serve as a vehicle for change. In the case of the Chinatown gangs, the community has only reacted with fear and flight whereas the larger society has tended to ignore the problem, preferring to look the other way when recreational facilities or youth programs are proposed.

Differential Association

The most prevalent theory about the causation of crime—that of differential association—was formulated by Edwin H. Sutherland and Donald R. Cressey (1939). The theory postulates that criminal behavior may be stated either in terms of the processes which are operating at the moment of the occurrence of crime or in terms of the processes operating in the earlier history of the criminal. Criminal behavior is learned, and a person becomes delinquent because of an excess of definitions favorable to violation of law over definitions unfavorable to violation. The objective situation is important to the occurrence of crime largely to the extent that it provides an opportunity for a person to act. On the other hand, if the person has been immunized in his or her socialization against violation of societal mores or laws, criminal behavior will not result, even if the opportunity presents itself.

To repeat, Sutherland and Cressey maintain that criminal behavior is learned, and this theory certainly is supported by the circumstances and environment in New York's Lower East Side where Chinatown is located. The Chinese teenager is exposed daily to behavior like vandalism, hanging out, fighting, mugging, truancy, and aggression. The point was brought out very clearly in a conversation with a Puerto Rican sociologist who lived in the Chinatown area and who went to the same schools used in this research. When he talked about Puerto Rican gangs of his childhood, his eyes lit up and his whole expression became animated. He confessed that he was "too cowardly" to take part in the gang exploits in the neighborhood, but he hung out with gang members because he was fascinated by their pranks, their deeds, and their fighting. He would listen in rapt attention as gang members boasted of their exploits, and secretly he admired and envied their bravado. Since he was a good student he served their purpose by helping some gang members with their school work and by being a good listener.

The primary code of ethics in the gangs is: Never "rat". This sociologist was witness to or knew about many gang activities, but he never told. He was suspended from school three times because he had information that the school authorities wanted but he would not reveal. After each suspension, his star rose higher with the gang members, and to this day, even as a college instructor, the sociologist believes firmly that his suspensions were worth the esteem he had gained in the eyes of his peers.

He lived in a housing project directly across the street from the junior high school in Chinatown used in this study. From his window he used to see marauding gangs throwing stones through the school windows and vandalizing school property. He also watched the gang fights that took place in the small park across from the school. These events were thrilling spectacles to the teenage boy, and if he had not been such a good student and had he not found satisfaction in this studies, he would have easily opted for the excitement of the gang life. The lure of being part of the gangs is very strong—especially at the pre-adolescent age. During this period, boys show a pronounced tendency to engage in team activities. It is of utmost importance for them to be part of a peer group (Furfey, 1928). If a Chinese immigrant teenager comes into a neighborhood where he is daily exposed to gang activities, and if his character and home defenses are weak, he may easily succumb to gang recruitment.

Delinquent Subculture

In his book, *Delinquent Boys: The Culture of the Gangs* (1955), Albert K. Cohen maintains that delinquent behavior is a subculture of its own. "The delinquent is the rogue male. His conduct may be viewed not only negatively, as a device for attacking and derogating the respectable culture; positively it may be viewed as the exploitation of modes of behavior which are renounced by middle-class culture incompatible with it ends, but which are not without a certain aura of glamor and romance." (140)

The subculture of the gangs stresses the willingness of the members to fight, to take on dangerous assignments, to eliminate rival gangs, and to enrich themselves at the expense of others. A reckless few soon build up their reputations and attract followings because of their "cool" and "courage", but none last too long or survive to enjoy their "gains". In spite of these gang norms, most of the Chinese gang members interviewed did not approve of what they were doing. They had guilty consciences. They knew it was wrong and detrimental to their own future. Once these youths reached a certain stage of maturity, they began to see the futility and error of their ways. This is a very optimistic sign that accounts for the exodus of most gang members at around age 18. These facts tell us that gang activity is not internalized as an accepted norm, nor is it in the community tradition to condone it. The residents live in terror and fear, but they feel impotent to deal with the situation. The dangers of reprisal are all too real.

Social Disorganization

Charles Cooley's (1918) theory of social disorganization is also applicable in the case of the Chinatown gangs:

> We are dependent for moral health upon intimate association with a group of some sort, usually consisting of our family, neighbors, and other friends. It is the interchange of ideas and feelings with this group and a constant sense of its opinions that makes the standards of right and wrong seem real to us. We may not wholly adopt its judgments, or that of any member of it, but the social interplay is necessary to keep the higher processes of the mind in action at all. Now it is the general effect of social displacement to tear us away more or less completely from such groups. When we move to town or go to another country, or get into a different social class, or adopt ideas that alienate us from our former associates, it is not at all certain that we shall form new relations equally intimate and cogent with the old. A common result, therefore, is a partial moral isolation and atrophy of the moral sense. (180-181)

These conditions certainly apply to the Chinese population in New York's Chinatown, where most of the residents are recent immigrants. Almost without exception, members of the youth gangs are immigrants from Hong Kong. These people have been uprooted and transplanted onto foreign soil. The values, the norms, the culture are completely different. The nuclear family is isolated from the kinship group, and primary relations break down. Even the nuclear family has undergone transformation because both parents must work long, hard hours in occupations that demand absence from the home for long periods during the day and evening. The school becomes the main socializing agent, but it is an impersonal and secondary institution. Long hours are spent in front of the television and the message of this medium is the advocacy of material acquisitions—values that are at odds with Chinese teachings. Young males, at the teenage stage in particular, must reach out to form ties with the peer group, and it is during this stage that they are most susceptible to the attraction of belonging to a group that promises camaraderie and the excitement of forbidden activity. Combine these factors with the lack of social control from the parents and kinship group who themselves are groping for adjustment in the new society, and the result is the classic conditions that lead to a breakdown of the moral sense.

The very reason that new immigrants go into Chinatown is to recreate a sense of the primary groups to which they are accustomed. Yet it is precisely within Chinatowns that the youths are drawn or coerced into gangs. Chinese youths who live beyond Chinatown are seldom found in gangs. They are removed from the gang recruiters and their strong-arm tactics. Distance separates them from the enticement and excitement of peer groups running together. Isolated teenagers in alien surroundings dare not step out of bounds, whereas within Chinatown they muster courage from the group. When parents learn their sons have been threatened or have become active in gangs, their first reaction is to move away or send their sons away, thus removing them further from the basic primary group—the family—as well as from the ethnic community, so that in fact we have a contradiction. Social disorganization results from the removal of immigrants from their primary group ties of the homeland, yet efforts to recreate these ties by gravitating to and concentrating in Chinatown have had the reverse effect of the neighborhood becoming a breeding ground for gangs. This is one instance where the ethnic community is more detrimental than helpful.

XI

Peer Groups

Although peer groups can be villains dragging confused, misled, and sometimes unwilling youngsters into gangs or otherwise leading them astray, peer groups can also be extremely supportive and helpful to the newcomer. This point was highlighted in the case of Won and Yip mentioned in the previous chapter. Yip was an exemplary student while his brother Won was a truant and a discipline problem. Yip had quickly found a friend who helped him in school upon his arrival in this country, whereas Won, the truant brother, had no one.

Peer Group Support System

Mrs. Virginia Kee, who has taught in the public schools of Chinatown for more than twenty years, particularly recommended a peer-group support system as the answer to the gang problem as well as to the pervasive phenomenon of absentee parents in Chinese immigrant families. She said:

> I've observed the teenage scene for many years, and I have noticed that when the immigrants first come, if they can build themselves a support system, they can be strong enough to withstand being drawn into, pulled into, or pushed into the gang system. But that support system must be built up and encouraged when they first come to school.

> When they come to the United States, the parents are so busy they don't know what is happening at school. They don't really understand this society. They can't give that same comfort to the youngsters because the parents themselves are struggling. How much can they give in the way of encouragement and support to the children? Very little, although the love and caring is

there. Somehow, the ones who do well, I have noticed, are the ones who can pull themselves together and provide a peer support system for each other throughout the difficult years. The person who does not belong to this type of situation will soon seek this type of support from the gangs.

I try to encourage the formation of these peer groups in my class. That means when they are in the playground, they will be there to help each other if someone tries to intimidate or extort money from them. They will be there together when they have a problem and they don't know how to solve it. They will tell each other where the library or post office is. They will share whatever information they have with one another. They will teach each other what tests count and which teacher is helpful. They will help each other with college applications. This way they learn from one another. A person is so much stronger when he has that.

Segal and Yahraes, in *A Child's Journey* (1978:234), writes "Willard W. Hartup, director of the University of Minnesota's Institute of Child Development, is among those who view the quality of a child's interaction with friends as a powerful diagnostic index. 'Among the most sensitive indicators of faulty development', he observes, 'are failure by the child to engage in the activities of the peer culture, and to occupy a relatively comfortable place in it'".

Because peer relationships convey so much about a child's potential for emotional difficulties, it is hardly surprising that there is embedded in them, too, the seeds of healthy development as well. 'There are some necessities in children's development,' says Hartup, 'that require interaction with coequals – that is, individuals who have the same kind of developmental status and competencies in the cognitive and social areas as they do. The relations between adults and children have evolved to serve a very special set of functions – to ensure basic survival, to help keep the child safe from physical danger and harm, and to help build relations with authority figures. But in some very critical areas of adjustment, relations with coequals are the key.

Many contemporary child development experts would agree. The imprint of peers on the child's personality is second only in importance to that of parents, and in some areas, it is actually predominant. It is largely through the child's interactions with peers that many of life's most important attitudes and behaviors are shaped in the young—for example, learning to find sexual expression, to display and modulate aggressive instincts, to live by ethical standards, even to overcome disabling fears and anxieties and gain a sense of emotional security. (Segal and Yahraes, 1978: 237)

Reverse Roles Of Parents and Children

The comments of both Mrs. Kee and Dr. Hartup about harnessing the positive aspects of peer influence are especially *a propos* to the Chinese immigrant family, in which, we have already observed, the parents tend to lose a great deal of respect and authority that they had in the old country when they come to the United States. As soon as the children come to this country, they enter schools and are exposed to American ways. They begin to learn English and are not as afraid as their parents to venture out. They are exposed to hours of television, and their eager young minds quickly absorb the message of the medium. The new ideas and ways of the American people are quite different from those of their parents, who must provide the rice for the dinner table by long, hard hours of work. Invariably, the father must take a job on a lower rung of the occupational ladder (*See,* Table 12-1) and he suffers from a loss of status and self-esteem. The parents simply do not have the same opportunity to learn English as do their children, so they are dependent upon their children to communicate with the outside world. The child takes the mother to the store, answers the telephone, interprets the gas bill, translates letters, and deals with many of the day-to-day situations with which the parents are totally bewildered and incapable of coping. Instead of the child looking to his parents for guidance, support and leadership, the roles are reversed (*See,* Fig. VII Chapter XII, "The Immigrant Family"). Under these conditions, parental respect and authority are undermined. To fill the vacuum left by the parents, peer groups become increasingly important.

In our questionnaire administered to recent Chinese immigrant high school students, we asked: When you have a problem like the ones given below, to whom do you go? We had anticipated that they would probably turn to different people depending upon the nature of the problem, so three types of problems were used as examples: school work, skin (medical), and future career. The responses are given in Table 11-1.

TABLE 11-1

Persons Turned to When Faced with Problem by Chinese Immigrant Students in High School Bilingual Programs

Problem	No One No.	%	Father No.	%	Mother No.	%	Sibling No.	%	Friend No.	%	Teacher No.	%	Total 100%
School Work	20	9	14	6	19	8	58	26	79	35	34	15	224
Skin Problem	41	19	18	8	98	46	29	14	26	12	2	1	214
Future Career	20	10	42	21	25	13	33	17	76	38	3	2	199
Total	81	13	74	12	142	23	120	19	181	29	39	6	637

Source: Student Survey Questionnaire, 1978.

More respondents turn to their friends or siblings except for medical problems. In that case, most children still look to their mothers. But whether it is an immediate issue of school work or one involving future career, the immigrant youths turn to their peers, and more often to their friends than to their siblings.

Drastic Departure From Cultural Norms

This phenomenon can be said to be a distinct departure from the Chinese cultural norm and it calls for major adjustments on the part of both immigrant parents and children. In traditional Chinese society, stress is put upon the vertical relationships within the family. Ties between parents and children are the strongest; they are family ties, hence permanent and immutable. One is born into a family and one's position within it is secure.

In the dominant American culture, the peer group exerts a very strong pull against the family at a very early age. To be psychologically normal in the Western sense, one must gradually detach oneself from one's parents and seek a niche among one's own peers. Whereas parental affection is taken for granted, peer acceptance is a horizontal relationship that must be worked at. There is a great deal of anxiety attached to being accepted and liked by one's classmates, playmates, colleagues, and friends. Family ties provide a cushion of permanence and security, but peer relationships are ever changing and changeable.

When their children begin to put distance between them, even to feel ashamed of them, the immigrant parents become upset and chagrined. Before emigrating, they enjoyed respect and obedience. After coming to this country they begin to sense that their children are slipping away from them, and their sorrow is great.

Friends

When asked, "Do you have a close friend?" only 33 out of 131 males and 22 out of 139 females said yes (See, Table 11-2). Through the high school years, most of the students we surveyed had friends of their own sex and very few dated (See, Table 11-3). Of the males, two-thirds had never or seldom dated. Of the females, one-half had never or seldom dated.

Immigrant youths are not as accustomed to the free and easy intermingling of the sexes as Western teenagers are. Only one generation removed from their parents, whose marriage may have been match-made with go-betweens, they are still shy and reserved. Though these young people may long for association with members of the opposite sex, they are still too inhibited to be comfortable in a dating situation. The awkwardness of the Chinese male on a date was brought out by Melford Weiss in his article, "Selective Acculturation and the Dating Process: The Patterning of Chinese-Caucasian Interracial Dating" (Tachiki, et al.,1971: 37-43):

> Chinese American girls report that getting-to-know-you chatter with most Chinese American boys is basically shallow and tends to revolve around common experiences as Chinese. Males are often considered to be egocentric and rarely to consider the girls as an equal partner in a common dating activity...Chinese American dating activities are often limited to evening hours and to private or predominantly Chinese settings with the drive-in movie a favorite...

TABLE 11-2
Friends of Chinese Immigrant Students in High School Bilingual Programs

	Males	(131)	Females	(139)
Type of Friend	No.	Pct.	No.	Pct.
Close Friend	33	25	22	16
Female Friend	4	3	60	43
Male Friend	59	45	11	8
American Born Friend	21	16	24	17
Foreign Born Friend	58	44	64	46
Black Friend	0	0	0	0
Puerto Rican Friend	0	0	2	1
White Friend	1	1	2	1
No Response	39	30	38	28

Note: Many students had more than one friend so that total adds up to more than 131 males and 139 females, and percentages add up to more than 100.

Source: Student Survey Questionnaire, 1978.

TABLE 11-3
Frequency of Dating by Chinese Immigrant Students In High School Bilingual Programs

	Male		Female	
Frequency	No.	Pct.	No.	Pct.
Never	50	38	43	31
Seldom	37	28	30	22
Occasionally	25	19	46	33
Frequently	9	7	12	9
No Response	10	8	8	6
Total	131	100	139	100

Source: Student Survey Questionnaire, 1978.

Nevertheless, dating is such an important part of high school years that these young people must feel the strain of the bicultural conflict.

Segregation

Immigrant teenagers tend to stick with others like themselves. The males chose foreign born Chinese females as friends. That some chose American born Chinese members of the same sex as friends is encouraging and refutes somewhat the contention that there is a sharp cleavage between the American born and the foreign born. One fact stands out with respect to socializing with members of other ethnic groups: few immigrant students had black, Puerto Rican or white friends. This separatism among the racial groups was especially evident in school visits and observations of the children and youths in the lunchrooms and at play. In the lunchrooms, the various ethnic groups did not mix at all: the Chinese children had their own tables; the black children sat with other blacks; and the Hispanics sat with their own kind. The sexes also sat apart although the tables were not delineated for boys or girls. The boys just naturally went to one end of the lunchroom, and the girls sat at the other end.

There was usually a great deal of horseplay among the students in the lunchroom while they lined up for their lunches. The Chinese immigrant children were no less boisterous than the others, hitting the fellows and teasing the girls. While standing on line, the Hispanic boys would tease the Chinese girls, but after they got their lunches, each group went to its own table, and the interaction between the races ceased while they ate.

After gulping down their lunches in great haste, the students would run out to the playgrounds to play ball, run around, or talk with their friends. Others would go to the gym to play ball. At the Chinatown junior high school gym, the Chinese students would throw a basketball into the basket at one end of the court, while the Hispanics and blacks shared the other basket. It was as if the baskets were marked "Chinese" and "Hispanic". An invisible boundary separated the groups. They simply did not mix.

The same held true for the Chinatown high school although the separatism was not so pronounced in the satellite community junior high. The Chinese students were scattered in all sections of the classes, so there was ample opportunity for them to mix with other groups. In checking through the class rosters, it was found that no more than six Chinese names appeared in any one section or class. There was no opportunity to observe any out-of-class interaction between the ethnic groups at the satellite community high school because the school ran on an end-to-end double session with no lunch period and no recess period. After school, the students went home.

The bilingual classes tend to separate the groups along ethnic lines. Since they are separated for lessons throughout the day, there is little opportunity for the various groups to intermingle socially. Drastic cutbacks in the New York City school budget during this period forced the elimination of many after-school programs that might have provided more opportunity for intermingling. These would have been intramural sports, recreational clubs, hobby groups, handicraft classes, school trips, dances, and other social events.

This tendency to stick with one's own group is a deterrent to reaching out to the larger society in which one must eventually find oneself. Unless one is content to be bound to Chinatown or a narrow circle of Chinese friends, adjustment to the wider society later is necessary but will prove more difficult after graduation than it was during the school years. Part of the responsibility for this segregation falls on the shoulders of the Chinese children and their parents who discourage social interaction with non-Chinese because they are suspicious of foreigners and fearful that their own ways may be undermined by contact with other groups. But the eventual consequences will be that the Chinese will find themselves ill at ease in any mixed social setting. As pointed out in my study *A Survey of Chinese-American Manpower and Employment* (1976), advancement and upward mobility beyond a certain level will depend more upon social factors than on competence. To be uncomfortable in a non-Chinese social setting is a psychological as well as an economic barrier to one's well-being later in life. Neither school nor parents should neglect the social aspects of a child's upbringing.

At the same time, social scientists must see how strong the force is to maintain one's ethnic exclusiveness, so they can appreciate the degrees of resistance toward assimilation.

Conclusions

Peer groups are assuming a much larger role in the lives of Chinese immigrant children and youth than they formerly occupied under traditional Chinese culture. Whereas children used to look to their parents and elders for direction and counsel, they now turn to their peers. In their choice of friends, Chinese immigrant children tend to choose someone of their own sex and ethnic group as well as someone who is foreign born like themselves. There is very little socializing or intermingling with other groups.

Dating is infrequent and probably an unfamiliar experience for the newly arrived Chinese young people in high school. Because of the tendency for ethnic groups to stick to themselves, the social isolation of Chinese children may create problems of awkwardness in a non-ethnic setting later in life. On the other hand, the tenaciousness with which even school children cling to their own ethnic groups is a sociological phenomenon that merits further investigation.

XII
The Immigrant Family

Throughout this study, our hypothesis has been that immigration is a powerful agent, causing changes that have a ripple effect upon all aspects of life. Even the most stable of Chinese institutions—the family—has metamorphosed in the new land of the United States, departing from the idealized, Confucian, traditional models described in fiction and in sociological studies about the Chinese family in China.[1] The families of the immigrants who came to this country have always been distinctive in that:

They have had a long history of dismemberment.
Females have played a larger and more independent role.
Families are smaller in size than the traditional Chinese family.
The births of children are more widely spaced.
There may be two distinct sets of children, one older and reared in China, another younger and born in the United States.
Family reunification in this country has been in relays.

DISMEMBERMENT

One of the most peculiar features of the Chinese immigrant family has been the prolonged separation of the men from their parents, wives, and children. As Charles Frederick Marden (1952) put it, such a family was mutilated or missing a member; it was not whole. The men were in this country while their wives and children stayed in China. Initially the men intended to come to this country for only a short while to earn sufficient money and then return to their family hearth in the homeland. Before this original intent could be modified, the exclusion laws against

[1]Studies by F. Hsu, "The Myth of Chinese Family Size", *American Journal of Sociology* 1943, and C.K Yang, *The Chinese Family in the Communist Revolution*. Cambridge, Mass: MIT Press, 1959 have revealed that the so-called traditional Confucian Chinese family was more of a myth than a fact.

Chinese immigration froze the situation, making it economically unfeasible or legally impossible for the women to come. As previously noted, Chinese immigration to the United States, for almost a hundred years, was predominantly adult males. In 1890, the sex ratio was 2679:100, or approximately twenty-seven males to every Chinese female (Sung, 1971). Even as late as 1980, the sex ratio in the state of New York was unbalanced with 106 males to every 100 females. Obviously, there was not even the slightest resemblance of family life for these men deprived of the conjugal relationships with their wives, the presence of their loved ones, and the comforts of home. The men led lonely, celibate lives. On the other hand, they were responsible for the support of their families in China. Duty and obligation kept their noses to the grindstone, and if they were fortunate they managed a trip or two back to their homes over the years.

Family separation characterized most of the Chinese families with members in the United States from the 1850s to the 1950s. Four factors brought about change. The first was the repeal of the exclusion acts against Chinese immigration in 1943, which also gave the Chinese the right to become naturalized citizens and to bring their wives and children in as non-quota immigrants. The second was the passage of the War Brides Act in 1946. The third was the communist overthrow of the Nationalist government in 1949. But the small quota for China of 105 per year continued to act as an insuperable barrier to speedy reunification. The mutilated family was still much in evidence in the 1960s, and conditions did not ameliorate until the fourth factor, the liberalization of the immigration laws in 1965, came about.

Writing in the *Washington Post*, columnist Colman McCarthy (1977) advocated "...looking at every piece of major legislation and every program in terms of what it does to the family". Former Vice President Walter Mondale said that nearly all the human problems he had seen were created by family breakdowns, and he called for "family impact statements", much like environmental impact statements. My contention here is that the discriminatory immigration laws enacted against the Chinese are a classical example of how legislation has severely affected Chinese American families to the extent of dictating their form, their size, their make-up, and family member interactions.

The mutilated family was an adaptation to the exclusion acts and highly restrictive quotas. On the other hand, miscegenation laws enacted in fourteen states with high concentrations of Chinese prevented the men from establishing interracial unions. In essence, a long-distance family was better than no family at all, and the Chinese suffered the separation, the sporadic conjugal relationships, and the lack of home comforts as the best-of-all-evils response to the laws. In turn, the other distinct characteristics of the Chinese American family, such as the smaller size, the two-tier offspring cohorts, etc., are corollary consequences of the dismembered family. Karl Marx has shown how technology impacted upon the social structure of society. Laws may also impact in the same way.

PROMINENT FEMALE ROLE

I have lived in and visited villages in southern China in the 1930s and the 1970s where the inhabitants were overwhelmingly women, children, and older folk. The able-bodied men were abroad, and their absence was conspicuous. The family income came in bi-monthly or quarterly checks from the United States. Women performed most of the tasks and made the family decisions. The children had never seen their fathers or had seen them only on their infrequent trips back to China. Even husbands and wives, separated by thousands of miles and lengthy intervals between trips, were strangers to one another. Parental bonds were stronger, held together by blood ties and the cardinal virtue of filial piety. Female influence in child-rearing was dominant. The children were surrounded by their mothers, aunts, grandmothers, and perhaps grandfathers returned from abroad. There were few male models to emulate; Freud would be hard put to explain his Oedipus complex in this kind of family situation where no father is around to compete with the son for the mother's attention.

The physical absence of the men created a departure from the prevailing patriarchial familial structure. Even if the immigrant family could not be labeled a matriarchial one, it was definitely female dominant. The women from such families enjoyed a modicum of independence and authority that their sisters in traditional families did not have. They had to make the daily decisions affecting the life of the family, and they learned how to handle money and deal with people outside of the home. Naturally, these women became extremely self-reliant. Their lives were centered

FIGURE V
Changing Husband/Wife Identity Roles

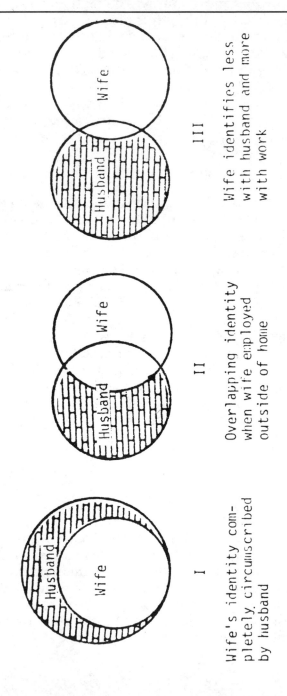

totally around their children and their parents-in-law. The husband-wife relationship was a minor aspect of the marriage to be played out occasionally during the husband's return trips to China. Nevertheless, in China the wife's identity was completely circumscribed by her husband. She would sever almost all her relations with her family and identify totally with her husband's family. She would serve his parents and bear his children who would take his name. Even though her husband was not present, it was her duty to maintain his home.

Fig. V shows the transformation of identity when the Chinese wife comes to New York City. Invariably she will immediately take a job in the garment factory. Now she has an identity outside the home, albeit an insignificant one. Her income gives her a measure of economic power, and she is in contact with people outside of the family. The dominant part of her identity is still with her husband, but no longer exclusively so, hence the overlapping of circles in Fig. V. In time, the progression may tend toward the evolving model of husband and wife having separate identities yet maintaining the marital bond between them. Already the transformation from Stage I toward Stage II is a radical change for the Chinese immigrant wife.

FAMILY SIZE AND SPACING OF CHILDREN

The mutilated family structure has spawned other peculiar characteristics in the immigrant Chinese family. One is family size. The number of children depended upon the frequency of the husband's trips home, and if these were infrequent, the number of offspring were correspondingly few. Traditionally, the Chinese have valued large families and many sons. Forced to live apart by the circumstance of U.S. immigration barriers and thus unable to have more children, immigrant families were invariably smaller. Not only were the children fewer, their births were more widely spaced. The years separating the siblings again inevitably depended upon the frequency of the father's return trips. Consequently, in many immigrant Chinese families the age gap between siblings is greater than usual. In fact, the parents may have sets of children widely spaced. The more common situation is an older set born in China when the father made his periodic trips home and another set born in the United States after the family was brought to this country. Though the siblings may be brothers and sisters born of the same parents, the age gap between them may be so great that they have little in common.

RELAY IMMIGRATION

If the men came first, and the wives and children joined them subsequently, one may characterize this phenomenon as relay immigration. The pattern of immigration is fairly common among other immigrant groups as well as the Chinese and is somewhat culturally or politically determined. The situation gives rise to a set of adjustment problems in addition to the one of transplantation because the immediate family members must get to know each other when reunited. One girl said, "At first, I could not bring myself to call this strange man 'Father'. The words stuck to my tongue." Sons who had been indulged by their mothers looked upon their fathers as intruders into their close family circle. Wives had to relinquish their control over the purse strings and their authority as heads of the household. The men had to get to know their women and children, some of whom they had never seen before. In spite of these stresses and strains, the family shell has withstood the battering, but there have been major alterations within the family.

STATUS AND ROLE

In the traditional Chinese family, every man, woman, and child has a definite place within a culturally prescribed hierarchy clearly determined by age and sex. If everyone knows his or her place and acts accordingly, order is assured. The grandparents or the elderly occupy the highest status rank by virtue of age and generation. The males stand considerably above the females of the same generation. Fig. VI diagrams the change in age and sex status hierarchy in the Chinese family after immigration. The father's status is invariably lowered. The working wife's or mother's status is raised to either slightly below the father or even slightly above if she happens to be the main provider. In the more egalitarian American society, the daughter's status is also raised to only slightly below that of the son's rather than being substantially lower. The grandparents are in an amorphous position. Being elderly, they generally cannot contribute economically to the family purse. More often than not, instead of being the fount of wisdom and experience, they become highly dependent and somewhat useless. Under such conditions, their status is lowered between that of the parents and the offspring.

FIGURE VI
Age and Sex Status Hierarchy in the Chinese Family

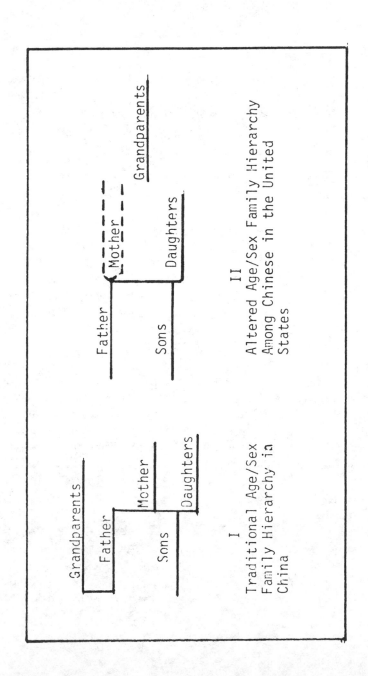

Grandparents

Father

Mother

Daughters

Sons

II

Altered Age/Sex Family Hierarchy
Among Chinese in the United
States

Grandparents

Father

Mother

Daughters

Sons

I

Traditional Age/Sex
Family Hierarchy in
China

In addition to status or position, people have roles to play and these roles delineate the way they relate to one another and to society at large. If a society is stable, the role changes are minor. If a society is in a stage of flux, the roles may have to be altered drastically to fit the environment and the circumstances.

Father's Lower Status

If the father has been the source of the checks that were sent regularly back to Hong Kong or China, he indubitably enjoyed the elevated status due to him as the family provider. He also enjoyed a high social status as a "guest of the Golden Mountain".[2]

As has already been established, the more recent immigrants tend to be among the professional class, but when they come to these shores, they find that they must take lower echelon jobs. The language barrier is the biggest hurdle they face. A lawyer, an accountant, a teacher, or a businessman in Hong Kong simply cannot pick up his former profession or business here. At the beginning, he must accept what work there is, and if he is dependent upon his relatives or friends to find him a job, the job is inevitably in the restaurant business (See, Table 12-1).

Note that only one out of ten fathers who held professional positions prior to immigration could find a similar one after immigration. Half the businessmen and five-sixths of the skilled laborers had to take lower-rung jobs, and it is obvious that these jobs (108) were concentrated in restaurant work. A very high proportion, 75 out of 262, did not respond to this question fully, indicating perhaps unemployment or reluctance to state what their jobs were. Such a come-down is not only disappointing for the man himself, but it also reduces his status in the eyes of his wife and children. One father interviewed used to be a pharmacist; he was unemployed. He considered himself a professional and was loath to accept a lower status job. A man's work is his identity. To step downward or backward must be a terrible blow to his ego and self-esteem. Another father interviewed used to own a fleet of taxis in Hong Kong. Now he runs a laundromat. He said on many occasions he regrets his decision to come here, but he consoles

---

[2] Few people in Hong Kong and China concern themselves with how the Chinese earn their money in this country. All they know is that the sum, when magnified by the favorable exchange rate, is generous, so they view this country as the Mountain of Gold.

TABLE 12-1

Parents' Occupations Before and After Immigration by Residence

	In Chinatown				In Satellite Community				Total			
	Father		Mother		Father		Mother		Father		Mother	
	Before	After	Before	After	Before	After	Before	After	Before	After	Before	After
Professional	5	0	1	2	5	1	1	0	10	1	2	2
Businessman	14	3	1	0	20	14	2	3	34	17	3	3
Skilled Laborer	24	5	1	0	6	1	1	0	30	6	2	0
Clerical Worker	4	0	2	0	7	0	1	0	11	0	3	0
Factory Worker	29	28	36	105	8	4	7	35	37	32	43	140
Restaurant Worker	18	77	4	1	11	31	1	1	29	108	5	2
Farmer	2	0	1	0	1	0	1	0	3	0	2	0
Seamen	18	1	a	a	4	0	a	a	22	1	a	a
Service Worker	16	10	0	0	9	12	0	0	25	22	0	22
Housewife	a	a	91	34	a	a	66	30	a	a	157	64
No Response	33	39	26	21	28	36	19	30	61	75	45	51
Total	163	163	163	163	99	99	99	99	262	262	262	262

Note: a Not applicable.

Source: Student Survey Questionnaire, 1978.

himself by saying that his children will have a better future in the United States. This way of thinking is a key to unlocking the acceptance of transitional difficulties for the Chinese immigrants: to sacrifice the present for a better tomorrow, not necessarily for oneself (and this is crucial) but for future generations, if need be. Irving Howe, in his book *World of Our Fathers* (1976:251), ascribed the same stoicism to the early Jewish immigrants. The fathers considered themselves a transitional generation. "With gratifications postponed, the culture of the East Side became a culture utterly devoted to its sons. Onto their backs it lowered all its aspirations and delusions expecting that the children of the new world would reach the goals their fathers could not reach themselves.... By providing consolations of the ideal, their visions gave the immigrant Jews strength enough to survive the miseries of the settlement. By releasing long-suppressed energies, their ambitions drove them to labor, sacrifice, obsession, and material conquest."

Working Wives and Mothers

The wives are not saddled as heavily with such ego problems. Most have never before gone outside the home to earn money. Table 12-1 shows that 157, or approximately 60 percent, were housewives before immigration, whereas almost all who could be identified as employed worked in the garment factories after their arrival here. Garment factory work is readily available, requires no language ability, is quickly learned, offers flexible hours, and is close at hand.

Because it is harder for a man than a woman to find suitable employment, or because a man may find it beneath his dignity to accept a lower-status job, when financial needs are pressing the woman of the house goes to work. In many cases, she becomes the main family provider until the husband resigns himself to the fact that restaurant work is about the best he can hope for. Garment factory work may net more than restaurant work considering the long hours that the newcomer works at her sewing machine. She is paid by the piece, and depending upon her speed and the time she puts in, she can gross upward of $200 a week during the busy season. This is a fantastic sum to a woman who has never earned money before, and it gives her a sense of increased status and power. The magnitude and pervasiveness of working women is apparent when one realizes that six out of every ten families in Chinatown has someone working in the garment factories.

This reversal of husband and wife roles has its repercussions within the family circle. It puts an immediate strain on the conjugal relationship at a time when the husband's self-esteem is low and when the entire family is trying to make adjustments to all of the other changes happening so swiftly in their lives.

ELEVATED FEMALE STATUS

Unquestionably, female status in the Chinese immigrant family has been altered by the present and important economic role of the mother, by her former independent role as head of the household in the homeland, and by her place in the hearts of her children. She commands an important position in the home. But it is the second generation female status that jumps immeasurably higher. The key is education. Girls have the same opportunity as boys to go through high school. They still do not enjoy the advantages given their brothers in college. The number of Chinese male students is continually higher than that for Chinese female students by an approximate ratio of three to one at the City College of New York. Nevertheless, their high school education will provide them with a ladder to greater freedom of choice and latitude than their mothers had. When asked which is more important, career or marriage, two-thirds of the girls surveyed answered "career".

Reversal of Parent-Child Roles

This study was confined to recent immigrant children and youth, so the Chinese cultural values and roles still persist in the home. However, as the children are exposed more and more to the American way of life, parental ties, control, and influence begin to fade. A reversal in parent-child roles is a frequent occurrence in Chinese American homes, especially those where the parents are not well educated and do not speak English. Right after immigration, parents and children are at the same starting line. Neither speaks English, but within a few years the children will have attended school and become fairly proficient in English. At that point, the parents will turn increasingly to their children for help. Instead of the parents leading the way and instructing the child, the roles are reversed. Some parents are quite helpless—especially the ones who have had little education—and they lean heavily upon their children. At the same time, because of cultural conflicts as the American ways seep into the immigrant families or because the parents are not knowledgeable, the children cannot turn to their parents for guidance or direction. Fig. VII shows how the traditional parent-child roles have been altered to a more egalitarian role or role reversal.

The educational level of the parents of the high school students surveyed is shown in Table 12-2 and is correlated with occupation. At least half of the fathers had a high school education or better, but only 32 out of 253 had been to college. The other half had

FIGURE VII
Parent-Child Role Reversal

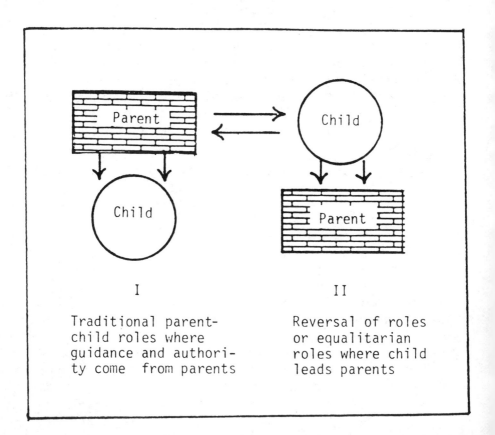

I

Traditional parent-child roles where guidance and authority come from parents

II

Reversal of roles or equalitarian roles where child leads parents

either an elementary school education or none at all. Overwhelmingly, the mothers in the survey group were poorly educated. Yet
almost all of the students surveyed aspired to college. The disparity of educational levels between immigrant parents and children
can be great and creates a situation in which the parent as a model
no longer holds. The children need substitute models, either in
their teachers or from leaders in the Chinese community. Unfortunately, role models or leadership in the Chinese communities
are sorely lacking.

TABLE 12-2

Parent's Present Occupation and Level of Education

	None	Level of Education Elem.	H.S.	College+	Total
Father's Present Occupation					
Professional	0	0	0	1	1
Businessman	1	1	5	10	17
Skilled Laborer	3	2	1	0	6
Factory Worker	3	12	15	3	33
Restaurant Worker	14	48	44	3	109
Seaman	0	0	1	0	1
Service or Unskilled Worker	3	8	8	3	22
No Response	5	21	26	12	64
Total	29	92	100	32	253
Mother's Present Occupation					
Professional	0	0	0	0	0
Business Woman	0	0	2	1	3
Skilled Laborer	0	0	0	0	0
Clerical Worker	0	0	0	0	0
Factory Worker	34	66	40	1	141
Restaurant Worker	0	1	1	0	2
Housewife or Service Worker	13	24	22	3	62
No Response	7	20	10	3	40
Total	54	111	75	8	248

Source: Student Survey Questionnaire, 1978.

FAMILIES WITHOUT PARENTS

If the wife/mother puts in eight to twelve hours a day at work, she will not also be able to provide the services she formerly provided for her husband and children. Nor will she be there to keep an eye on the children. As discussed previously, the most noticeable phenomenon in the Chinese immigrant family is the lack of parental presence. Table 12-3 tabulates the number of hours or days that the Chinese high school immigrant students see their parents. For example, 82 percent lived with both mother and father, but 32 percent did not see their fathers from one day to the next and 21 percent never even caught a glimpse of their mothers. If the father worked in a restaurant, his hours were usually 10:00 a.m. until 11:00 p.m. or midnight. On his one day off, he would sleep late and perhaps manage to see his children for a few hours after school, most likely at the evening meal.

The mothers worked equally long hours; that they saw their children more often than their husbands did was due to the fact that they frequently took their children to the factory with them or at least would come home to prepare the evening meal. It was disturbing to note that 17 percent of the high school students never saw their mothers—not even for a single day—from one week to the next. This conspicuous absence of parents from the immigrant Chinese home made it extremely difficult to interview the parents. Even when evening or weekend appointments were scheduled, we frequently had to return many times because the mother would suddenly be working overtime or be called in on Sundays to get out an order.

When some children were asked how they felt about their parents not being home, they said they felt lonely, ignored, and neglected. The mother's absence was most keenly felt, and many made the comment that their mothers loved money more than they loved their children. They understood the need for their mothers to work, but they were critical of her long hours away from home. When asked if the parents kept close supervision over them, 53 percent of the male high school students and 66 percent of the female said yes. The remainder said no. When asked who disciplines them, the following picture emerged (Table 12-4).

Obviously, the mother is the main disciplinarian in the home, but it is disturbing to note that 29 percent of the teenage males are disciplined by no one. This lack of parental supervision, guid-

TABLE 12-3
Chinese High School Students' Contact with and Closeness to Parents

	Father No.	N=270 Pct.	Mother No.	N=270 Pct.
Live with Parents:				
Yes	222	82	232	86
No	27	10	21	8
No Response	21	8	17	6
Hours See Parents Daily:				
0	86	32	57	21
1-2	40	15	10	4
3-5	96	36	87	32
6-8+	48	18	116	43
Days See Parents Weekly:				
0	58	21	45	17
1	40	15	10	4
2-5	31	11	19	7
6-7	141	52	196	73
Closeness to Parents:				
Distant	17	6	5	2
Not Close	46	17	25	9
Somewhat Close	78	29	78	29
Very Close	106	39	147	54
No Response	23	9	15	6

Source: Student Survey Questionnaire, 1978.

ance, or presence may not have an impact, but I fear that the seeds sown will sprout in later years. Already, we may be seeing the results of it in the eruption of Chinatown gangs.

There were, however, some positive conditions and strengths within these families that should be noted. Despite the fact that many of these children hardly knew or saw their fathers, they still felt somewhat close or very close to them. They felt even closer to

TABLE 12-4
Disciplinarian in the Family

	Males		Females	
	No.	Pct.	No.	Pct.
No One	24	29	14	16
Father	15	18	12	14
Mother	37	45	53	60
Other	7	8	9	10
Total	83	100	88	100

Source: Student Survey Questionnaire, 1978.

their mothers (*See,* Table 12-3). These feelings are a strong hold-over from the cultural values instilled in them to honor and respect their parents. When asked: "How often do you agree or disagree with your parents?" the girls were found to be more compliant, but neither sex was at great odds with father or mother. In this instance, we are referring to immigrant children and not American born children of immigrant parents where the generation gap is considerable.[3]

Even when the high school students interviewed had strong disagreements with their parents or when they were somewhat ashamed of how their parents looked or behaved, they would invariably end up saying, "But he's my father", or "She's my mother". Those pronouncements settled the matter. Parental bonds were ironclad. Children were reluctant to go against their parents' wishes or to incur their displeasure. Again, this reluctance is a holdover of Chinese values where filial piety is the cardinal virtue.

LOSS OF WIDER KINSHIP OR CLAN SUPPORT

The average Chinese family may not be the extended kinship unit described by Olga Lang (1946) or Lin Yutang (1935), but stem or

---

[3] Substantiation of this fact comes from the author's dealing with young people in her more than ten years of teaching at the City College of New York and her contacts with Chinese families.

nuclear families generally live close enough to one another in China, Hong Kong or Taiwan to see one another frequently, to be able to call upon each other in times of need, or to derive the sense of security inherent in kinship relationships. When a Chinese family migrates to the United States, it seeks the proximity of kinfolk by crowding into Chinatowns. Family ties still hold, but many of the props have been pulled out by economic conditions and American values.

One complaint heard frequently is that people have no time for one another anymore. For economic survival, everyone works long hours. Restaurants are open seven days a week, and their evening

TABLE 12-5

Agreement or Disagreement with Parents

Agree with Parents	Males		Females	
	No.	Pct.	No.	Pct.
Never	19	15	7	5
Sometimes	40	33	44	34
Half Time	41	33	43	34
Always	23	19	34	27
Total	123	100	128	100

Source: Student Survey Questionnaire, 1978.

TABLE 12-6

Five Ranking Areas of Disagreement with Parents

Males	Females
1. Spending money	1. Disobedience
2. Disobedience	2. Spending money
3. Parents too old-fashioned	3. Dating
4. Chores	4. Coming home late
5. Coming home late	5. Parents expect too much

Source: Student Survey Questionnaire, 1978.

and weekend hours take away time that parents ordinarily spend with their families. The piece-rate arrangement in the garment factories pits the women against the clock in their race for the dollar. The one day they have off is spent catching up with essential household and personal chores. Time is a luxury; no one can afford to stop and chat, to exchange pleasantries, to listen to another's concerns and problems, or even to be sociable. Life is a treadmill, and each person is fully involved in, and intent upon, staying on the belt. Many of the little niceties of human relationships are sacrificed to the work demon.

"People change a lot when they come to this country", is a statement commonly heard. "They become selfish." Whatever the reason, kinfolk are not as willing to lend a helping hand as they were in the homeland.

The family or village associations, once the rallying points of common ancestry and identity, are fast losing ground as viable institutions. Controlled by elders who cannot and have not kept up with conditions created by the recent huge influx of immigrants, these organizations are declining and disintegrating. The younger people no longer belong or participate. In fact, they don't even have time for their immediate family, much less for their extended family.

THE FAMILY ABODE

The physical environs of the family are no less important a factor than the makeup or status roles of the members. A description of the two communities from which the subjects and respondents of this study were drawn was already detailed in Chapter IV. The following relates what was learned when the homes of some of the students interviewed were visited.

Case One

Wendy Chin (all names are pseudonyms) was thirteen years old at the time of the interview and attended the Chinatown junior high. She had been in the United States one year. Her father came first; her mother came with the son two years ago; Wendy and her sister came last. They were originally from the mainland, but had lived in Hong Kong for ten years while waiting for their papers. The family lived in a fifth floor walk-up apartment on the fringes of Chinatown bordering on the old Jewish community. They paid a little over $100 a month for a four-room apartment, but they had to pay $800 key money for the privilege of moving in. There were two small bedrooms, one large kitchen, and one elongated entranceway used as the living room. There was a modern toilet, but no bath tub or shower. Obviously, the apartment had been fixed up recently, but there were two large leaks in the ceilings of the kitchen and living room, and water had loosened large chunks of plaster. The apartment was one of ten in the building owned by a Chinese landlord.

The apartment was very clean inside, but the hallway was dark and the stairs rickety. Yet Mrs. Chin was very happy that her son had found this place, and one could see that the family members were close and overjoyed that they were now all united in this country. Mrs. Chin worked in a garment factory hanging up skirts and buttoning up garments. She earned about twenty dollars a day. Mr. Chin was not at home. He left for work in the suburbs at 10:00 or 11:00 a.m. and returned after midnight.

Case Two

Su Ling, age thirteen, also from the Chinatown junior high, kept putting off the home visit. In most of the family visits, the interviewers had to resort to the door-to-door salesman's technique of putting a foot in the door and trying to talk their way in. Most of the students refused to say where they lived. It seemed as if they were ashamed of their homes, and I could see why Su Ling felt that way. I saw Su Ling walking home from school, so I followed her. When she got to the door, I asked her to invite me in. She consented reluctantly, but told me I could only stay for a short while.

There were two bedrooms in the three-room apartment and a tiny hallway space. The living room was about eight feet square. The parents used one bedroom and six children (boys and girls alike) slept in three bunkbeds in the other. The bunkbeds lined the walls of the room like an inverted U, and if all six children were to jump out of bed at the same time, they would not have space to stand. The room had only one light fixture on the ceiling, thus it was utilized only for sleeping. A seventh person slept on the living room couch. There was a television, and the tiny hallway held a sewing machine for the mother to work with at home.

Su Ling said her mother would be very angry at her if she knew that the girl had let someone into the house, so I did not linger long.

Case Three

Yuet Han, a young fellow of fourteen, was also from the China-town junior high and had been in this country for about six months. His family operated a fish store in the heart of China-town, so I dropped in on him one day after school. He was help-ing out by waiting on customers, and business was brisk. Yuet Han pointed out his mother, but I could not talk to her while she was waiting on customers and cleaning the fish. I asked where the family lived. Yuet Han pointed to the back of the store. Pro-priety prevented me from intruding further into their private lives when the family was so busy at work. Again, I did not see any male figure who could be the father.

Case Four

The first time my research associate, Dr. Rose Chao, went on a family visit, she was so upset she called me immediately after-ward to say that she wasn't going to make another visit unaccom-panied. The shock of what she saw was vividly described in her preliminary report:

> The winter of 1977 was one of the coldest in New York's history. That winter, the Chus, a family of six, slept in their tiny kitchen, about 8' by 10', in their three-room sixth-floor walk-up. In the kitchen there was a televi-sion, four chairs, a kitchen table, and two refrigerators. One was broken and served as a storage cabinet since there was none in the kitchen. A tiny gas stove stood inches from the door with an old sink next to it. There was an electric heater in the center of the room. I was alarmed to find only one electric outlet in the kitchen. It was heavily overloaded with plugs. Since the Chus apartment was on the top floor, the unmelted snow, ac-cumulated during the two previous snowfalls, had made the ceiling in the apartment very damp. In a corner of the kitchen ceiling near the pipes there was a steady drip.

> The front room in the apartment overlooking the street had not been used the entire winter; the temperature in that room only differed a few degrees from the temper-ature outside. There was no heater in this room. Mrs. Chu kept the window next to the fire escape opened a

crack because of the fear of fire. There had been a fire in the building a few blocks away several months ago. Mrs. Chu wanted to be able to open the window so that the family could get out quickly in case of fire. Fear of burning to death was greater than the discomfort of the bitter cold.

Dr. Chao went on to tell how a rat ran across her feet as she was sitting in the apartment. She shuddered to think of the health and physical hazard these rodents could pose, particularly to the little baby.

More case histories of family living quarters in Chinatown would only be repetitious. The housing stock in Chinatown is ancient and dilapidated. The adjacent area into which the new immigrant families are moving is the infamous Lower East Side. The rents are kept low by rent control, but made expensive by key money. The demand is so great that shortage of housing is acute. It is the overcrowding that stands out as the most glaring problem. Perhaps the crowding is not so keenly felt by the immigrants who have just come out of a "sardine can" like Hong Kong. Nevertheless, the lack of space and privacy must take its toll on health and nerves.

Housing facilities in the satellite community were many times better than those in Chinatown. As mentioned previously, the houses now occupied by the Chinese families were built during the 1950s and 1960s. They are solid two- to three-family brick attached homes with front and back yards. Some are older frame houses, but they have been well maintained by their owners. The newer houses, rows and rows of them, are almost all the same. There are two six-room apartments on the upper floors, a garage and a three-room unit on the street level. These homes sold in the late 1970s for $90,000 and up. Those renting the six-room units paid from $350 to $385 a month. In comparison with apartments in New York City of the same quality, the rentals could be considered reasonable. In general, the furnishings in the homes were modest and more functional than decorative. Invariably, there were bicycles in the hallway. Books and toys, which were noticeably lacking in the Chinatown homes, were frequently in evidence in the satellite community homes.

The higher rentals or cost of purchasing a home meant that the immigrants who went into the satellite Chinatown had more financial resources available or they were willing to spend more of their family income on housing than were the New York Chinatown families.

Case Five
The family arrived two and a half years prior to the interview, but the father had been here previously (again, we see the relay immigration pattern). The father had a graduate degree in business administration, but here he owned and operated the local grocery store. The wife had been a nurse in Taiwan. The two boys, ages nineteen and sixteen, were in high school. The family was Mandarin-speaking.

It was obvious that there was a great deal of discontent in the family. The mother wanted to resume her nursing career, but knew it was an unattainable dream because she could not speak English. Besides, she had to help her husband in the store. The teenage sons wanted to play ball with their friends after school, but they had to help their parents and resented having to work. The father felt that his sons were lazy and that his wife was not giving him the moral support he needed. He complained that, after living alone in this country for several years, he finally, managed to bring his wife and sons here, but their expectations of the United States were much greater than could be met. Instead of being grateful, they were disappointed. He felt that with his M.B.A. degree he should have done better.

Case Six
Mr. Wang owned an efficiency apartment complex of twenty-five apartments in Taiwan, which he rented to United States military personnel. In Mr. Wang's case, the relay immigration pattern was reversed. He sent his wife and children to this country first, and he came a year later. He was very excited at the prospect of coming to the United States, but once here the only job he could get was as a salad chef in a large midtown Manhattan hotel. He did not sell his apartment complex in Taiwan, so he was still collecting rent there to subsidize his living expenses here.

Fewer mothers in the satellite community worked, thus they had more time to spend with their children and among themselves. Dr. Chao reported that she was often welcomed in her home visits because the mothers hoped she would make a fourth in their mah-jong games.

Considering the differences in the family background between the immigrants who lived in the two communities, it is very difficult to make valid comparisons about adjustment and adaptation. It seems that the recent immigrant families living in the satellite communities went directly into that neighborhood without first being routed through Chinatown. They tend to have more financial resources, to be better educated, and to speak Mandarin instead of Cantonese. Therefore, we are comparing two different classes of immigrants: those who are able to afford the $350 rentals or the purchase of a $90,000 home, and those who must squeeze into the rundown tenements of Chinatown. If there is any truth to the commonly maintained premise that socioeconomic class is an almost infallible indicator of success or failure in the American educational system, then the immigrant children living in the satellite Chinese community will have an inherent advantage in their achievement record in school and their adaptation to a new life in the United States.[4] We may not be able to make a valid comparison of the extent and rate of adjustment of immigrant children in the two communities for this reason, but at least we will have uncovered this difference and taken this factor into account.

FAMILY INCOME

At the time of this writing, income figures broken down for Chinese by neighborhoods were not yet available from the 1980 census. The closest approximation would be median household income by census tract, but these figures are for the total population. Thirty percent of the population that comprise the Manhattan Chinatown tracts are Chinese, so these tracts can serve as guidelines. The same cannot be said for the satellite Chinatown tracts, thus they are not presented here.

It is quite apparent from these figures that Chinatown families are poor. Median income means that half of the households have less than the amounts listed above, and more often than not represents the income of more than one earner. For purposes of com-

---

[4] Prof. W.W. Charters maintains that social class of the parents predicts with almost certainty the success or failure of the offspring in the American educational system. He said that this has been so consistently confirmed by research that it can now be regarded as empirical law. *See,* W.W.Charters "The Social Background of Teaching".

TABLE 12-7

Median Household Income for Census Tracts
in Manhattan's Chinatown, 1979

Tract No.	Median Income	Tract No.	Median Income
2.01	$ 7,311	25	$ 7,111
2.02	8,106	27	14,527
6	8,233	29	10,523
8	10,936	30.01	6,992
16	10,194	41	8,527
18	8,093	43	10,146
22.01	10,025		

Source: U.S. Census Bureau as quoted in ILGWU, *The Chinatown Garment Industry Study*, 1983. Table A-12.

parison, the median household income for the borough of Manhattan in 1979 was $13,905.

In general, when immigrant groups first arrive in this country they are poor, and the poor are handicapped economically, socially, and academically. "But being poor is also a state of mind", wrote Irving Howe (1976:258) of the Jewish immigrants. "All the evidence we have suggests that the children of the Lower East Side rarely felt deprived. They certainly knew that life was hard, but they assumed that, until they grew up and got a grip on things, it had to be hard".

In his study of Puerto Rican and Mexican immigrants, however, Oscar Lewis (1968) felt that there is a "culture of poverty" that is perpetuated from generation to generation. "By the time slum children are age six or seven, they have usually absorbed the basic values and attitudes of their subculture and are not psychologically geared to take full advantage of the changing conditions or increased opportunities that may occur in their lifetime".

Lewis contends that there are clusters of characteristics in conjunction with their functioning and patterning that define the culture of poverty. Among them, on the level of the individual, are strong feelings of marginality, helplessness, dependence, and inferiority. On the group level, there are a weak sense of group identity and a low level of organization within a highly stratified society. Fatalism and a low level of aspiration are key traits of the culture of poverty. Lewis maintains that these traits have evolved and are perpetuated as coping mechanisms to deal with deprivation and frustration.

Is the culture of poverty evident in the Chinese community? Some of the individual characteristics are present, but group identity is strong and the culture is rich. Aspirations are high and so are hopes for the future. The area teems with vitality and activity. The people are hard at work for long hours at low-paying jobs. They have been resourceful at devising means of livelihood for themselves in the restaurant, garment and tourist industries. They save whatever they can from their meager earnings, but their present frugality means shoring up for the future. The drawback is they are penalized for these virtues because they do not apply for welfare and are seldom granted funds for social services to which they are entitled. For example, Title I funds to schools in economically disadvantaged neighborhoods were denied to the Chinatown public schools because only a handful of families were on public assistance—the criterion for Title I funds. Yet, more than in any other area, these schools were shouldering the extra burden of easing an immigrant group into American society. Besides, as mentioned previously, enrollment for these schools far exceeds capacity.

EVOLVING WITH THE AMERICAN FAMILY

The changes that have come about in the Chinese immigrant family are not merely changes resulting from their transplantation alone. In addition to the decreasing size and realignment of family relationships, the immigrant families are caught up in the tide of changes taking place in the American family as well. In the evolving American family, the affective and nurturing-of-young functions have superseded the biological function. A strong emotional attachment between husband and wife is the fundamental requisite of family formation. This takes precedence above all, and when the bloom of marital love wears off, the union tends to disintegrate. In today's liberated society, extra-marital sex is easy to come by and is no longer frowned upon. The procreation of children has become an inconsequential aspect judging by the rate of abortions performed. When children are involved, however, their nurturing and upbringing are strong factors in holding families together, and when men and women want children, they still wish to bring them up in a family environment.

The American family is seldom a producing economic unit but rather a consuming economic one. Just as many social activities take place outside the home as within it, and family ties are loose and tenuous. Recognizing the weakening functions of the American family, President Jimmy Carter wanted to promulgate a strong family policy, but when he tried to convene a national family conference, the pre-conference planners could not even agree on the definition of a family. Moreover, the Census Bureau revealed that more than one-fourth of all American households consists of persons living alone or with nonrelatives, and that by 1995, the proportion of nonfamily households will rise to one out of three. The undertow of such a strong current toward family disintegration cannot help but pull the Chinese immigrant family along and effect more changes in it as acculturation into American society takes hold.

XIII

Adjustment

SOCIAL ADJUSTMENT

The determination of whether one is doing well depends upon the yardstick applied. This study has dwelled heavily upon the sociological aspects of adjustment. Children and youth were observed and studied in their schools, their homes, their communities, and among their peers. These are group environments. The child relates to the group to see if he fits within the societal norms and expectations. Do his performance and behavior interfere with those around him? If there is no perceivable dislocation or disorganization caused by these children in the school, home, and community, can we say, "All is well"? If disruptions or eruptions have occurred, does this signal social change or must the deviant behavior be brought back into line with the collective interests of the group in question?

TEACHER AND PARENTAL EXPECTATIONS

What is expected of children who are immigrants from another culture in an American setting? The expectation—and even the law mandates it—is that children under sixteen must attend school. If the child shows up in school every day, does his lessons reasonably well as judged by test scores, commits no infraction of the rules or regulations, and causes no trouble, then he is deemed a well-adjusted child. Chapter VI described the Chinese children in a school setting. In spite of the language difficulties experienced, in spite of the strange customs and surroundings into which they are thrust, the overwhelming majority seem to be doing well academically. Their attendance exceeded ninety percent. The teachers are delighted with their Chinese pupils, for they are obedient and respectful, they make little commotion and even less trouble, they do as they are told, and they make the teacher's job very easy.

This type of behavior is already part of the Chinese children's upbringing and has merely been transferred from the Chinese school to the American school. For American teachers who are accustomed to less pliant students, the change offers a welcome respite, although many teachers said they wished for a less rigid teacher-pupil relationship. In the eyes of teachers and students alike, by and large, Chinese immigrant children are performing very well in school and do in fact exceed expectation.

Children are expected to obey their parents, to please their parents by doing well in school, to help with family chores, and, if necessary, to help toward family financial support. In these respects Chinese immigrants again experience no discontinuity with the ways in which they have been brought up, with the exception perhaps of going to work outside the home. As shown in Chapter XII, despite frequent parental absence in the immigrant home, the children identify strongly with their parents and with their families. This identification and attachment may weaken as the immigrant child begins to absorb American values and the American way of thinking, but shortly after immigration the maintenance of that sense of family loyalty, duty, and obligation marks them as dutiful, well-behaved children. As roles are reversed however, as the child begins to guide and support the parents, the gap between parent and child will widen and create problems.

DROPOUT AND TRUANCY

Using school dropout as an indicator to measure adjustment, we again come to a favorable conclusion. Table 6-5 showed that the dropout rate among bilingual high school students was low. Not only do the youths continue with their education beyond the compulsory age of sixteen, but the high schools continue to enroll students twenty and twenty-one years of age. Moreover, and almost without exception, the high school graduates indicated that they would go on to college.

Truancy and cutting are usually the first symptoms of adjustment problems. If the cause of the truancy can be uncovered, as was attempted in the Chinatown high school by a very conscientious guidance counselor, problems can be brought to the surface and dealt with before they become more serious. For example, this guidance counselor would call the family after the third day of absence from school. Many times the parents do not know the child is absent, and alerting them usually means the parents will deal with the situation immediately. Once a dialogue is established between the guidance counselor and the parents, both will try to help the child. Two cases come to mind to illustrate this point, but such cases were not common.

Case One

Male student, seventeen years old, in the eleventh grade, started to cut physical education classes. The persistent cutting signaled a problem. The guidance counselor called the boy's father and asked the student to come in for a chat. After a few sessions with the counselor, the boy revealed that he was leaving school early to avoid the gangs who were threatening him after school. By sneaking out early, he thought he was solving the problem. Further questioning uncovered the fact that he was not eating during his lunch period either. Instead, he went to the library, where he thought he was safe. The boy's grades were suffering from the tension engendered by this fear, but he was attempting to handle the situation by himself instead of letting his family and school counselor help him. This tendency to keep problems to themselves, to evade the situation or to withdraw from dealing with the problem directly is fairly common among immigrant children. Unless an astute observer recognizes the telltale signs, the problem may go undiscovered until it is too late.

Case Two

Young girl, seventeen years old, in the United States nine months, had been absent from school three days. The counselor looked up the girl's academic record and found that she had been doing quite well in spite of her short period of time in this country. When contacted, the father said the daughter had decided to quit school and go to work. The counselor did not accept this explanation. She asked the girl to come back to school for a chat. The girl came in dressed completely in black. She was pale and haggard. No one in the family had died, but symbolically she was mourning her mother, who had gone back to Hong Kong with her youngest brother. In their grief, she and three siblings had quit school and gone to work in the garment factory with a single purpose in mind; they would work until they had saved enough money for plane fare to be reunited with their beloved mother.

In this family, the common pattern of relay immigration was again evident. The father had come first and after many years had sent for his family. The mother, however, did not like the United States. It was not clear why the mother left with the youngest boy. The children, who were very close to their mother, blamed their father for "chasing her away". To punish him, they dressed in black mourning clothes.

In her talks with the guidance counselor, the girl confessed that she wanted to finish school and go on to college. When made to see that the chances of her or her siblings ever completing their education in Hong Kong were slim, she began to view the prospect of living in the United States in a different light. The girl was referred to a pyschological counselor from Columbia University doing fieldwork at the school, who helped her to see the situation from her father's viewpoint as well as from her own. With the broadened perspective, she resumed her studies and her resentment against her father subsided.

Again we see an example of refusing to admit to a problem in order to come to grips with it. Here, it was the father who said his daughter wanted to quit school and work. If the guidance counselor had not persisted, this case would have smoldered later to erupt when the children departed. A similar situation occurred in Bip's case, detailed in Chapter X. The father refused to ask for help from the community agencies because he was afraid of losing face. When claims are made that all is well, further probing may reveal that indeed all is not well. It takes an astute observer attuned to the cultural nuances of denial to find whether there really are problems. That is why the guidance counselor may be indispensible for Chinese immigrant students. A competent counselor who can speak their language and who is familiar with the cultural leanings can immediately spot a budding problem and deal with it before it gets out of hand, especially since the Chinese try to cover up their differences and stoically endure rather than attempt to deal with their problems. As evidenced in the cases described, the counselor in the Chinatown high school's bilingual program defused many psychological bombs before they exploded.

BEING PART OF A GANG

The most glaring outward manifestation of maladaptive social behavior among immigrant youths is the rapid increase in gangs and their vicious activities. As was noted in Chapter X, gang membership is made up almost exclusively of immigrant youths. This author believes that the manifestation of New York's Chinese gang problem is not so much rebellion against society as the inducement of big money and the need to belong to a group for protection. The fact that gang members must threaten and coerce others to join their ranks indicates that being a member is not always a voluntary act. Many join out of fear, and fear blocks their exit from the gang. Sometimes a gang member may swagger about, but when asked whether he would like his younger brother to join, his strongly negative answer reveals his true feelings.

Money is the drawing card. Hundreds and sometimes thousands of dollars are dangled before the naive teenager who, as a recent immigrant, may have had all his supports pulled out from under him. He can't speak English. He can't catch up with his school work. The future job prospects look bleak. He has to work long, hard hours. The family quarters are cramped, and his parents are away most of the time. His close friends are thousands of miles away, and he hasn't formed close relationships with new friends. He is beaten up and threatened on one hand and enticed by promises of power, money and status on the other. Money may spell security and fun, and he grasps at it hungrily.

The excitement and glamour of belonging to the Chinese gangs are short-lived. A social worker who works with the gang members says the age span for most is fourteen to eighteen years old, and the membership turnover is high. Sometimes there is a wholesale depletion of the ranks, which explains why recruitment efforts are vigorous and vicious. Within a short time, peripheral members try to ease out of the gang. They may be sent out of town by their parents, the family may move out of Chinatown, or they may seek help from youth agencies. Those who stay in beyond their twenties generally are hard-core members, but even they become tired of the kind of life they lead.

In an interview with the editor of *Canal Magazine* (1978:1), even the notorious leader of the Ghost Shadows, Nicky Louie, admitted as much. He became a gang member at fifteen. By twenty-three he was tired, empty, and spent. Ambushed twelve times and close to death on a number of occasions, he still has some bullets rattling around in his lanky frame. When asked what he thought of youth gangs now, he replied without hesitation:

I hope all the young people should think clearly before

they act. Being superior is only a brief thrill. Nobody can be the champ forever. Yesterday I was the master of Mott Street. Today, it is somebody else. Who is to guarantee that he won't be pulled down from the stage? This kind of fighting has no ending to it, and it's meaningless. I, myself, am the perfect example of this. An exciting life cannot compensate for my emptiness. I gamble heavy, but it is only a way to paralyze my mental state. The few friends that were with me when I first started out, some died, some in jail. I even had to break up with my beloved. For these couple of years I actually gained nothing.

He did gain money. From 1976 to 1977, he said the gang took in as much as $10,000 a week. But even this kind of money loses its appeal in a short time for those who have a strong moral foundation grounded in Chinese culture. Knowing these facts about Chinese gangs, effective measures can be taken to stamp out antisocial activities. More effort must be made to provide fellowship for the young teenagers in a wholesome, constructive atomsphere, and more effort must be made to deal with the insecurities of the young immigrant during the adjustment stage. But only when the enticement of big money from the gambling establishments is curtailed, can these other remedies stand a chance of competing successfully against the gangs.

Female Deviants
This study first tried to match well-adjusted with maladjusted immigrant children, but that approach was abandoned when the teachers, guidance counselors, and principals had little but praise for the progress the children were making. Even more difficult than finding boys with problems was finding any type of irregular behavior from the girls. Female rebellion is generally manifested by running away from home or by promiscuity, but it was impossible to obtain data on either. The girls were very shy and reluctant about talking at all.

The girls from Hong Kong and Taiwan do not flaunt sexual attractiveness. They are reserved and demure. It was found, from observing the girls in the lunchroom and on the playgrounds, that they tend to stick together. Even dating is very limited (See, Table 11-3). In conversation with some of the teachers, however, it was learned that sexual behavior is more pronounced among American born Chinese, but these are outside the purview of this study. A few girls, however, do attach themselves to male gang members, and these numbers are on the rise.

PSYCHOLOGICAL ADJUSTMENT

Stepping outside of societal bounds can be interpreted as social maladjustment, and it is readily recognized because it is disruptive and infringes upon the lives of other people. Psychological maladjustment is individual and personal, and to most people it is of less concern. If a child makes no demands, sits quietly, seldom opens his mouth, and withdraws when confronted with a problem, he may pass completely unnoticed and may even be praised for causing no trouble. To most parents and teachers, this is a "good" child. Chinese culture tends to reinforce this kind of behavior. It places a high value on self-control, endurance, tolerance, "face", responsibility, and achievement via conformity. Harmony is the keystone. Priority is placed upon the well-being of the group rather than on the individual, so their individual rights, concerns and happiness are downplayed for the larger good of the family, the clan, the village, or the nation. The Chinese child is socialized to accept this priority as the proper order of things.

STANDARDS OF BEHAVIOR

The Western mind finds some of these ideas strange. In American terms, normality is measured by different yardsticks. A child is well-adjusted when he is on good terms with his parents but not too close to be termed dependent, gets along with his peers, is outgoing and independent, can handle problems in a rational manner, has an optimistic outlook on life by expecting improvement and advancement, and performs at a level comparable to that of his peers.

By Chinese standards, a "good" child is one who may not necessarily be affectively close to his parents, but who fulfills his familial obligations to them, respects and obeys authority, emulates adult behavior as soon as possible, is a conformist rather than a maverick, studies hard and values hard work, has a more realistic outlook on life by willingness to accept what is, and will strive to outperform others.

Since there is a wide divergence of standards of what is desirable and acceptable behavior and outlook, it would be folly to attempt to measure against the American norm the psychological well being of a group of recent immigrant children brought up with different concepts of one's purpose in life. The researchers relied, by and large, upon observations and interviews to see if they were frightened, withdrawn, bewildered, sad, uncooperative, hostile, angry, or defiant.

In general, children at the grade school level experienced but a brief transitional period. Most of the teachers queried said that six months to a year was all that was needed for the children to be able to get along comfortably. In fact, the parents were concerned that their chidren were losing their ability to speak Chinese and their cultural heritage too rapidly. The researchers found the children to be spontaneous in class and quite outgoing in the playground. The one notable feature of their behavior was that they stuck to their own ethnic groups. If there was any interaction, it was abrasive rather than friendly. The Hispanic or black boys loved to tease the Chinese girls or playfully make them angry. The Chinese girls generally stayed in groups or in pairs and would avoid the boys as much as possible.

As mentioned previously, the blacks, Hispanics, and Chinese all sat at their separate tables in the lunchroom and played among their own groups in the playground, with little intermingling. The Chinese immigrant children regarded the other ethnic groups with a great deal of disdain. They felt that the others were too boisterous, too disruptive in the classroom, and too uninhibited in their personal relations. They felt very uncomfortable when they saw boys and girls kissing and hugging each other, and they would show their annoyance when other students were disruptive in class.

Since whites, other than Hispanics, were a minority in most of the schools researched, the Chinese immigrant students had less contact with other white students than with the Hispanics, who were usually the predominant group. This tended to insulate the Chinese from experiences they would no doubt encounter later in life—that of racial slurs, name-calling, prejudice and discrimination from whites. As long as the Chinese were the majority group or a sizable number in the schools, racism against them would not have affected them, at least not during the time of this study.

For many reasons, the high school students seemed to have greater difficulty than the younger ones in their adjustment. Of course, their lessons were more advanced, they were more deeply set in their ways, and they were not as flexible as their younger compatriots. The language was harder for them to learn and many had to work after school to contribute to the family purse as well as attend school.

If limited resources were available to help the immigrants in their transition, my recommendation would be to allocate it to upper-level school programs for personalized tutoring, guidance and counseling, and perhaps programs for work-study. The immigrant youths already work and study, but a work-study program should introduce these young people to jobs outside the traditional occupations beyond the community. This would serve to widen their horizons and bring them into contact with the larger American society.

AREAS OF ADJUSTMENT DIFFICULTIES

When asked to rank common areas of difficulty in their adjustment, students mentioned language as the problem most keenly felt by a very large margin (119) over the next category, which was worry over college or future (44) (See, Table 13-1). Following fairly close were being picked on and gang threats. The students perceive these areas as their major concerns, but it is evident that these concerns are immediate ones. In order of priority, therefore, the high schools should provide more intensive language training, college counseling, and protective measures to safeguard the students from harassment and danger. For recent immigrant children, at least, having differences with parents is a minimal problem. The parent-child relationship is still emotionally close in spite of parental absence. Getting used to new foods and new customs are not troublesome problems. If the language barrier could be dealt with effectively, a major portion of their adjustment difficulties would be solved.

One big plus in the reservoir of personal resources that enables immigrant children and youth to deal positively with their transplantation is the favorable attitude they have toward immigrating to the United States. Coming to this country may have been the culmination of years of effort on the part of the family and is a high watermark of achievement. When asked if they wished to go back, few said yes, although some said they would like to go for a visit. They may be critical of certain aspects of life in the United States, but they want to stay here. As long as these immigrants

TABLE 13-1
Adjustment Difficulties of Chinese Immigrant High School Students

Area of Difficulty	Rank Order — Difficulty in Adjustment				
	One	Two	Three	Four	Five
Language Barrier	119	32	15	10	30
Worried about College/Future	44	35	38	33	39
Picked on	33	19	10	13	26
Gang Threats	25	12	14	7	17
Feelings of not Belonging	15	15	20	18	23
Financial Worries	12	32	30	23	17
Future not Bright	12	12	16	20	35
School Work	11	18	20	19	21
Different Customs	9	18	17	15	27
Powerlessness	8	8	13	22	27
Not Used to Food	7	4	12	8	26
Differences with Parents	3	8	14	11	20

Note: Students were asked to rank the list of difficulties in left-hand column above in the order in which they experienced the most problems.

Source: Student Survey Questionnaire, 1978.

TABLE 13-2
Things Liked Most About Living in the United States

	Rank Order		
	One	Two	Three
Chance for Education	160	29	38
Chance to Make Money	46	59	69
Better Chance for Children	15	61	67
Political Freedom	23	22	72
More Material Comforts	13	26	77

Note: Totals do not add up to number of students surveyed because of no response or more than one reason given for same rank order.

Source: Student Survey Questionnaire, 1978.

measure their conditions here against what they so recently left behind, they are happy just to be in the United States, which is the obverse of the theory of relative deprivation (Stouffer, *et al.*, 1949). When asked what they liked most about living in the United States, the high school students chose chance for education as their number one choice by a wide margin (*See*, Table 13-2), and this high motivation to get an education contributes to their high academic achievement.

OUTLOOK

The outlook of the high school students surveyed was ambivalent. More than half of both sexes were satisfied with their school work. Almost all planned to go to college – surprisingly, more girls planned this than boys. They were more uncertain about being able to find a good job and even less certain about being able to earn a good income (*See*, Table 13-3). This outlook may be quite realistic; despite the fact that the educational attainment of the Chinese in the United States is exceptionally high, the positions they hold and their income are not commensurate with educational level.

TABLE 13-3
Outlook of Chinese Immigrant High School Students

	Yes		No		NR	
	No.	%	No.	%	No.	%
Males						
Satisfied with School Work	71	54	50	38	10	8
Plan to Go to College	108	82	14	11	9	7
Able to Find Good Job	67	51	42	32	22	17
Able to Earn Good Income	53	40	42	32	36	27
Females						
Satisfied with School Work	73	53	51	37	14	10
Plan to Go to College	121	88	13	9	4	3
Able to Find Good Job	85	62	34	25	19	14
Able to Earn Good Income	68	49	40	29	30	22

Source: Student Survey Questionnaire, 1978.

The feelings and beliefs of the same high school students were mixed (*See*, Table 13-4). By and large, they felt that they could succeed if they tried. Surprisingly, 60 percent did not feel that they were better off in the United States, in contradiction to the feeling that they did not want to go back. Their aspirations were not low; only 28 to 29 percent would be satisfied if they just had enough. The girls were rather uncertain on this question, as demonstrated by the large number who did not respond. About two out of five students felt that they were not discriminated against, although these data may be misleading. As pointed out previously, the subjects of this study were in schools with large numbers of Chinese, and in some instances they were numerically the majority group, giving them a sense of security. Feelings of inadequacy were not pronounced; only about a third felt inadequate. On future outlook, 9 percent said it was very bad, 39 percent said it was fair, 32 percent good, 10 percent very good, and 5 percent said it was excellent. Although this curve leans towards the pessimistic side, it is a fairly normal distribution.

TABLE 13-4

Feelings and Beliefs of Chinese Immigrant High School Students

	Yes		No		NR	
	No.	%	No.	%	No.	%
Males						
Can Succeed if Try	86	66	43	33	2	1
Better Off in U.S.	53	40	78	60	0	0
Satisfied with Enough	38	29	85	65	8	6
Chinese Discriminated Against	53	40	77	59	1	1
Feel Inadequate	43	33	86	66	2	1
Females						
Can Succeed if Try	98	71	40	29	0	0
Better Off in U.S.	56	41	82	59	0	0
Satisfied with Enough	38	28	85	62	15	11
Chinese Discriminated Against	61	44	76	55	1	1
Feel Inadequate	53	38	84	61	1	1

Source: Student Survey Questionnaire, 1978.

VALUES

How much of the Chinese values did the immigrant retain, and how much of the American values had they already absorbed? (*See*, Table 13-5) Filial piety is still strong, but duty to the family has already been diluted. The idea that boys are better than girls is completely debunked by the girls and even to a large extent by the boys. The majority of both males and females wanted to keep the Chinese customs. The most noticeable features are the heavy emphasis on getting a good education, the belief in hard work and the feeling that work comes before play. These are the cultural strengths that will stand the immigrants in good stead. Strengthened by the belief that they can succeed if they try, the immigrants come with firm convictions to support them in their struggle.

TABLE 13-5
Values Believed in by Chinese Immigrant High School Students

Values	Males			Females			Total		
	Yes	No	NR	Yes	No	NR	Yes	No	NR
Filial Piety	74	49	8	81	45	12	155	94	20
Duty to Family	48	66	17	61	61	16	109	127	33
Male Priority	55	68	8	13	116	9	68	184	17
Keep Chinese Customs	65	47	19	90	35	13	155	82	32
Prize Education	102	21	8	110	16	12	212	37	20
Hard Work	104	19	8	118	10	10	222	29	18
Don't Get Involved	57	59	15	66	55	17	123	114	32
Work Before Play	90	33	8	101	29	8	191	62	16
Parents Non-Interference	39	76	16	39	88	11	78	164	27
Learn American Ways	70	45	16	63	59	16	133	104	32
Money is Important	73	47	11	70	56	12	143	103	23

Source: Student Survey Questionnaire, 1978.

The belief that one should not get involved is about fifty-fifty, with more leaning to becoming involved in organizations, community affairs, and political issues. This is a departure from the Chinese tradition. More students still conceded that parents have the right to interfere in their children's lives, a strong retention of Chinese ways. There is an ambivalence in the responses to keeping Chinese customs and learning American ways. The students want to do both in about the same proportion although the girls are more pro-Chinese. There is no conflict in many areas, among them speaking Chinese and English, eating with fork or chopsticks, observing Chinese manners at home and American manners outside. One can do either depending upon the circumstances, but some very real conflicts, such as those used as examples in Chapter VIII, do exist.

Is money important? A yes answer would indicate acceptance of material values, but in comparison to hard work and education, money placed much lower in value. It is when these values are reversed, as in the case of gang members, that deviant behavior results.

ACCEPTANCE OF FATE

In working with Vietnamese refugees, psychologist Dr. Walter Slote marveled at the equanimity with which some overcame their trauma in flight from the country in 1975. Upon interviewing them, he learned that some of their resilience came from the acceptance of fate inherent in their belief that some events are beyond individual control, and one should just make the best of it. Among their beliefs is one that is accepted also by some in Western culture—astrology. If one's fortunes and misfortunes are preordained by the positions of the stars and planets, then one accepts the situation until the celestial bodies realign themselves.

A second belief is geomancy, the notion that the surroundings, the ancestral graves, the placement of furniture, and the direction of the house must be in alignment with nature and the natural spirits. If things are out of line, fate takes a downward turn. If things are in harmony, all goes well.

A third belief is called *fook dock* or benevolence from virtue. One accumulates credits or demerits in heaven five generations before and five generations after one's lifetime. A misdeed or unethical conduct by one's great-great-grandfather may be settled against the great-great-grandson five generations later. Spiritual control is exerted against an individual who is tempted to do wrong. He is restrained by the thought that he is responsible not only for his own fortunes, but that he may affect the destiny of his progeny for five generations to come. Dr. Slote found that many refugees shrugged off the ordeal by saying, "One of my ancestors was at fault for my plight now". In this way, the responsibility is displaced, and even one's own folly may be blamed on someone else; thus is the burden of guilt shared.

A fourth belief, that embodied in Taoism, advocates acceptance of fate and preaches non-action, for life is an endless cycle and everything will come around again.

> Bend and you will be whole,
> Curl and you will be straight,
> Keep empty and you will be filled,
> Grow old and you will be renewed.
> Bad fortune is what good fortune leans on,
> Good fortune is what bad fortune hides in.

> — Book of Tao —

A fifth belief comes out of Christianity. A very comforting statement, generally uttered in adversity, is "It is God's will". If we believe that God in His infinite wisdom has decreed these things to happen, then it must be for the best. A strong spiritual faith is a great reservoir of strength, and the Vietnamese tap into all these sources. The first four beliefs are also part of the Chinese cultural heritage, for many of the Vietnamese refugees are Chinese ethnics. These inner defenses help them surmount difficulties that overwhelm individuals trying to cope by themselves.

SURVIVAL FIRST

Aside from the positive forces mentioned above, which may provide strength and hope to the immigrant families during the difficult period of transplantation and adjustment and may soften the psychological blows, there are a number of negative factors that may mask maladjustment. One is that neither parents nor children have much time to dwell upon their emotional problems. The parents are so exhausted from their work and struggle to establish themselves economically, they simply do not have the energy to think about the more meaningful purposes of human existence. It is survival first. Until they are more secure in the most basic needs of food, clothing, and shelter, they cannot afford to think of whether they are content with their lot.

The children's days are packed with school, chores, and work. Their first concern is survival in school, and immigrant children must exert extra effort to compensate for the language barrier. Other issues, such as feeling discriminated against, alienated, uncertain about their identities, and even rejected must be relegated to a later period when the basics have been satisfied.

"FACE" AND ENDURANCE

Evidence of maladjustment may be hidden. "Face" is a very strong cultural trait among the Chinese. To say that one cannot handle one's own children, that one cannot get along with one's spouse, that one feels inadequate is shameful indeed. Add to this the fact that endurance and tolerance are highly valued Chinese character traits. Even if a person is experiencing difficulties, the more tolerance and endurance exhibited, the more character the person shows, so he wears his cross like an achievement badge. To such a person, obstacles are but challenges to be overcome. The smooth path is for weaklings; the rocky road builds character. As long as there is hope, the hardships of the present can be borne stoically.

PSYCHOLOGICAL BREAKDOWN

The ultimate in psychological breakdown would be reflected in commitment to a mental institution or in suicide. Attempts to find statistics on the former were unsuccessful. Figures for suicides for the Chinese in New York were available, however, from a study by Tom Tam (1978). The data are presented in Figures VIII and IX. Fig. VIII gives an historical perspective and shows how the male suicide rate declined drastically when passage of the 1965 Immigration Act permitted the reunification of families. The drop in suicide rate is even more dramatic from 1950, when the male suicide rate was around 30 per 100,000. The present rate of 10 per 100,000 is comparable to the average U.S. suicide rate.

Fig. IX breaks down the suicide rate by age groups and sex for the United States and New York City, and it is immediately apparent that the rate for Chinese young people is very low. However, the cases in New York that have come to my attention over the past several years all involved teenagers or college students.

FIGURE VIII
Suicides Rates per 100,000 for Chinese in the United States, 1962-1973

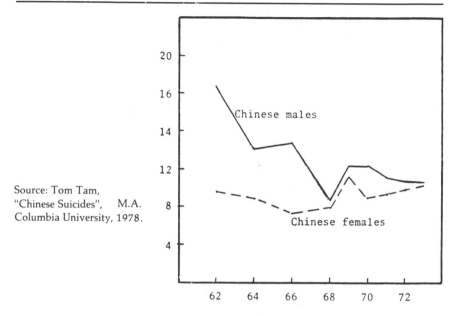

Source: Tom Tam,
"Chinese Suicides", M.A.
Columbia University, 1978.

FIGURE IX
Age Specific Suicide Rates per 100,000 Population Chinese and New York City, 1974-1976

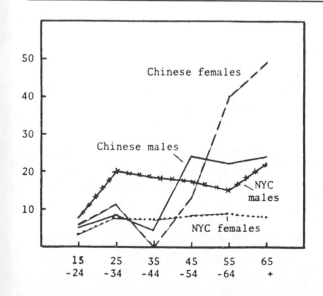

Source: Tom Tam, *Op. cit.*

The most shocking case occurred on November 10, 1978. Two immigrant sisters, ages seventeen and thirteen, jumped off the roof of their house because their father had forbidden the older sister to date a Puerto Rican boy (New York Times, 1982). Three other cases involved outstanding students from middle-class families. All three felt that they had not performed up to the expectations of their parents, and all three ended their lives in a dramatic fashion. One jumped in front of a train, one drank lye, and the third jumped from a twentieth floor window. These three were second generation American born Chinese, not immigrants.

Alfred Adler's theory that suicide is veiled aggression comes close to explaining methods and reasons for suicide among teenage and college-age Chinese youths (See, Tam 1978). These offspring were lashing out at their parents' cultural strictures. They wanted to hurt others by hurting themselves, and they committed suicide in the most melodramatic manner possible. Tam found that in traditional Chinese societies, the suicide rate for the young was high and for the elderly was low. The opposite was true in industrialized Western societies. However, the National Center for Health Statistics reported that suicide among the young (age 15 to 24) in the United States has risen dramatically from 5 per 100,000 during the 1940s and 1950s to 12.7 in 1978 (See, Williams, 1982).

Tam's study provided information up to 1976. Table 13-6 gives more up-to-date figures for Chinese suicides in New York City.

THE ONES ON THEIR OWN

In all six schools used in our study, the students had the advantage of not being alone in their transition. The schools were chosen because they had large Chinese enrollments. On the one hand, this facilitated the research; on the other hand, the students were studying in a setting not totally foreign. There was enough of the familiar to ease the adjustment, and there were enough immigrants in the same predicament to lend some comfort. It is easier to accept a bad situation when all are in the same boat. Besides, in these schools, the teachers and staff were understanding and supportive. There was recognition of the students' language difficulties, as evidenced by the offerings of English as a Second Language, orientation classes, and even bilingual classes.

TABLE 13-6

Suicides for Chinese in New York City, 1976-1980

Age Group	1976 M	1976 F	1977 M	1977 F	1978 M	1978 F	1979 M	1979 F	1980 M	1980 F
15-24	2	1	1	0	1	4	0	0	1	0
25-34	0	0	0	0	1	2	4	0	2	0
35-44	1	0	2	0	0	0	0	3	1	1
45-54	1	2	1	3	0	0	1	2	0	3
55-64	0	1	1	3	0	0			1	0
65-74	0	0	0	0	2	0	1	0	1	0
75-84	0	0	0	0	0	0	0	2	0	2
85 plus	0	0	0	0	0	0	0	0	3	0
Total	4	4	5	6	4	6	6	7	9	6

Notes: [1] Suicides are not always reported as such. Incidences may be higher than figures indicate.

[2] The numbers rather than the rates are given because the base population of Chinese in New York was not available.

Source: New York City, Department of Vital Statistics.

But what of the dispersed immigrant children who do not have such help? Since none was interviewed or observed, the study may be faulted for this reason, but the logistics would have been monumental. Some schools may have had one or a few immigrant students. In such instances, the school authorities would not allow any records or personal data to be revealed.

For these children the primary problems, besides that of language, would be feelings of loneliness and isolation. Another would be dealing with name-calling and racism. In the Chinatown and satellite Chinatown schools, there were enough Chinese to ward off racial slurs, but the dispersed may be the one or the few in an entire school. The racial minority experience is another dimension that is new and puzzling to the newcomer. With which group should he align himself? Which groups will accept him in their games, in their cliques, or in their circle of friends? The lone immigrant student is the odd man out, and if the child cannot make some attachment, he will feel rejected.

In sum, the psychological adjustment of Chinese immigrant children and youth is affected by their strong desire to come to this country, the opportunity to get an education here, their willingness to work hard, the realistic outlook they have on life, the cultural traditions from the Orient that sustain them, the fact that the immigrants must concern themselves with satisfaction of the basic needs first, and the belief that character is strengthened by tolerance and endurance.

In time, the above factors may be modified by the process of Americanization. The euphoria of coming to this country will wear off. Inroads will be made into the value placed upon tolerance, endurance, hard work and acceptance of fate. The economic position of these immigrants will improve. The reference group will shift from their own ethnic group to white Americans, so their standards will change. A sense of satisfaction will then depend upon the extent and degree to which these young immigrants attain their aspirations.

SUMMARY

Adjustment of Chinese immigrant children and youth was examined within the social context and the psychological context. In other words, do these children and youths fit into society's expectations, and do they feel comfortable within themselves? The children do measure up to teacher expectations, as evidenced by their school records, their low truancy and dropout rates, their good manners, their attendance rates, and the numbers who are college bound. They do measure up to their parents' expectations by studying hard, by working and contributing to the family income, and by maintaining close ties with their parents in spite of parental absence.

Maladaptive behavior has been manifest in the formation of gangs and in their various vicious activities. The apparent contradiction between the large number who do well and the small number who are deviants can be explained by the fact that those who can keep up with their school work remain in school. The gang members are not in school. Data on female deviants were hard to come by, so it seemed that their numbers were few.

Psychological normality is measured by different yardsticks in the American and Chinese cultures. There is a considerable divergence in standards of what is desirable and acceptable behavior.

For example, for adults to be extremely close to one's parents is interpreted as immaturity in Western eyes but is considered a cardinal virtue in Chinese eyes.

The three ranking areas of difficulty most commonly felt by high school immigrants were language, worries about college and the future, and fear of gangs and being picked on.

Factors that may have softened the shock of immigration are: the immigrants wanted to come to the United States, they feel they can succeed if they try, they are willing to work hard, they prize education, and their beliefs predispose them toward acceptance of fate.

Two negative factors that may mask psychological maladjustment are: the immigrant families are too busy trying to meet the basic needs of survival to think about anything else, and they may be masking their problems by denying that they even exist. Psychological breakdowns were not mirrored in the number of suicides reported for young Chinese, and data were unavailable on mental health institution admissions.

XIV
Conclusion

One of the main purposes of this study was to generate as much information as possible about the Chinese in New York City. The literature—even that pertaining to the Chinese in the country as a whole—is scanty and still evolving. Specific literature dealing with Chinese immigrant children is almost non-existent. More scholars and authors are writing about the Chinese at present, but the tendency is to dwell in the historical past and to base their assumptions on past experiences. Even the protest literature which proliferated during the 1970s was based upon the highly discriminatory treatment meted out to the Chinese in years gone by. Our history is part of our heritage, but urgently needed is information to deal with the rapidly growing Chinese population fed by the immigrant stream from the Far East. The Chinese community is changing at a very rapid pace, and conditions true today may be outdated tomorrow. Yet, few writers are dealing with the contemporary scene. They prefer conducting their research through secondary sources based upon outdated information, for fieldwork is exhausting, exasperating, time-consuming, and highly risky when there is little precedent and little corroborating material to go by. This contribution to the literature, therefore, is the primary research.

Fact-finding then becomes an end in itself, and accurate reporting of what is happening among Chinese immigrant children, their families, and their communities is basic to further research and theorizing. It is hoped that this study has contributed to the knowledge about the Chinese and has shed some light on the actual experiences that Chinese immigrant children undergo in their adjustment process. Toward these ends this study has:

1. Provided vital background information about the Chinese population, the rate of immigration, the historical forces that brought about the Chinese immigration pattern, population dis-

tribution patterns, the internal forces, structure, and institutions of the Chinese communities in New York City, the school environment and curricula with which the immigrant must deal, and their home lives.

2. Updated the statistics on the numbers of Chinese immigrants, especially the youthful population, entering the United States.

3. Uncovered sources of statistical data pertaining to the Chinese of which many people are unaware. Examples of these are crime statistics, birth and suicide rates, and school enrollment figures.

4. Painted a word picture to describe the kind of situation Chinese immigrant children and adolescents encounter when they arrive in this country. By knowing what to expect, it is hoped their children, their families, and those dealing with the newcomers can better anticipate problems that will arise.

5. Brought out those aspects of Chinese culture that are transferable to an American setting and those that have stood the immigrant children in good stead. Examples of these are the high value placed upon education, the belief that hard work will bring rewards, the respect for authority, and a positive attitude that America is still the land of opportunity. Incidences of maladjustment or deviant behavior invariably confirm a departure from the above Chinese cultural values.

6. Pointed out specific areas where experiences and cultural background are not transferable and must be learned anew. First and foremost among these is the learning of the English language; until some competency is gained, the immigrant will feel impotent. Conflict in cultural values and customs poses equally mystifying problems to the new arrival and may be a source of confusion and embarassment. Learning to deal with the different ethnic groups is puzzling to the Chinese person who has seen none other than Chinese faces, so he tends to stick with his own people.

7. Related the attempts on the part of schools and the communities to deal with the huge influx of immigrant children and made

critical comments on the effectiveness of such programs as English as a Second Language, bilingual education, and after-school centers. Noted that few isolated social service agencies have been funded by local and federal governments to deal with the special problems of the newcomers, but the need greatly exceeds the availability of service.

8. Shown how interpersonal relationships and roles have been altered within the family to meet the changing needs of the new society. Examples of these are the reliance upon peer-group support rather than the parental guidance and the reversal of roles between husband and wife or parent and child. The Chinese family, after it arrives in the United States, is invariably altered by the economical and social exigencies of the American way of life. Employment opportunities for the fathers are very limited and mothers must work. As a result, parental absence is a common feature of the new life. The children shoulder heavier burdens as well, so there is little time for recreation or socializing.

9. Presented a behind-the-scenes account of how gangs recruit and maintain their numbers and how they have terrorized the Chinese community.

10. Indicated the extent and areas of social and psychological breakdowns and, conversely, the strengths and inner resources within these young immigrants to deal successfully with their transplantation.

ROLE OF THE SOCIAL INSTITUTIONS

The structural framework of this study was to examine three major social institutions—community, school, and family—to see what their roles are in relation to helping Chinese immigrant children cope with and adapt to a new life in a new homeland. Without question, the transition from a Chinese setting to an American one is a stressful experience. Generally, too much emphasis is placed upon the individual's coping ability to deal with the external demands of the environment, and not enough attention is paid to the influence of social structural variables on personal and social adaptation. In fact, as David Mechanic (1974:34) said, "Major stresses of life are not amenable to individual solutions but depend on highly organized cooperative efforts that transcend those of any individual man, no matter how well developed his personal resources". Mechanic defined institutions as the collective and accumulated experiences that have become a fixed part of a society's culture to deal effectively with life's problems. "Group organization and cooperation allow for the development of mastery through specialization of functions, pooling of resources and information, developing reciprocal help-giving relationships and the like.... The effectiveness of individuals in many spheres of action is dependent almost exclusively on the maintenance of viable forms of organization and cooperation that allow important tasks to be mastered.".

The Community

The very existence of a Chinatown in New York City into which the newly arrived immigrant family can gravitate already serves to alleivate a large number of potential problems. The fears, the anxiety, the insecurity are mitigated to a considerable degree when one can go into a cultural milieu not too different from that which one left behind. The community performs a vital function as a cultural decompression chamber and in many ways it has met important needs of its increasing population.

For one, its boundaries expanded to accommodate the increasing numbers who want to live there, but it is overcrowded and it has already run out of space. Consequently, satellite Chinatowns have come into being, testifying to the need of the new immigrants to band together to live in proximity with one another. So far, the tourist industry, the food industry, the garment industry, and the retail shops have been able to provide employment to the newcomers. The community is a social and recreational center. Social service agencies have sprung up to meet the needs of the residents, and in many ways they have supplanted the former mutual aid organizations based upon kinship and place of origin.

Unfortunately, the buildings and physical surroundings of Chinatown are ancient, dilapidated, and overcrowded, and vested interests are resistant to change and cannot offer enlightened leadership. Conditions are changing so rapidly that it is difficult to keep up with the pace. Nevertheless, the community has served to mitigate many of the immigrants' problems.

The School

Three chapters of this study were devoted to the role of the school because most of the immigrant children's waking hours are spent within the walls of this institution. The school's primary function is to teach and prepare the children for their future roles in society, but with immigrant children there are the added hurdles of the language barriers and cultural differences. Only within recent years has the United States educational system recognized the special needs of limited English speaking children, so that special programs like English as a Second Language or bilingual education classes have been instituted in the Chinatown schools just since 1975.

Counseling programs set up under the bilingual education programs have been extremely helpful to the Chinese immigrant children in helping them deal with their personal problems. Teachers have been especially supportive of the Chinese children because they are studious, respectful, and obedient. In as much as education is highly valued in Chinese culture, the students' good academic performance may be a continuity of the value goal. School performance was measured by academic record, conduct, attendance, and dropout rate. Marks for these concrete indicators were high and can be taken as clues to a healthy and postive adjustment.

The schools not only perform their functions of educating and socializing the children, but in many instances they assume the role of surrogate parents as well. Oftentimes, two out of the three meals each day are taken in the schools, and after-school centers care for the children. In essence, the schools, too, play an important role—if not the most important role—in providing the immigrant children with institutionalized ways to deal with their new experiences.

The Family

The research reveals that the immigrant family has undergone the most drastic changes as a result of being transplanted. The status and roles of family members are changed or reversed. Parental absence is a pervasive phenomenon. The birth rate has declined noticeably. This smaller social unit has not adapted as well as the larger ones. Some of its functions, such as providing supervision, meals, and medical attention, have been relegated to the school. As a result, peer groups have increased in importance, and peer-group influence can be for the better or worse.

GANGS AS INDICATORS OF MALADJUSTMENT

Gang involvement is the most glaring concrete indicator of maladjustment. Fortunately the numbers involved are small—at the most about 300 out of a total Asian student enrollment of over forty thousand in New York City. However, this small number has created havoc out of proportion to their numbers.

The theory of differential association for criminal behavior has applicability here. The theory postulates that criminal behavior is learned, and a person becomes delinquent because of an excess of definitions favorable to violation of law over definitions unfavorable to violation. The objective situation is important to the occurrence of crime largely due to the extent that it provides an opportunity for a person to act (*See*, Chapter X).

Nowhere was this more evident than when gang violence declined as soon as Atlantic City offered nearby legalized gambling. When business in the gambling houses fell off, money for support of the gangs dried up and gang activity dropped as well.

Cooley's theory of social disorganization operates with respect to gang involvement also, but not totally. Disorganization may come about as a result of conflict and confusion about which norms, rules, and values to follow, but it seems that the moral standards of the Chinese immigrant teenagers remain high. Those who live outside of Chinatown might, in fact, experience more social disorganization, but few exhibit antisocial behavior. It is only when the opportunity presents itself for criminal behavior in Chinatown that disorganized and alienated youths are sucked into the gangs.

ADJUSTMENT

As stated in Chapter XIII, the yardsticks applied to the determination of whether immigrant children and youths' transition is smooth or rocky have been the concrete manifestations of school performance, social behavior, and gang involvement, the rationale being that actions and results speak for themselves. Subjective opinions were also elicited from the high school students through a survey questionnaire, which probed into the students' opinions and attitudes. A number of sociological theories may well explain the satisfactory adjustment that the Chinese children have made in their new homeland. The first is the reference group theory, which postulates that "group situations generate differential effects of significant consequence. Group interaction is seen as the major determinant in attitude formation, attitude change, and other phenomena of vital consequence to the individual." (Sherif in Coser and Rosenberg, 1969:284).

Most of the Chinese children have come from Mainland China, Hong Kong, Taiwan, and Vietnam where they lived under either totalitarian forms of government or colonial governments. They may have lived through the horrors of the Vietnam War, the Chinese civil war, or the Cultural Revolution. Material goods and food were scarce. Their economic future was limited as were their educational opportunities. Emigration to the United States must have been a much sought-after goal. Looking backward to their mother country as a reference point, they cannot help but compare the two and feel that coming to the United States was a godsend.

However, if upon their arrival they were incarcerated in a place like Ellis Island or Angel's Island to be suspected or questioned about their right to enter the country; if the laws of the country restricted them and made them feel like criminals for being here; if upon landing they were met with hostility, prejudice and discrimination; if they knew that they would be relegated to permanent inferior status and a limited economic future; if they were separated from their families and loved ones without hope of reunification in this country, then one set of intolerable conditions would be substituted for another, and the immigration experience could not help but be a negative one, as it was in the past.

On the other hand, if the immigration laws made it easier to obtain visas; if being Chinese was no longer a reason for being excluded; if the civil rights laws had improved the position of minorities and prejudice and discrimination were no longer blatantly practiced; if the country offered peace and stability, more personal and political freedom, better educational opportunities, hope for the future, more material goods and comforts, and even heightened appreciation for ethnic differences, then the trauma of pulling up roots would be mitigated by the more positive reception in the host country.

The above conditions make reference to the theory of symbolic interactionism. The immigrant defines the situation and indicates to himself that the social climate is receptive and an improvement over what was left behind. It follows that his reaction will be more positive and that he will try hard to grasp the opportunities suddenly made available to him. Having been deprived, he is more appreciative of the opportunities presented. That is why newly arrived immigrants work harder and the children study more diligently.

The theory of relative deprivation also has applicability here, but in reverse. Although the residents of Chinatown—by American standards—are living in dilapidated slums, lack recreational facilities, work long hard hours and earn little, in comparison with the conditions they left behind they feel their arrival in this country, in and of itself, is the attainment of a cherished goal. They have hopes for the future, and a substantial majority of high school students believe that they can succeed if they try.

INTEGRATION YES, ASSIMILATION NO

In this study, no attempt was made to deal with any of the theories of assimilation such as Milton Gordon's (1964) seven-stage assimilation process, because they are not applicable yet. Newly arrived immigrant children are only in the initial stages of adapting. They still identify completely with their own ethnic group; the umbilical cords are still strongly attached. They are trying to bridge the cultural gap, but this cannot even be described as the first stage of acculturation. Integration may be the more appropriate term to use. As defined by Sommerlad and Berry (1970), "Integration implies interaction between minority and host society resulting in change in cultural amalgam without loss of cultural identity. Assimilation is a unilateral process. Integration is a mutual process. Once an individual identifies with the host society he tends toward assimilation. If he identities with his own ethnic group, integration results.

CORROBORATION OF DATA

To persistent believers in the pathology of the immigrant experience, the data presented here may appear overly sanguine, but a number of other reports have confirmed the high academic attainment of Asian and Oriental children, of which a large proportion are Chinese. Dr. Jayjia Hsia (1983), Assistant Vice President of the Educational Testing Service of Princeton, wrote: "We have a large battery of tests on more than 1,000 Berkeley school children who are Japanese and Chinese, about half of whom are fairly recent immigrants from Hong Kong or Taiwan. I find that all of these groups are well above the California norms on the nonverbal tests, and the American born are above the norms even on the verbal tests and on tests of scholastic achievement.

"Feinberg (1981) reported unexpected numbers of Asian Americans who were valedictorians or recipients of top academic honors in the greater Washington D.C. area high schools....In schools which served predominantly white middle-class suburban students, as well as inner city schools with most disadvantaged pupils, Asian Americans of Korean, Vietnamese, Japanese, and Chinese origin carried off top awards in June, 1981."

Already mentioned at the beginning of this book is that a disproportionate number of the prestigious Westinghouse scholarships are awarded to Chinese immigrant youngsters every year. One of the most important reasons why the parents immigrated to the United States was for the sake of the children. They came to open up a brighter future for their progeny. Education was the cultural medium of mobility, and the parents push the children hard in this direction.

RESILIENCY OF CHILDREN UNDER STRESS

For more than thirty years, Dr. Robert Coles, Pulitzer Prize winner, pediatrician and psychiatrist, has been studying children under stressful conditions to see how they cope. He is the author of more than thirty books; his best known one is *Children of Crisis* (1964), in which he wrote about how children in the South dealt with the stressful experience of being vanguards in the desegregation of public schools. Dr. Coles expected emotional scars and psychological damage to come from their experiences. On the contrary, Dr. Coles concluded that there is extraordinary resilience, courage, and stamina in children. He also maintains that children often emerge from their painful ordeal much stronger in mind and in character. Were these children exceptional? "No", said Dr. Coles. "They were ordinary children caught up in extraordinary situations."

The subjects of this study—Chinese immigrant children, teenagers, and youth in New York City's Chinatowns—have also exhibited extraordinary resilience, courage and stamina in their transplantation from Chinese soil to American soil. But they were fortunate in that they were aided and supported in their coping process by social institutions that offered them collective solutions to the new challenges facing them.

The Future

Forty-seven percent of immigrants entering the Unites States in 1986 were of Asian ancestry. The 1980 census counted over 806,000 ethnic Chinese in the United States. By 1990, this number may increase to 1.3 million and by 2000 it may be close to 1.7 million, according to a projection by the Population Reference Bureau in Washington, D.C. This phenomenal increase will come mostly from immigration, so that the immigrant experience is the most pervasive influence upon the Chinese population in the United States, and the immigrant experience will continue to exert an inordinate impact upon the group. However, Chinese immigration to the United States hinges upon a number of macro developments beyond the control of the Chinese themselves, and these developments will underpin how the Chinese fare and react to these forces.

The first is adverse U.S. economic conditions, and these will be reflected in two ways against the Chinese. One will be through restriction of the immigration laws, and the other will be a change in the relatively tolerant attitude toward foreigners and minorities that prevailed during the Sixties and Seventies. During debate over the Immigration Reform Act finally enacted in 1986, there were strong currents of sentiment toward restriction of Asian immigration by modification of the second and fifth preferences. Fortunately these were not changed. If they had, Chinese immigration could have easily been cut by one-half. If Chinese immigration had been curtailed, the decrease in the rate of influx would have a strong ripple effect upon the lives of the entire Chinese community in the United States. We would begin to see more growth in the satellite Chinatowns and less explosive growth of New York's Chinatown proper. Immigrant Chinese student enrollment would decline, which would result in less demand for transitional programs such as bilingual education, English as a Second Language, and guidance couseling. Those who arrive would have to fall back upon the "sink or swim" approach, which would make their adjustment process more difficult. The communities would be able to take a breather from the dizzying rate of increase and to examine their problems and come up with some solutions. Without the intense competition for jobs and economic survival from a continuing stream of incoming immigrants, wage rates might improve slightly for those already here. These are but a few examples of the ripple effect that might come about with any restriction of Chinese immigration.

Should economic conditions worsen further, racism and hostility may again rear their ugly heads if immigrants and minorities are viewed as competitors for scarce jobs and resources. This time, the hostility may emanate from blacks, who have been disproportionately affected by high unemployment and who feel that they are Americans whereas the immigrants are foreigners.

As conjectured earlier, the adjustment process of the Chinese immigrant children in New York City was facilitated by the improved social climate of the Sixties and Seventies that resulted in generous funding for programs for ethnic minorities. The Eighties are witnessing a drastic reversal of this policy. For example, federal support for bilingual education stood at $161 million in 1981. It diminished to $138 million in 1982, and the Reagan administration pressed hard to reduce it to $95 million for 1983 (Holsendolph, 1982). Commitment to affirmative action is all but nil, and minority issues have been relegated to the farthest recesses of national concerns. Since the social climate is worsening for ethnic minorities, their well-being cannot help but suffer. According to John Acompore of the Office of Bilingual Education in New York City, federal funding under Title VII of the Bilingual Education Act has continually eroded over the past ten years.

The second macro development is the political uncertainties surrounding Hong Kong and Taiwan. Fears that the colony of Hong Kong is going to be reclaimed by China from Great Britain in 1997 when the lease on the New Territories expires has caused Hong Kong real estate and business to nose-dive and the residents to think of emigration. As for Taiwan, the threat is ever present that Mainland China will reclaim that island as well, also setting up strong push factors toward emigration. The desire of many is to come to the United States, the forces operating toward migration from both islands will be strong, thus sustaining the continued heavy influx into the United States.

The third development pertains to Vietnamese refugees, many of whom are of Chinese ethnic origin. Those with close affinity to their Chinese heritage will identify more with the Chinese community when they arrive in the United States. They add a new dimension to the Chinese American scene. They are especially noteworthy because their numbers are considerable. In 1980, the census counted 262,000 Vietnamese. By 1982, this number had almost doubled because the refugee quota is more liberal than the immigration quota. How many of these are ethnic Chinese is not certain, but those who came in 1979 as "boat people" were predominantly Chinese. They are categorized as Vietnamese, but they generally gravitate toward the Chinese communities bringing with them their unique experiences and cultural dissimilarities. By sheer force of numbers, they cannot help but affect the make-up, the outlook, and the direction of the more traditional Chinese American communities.

A fourth development is the beginning influx of immigrants from the People's Republic of China. Formerly, when China's borders were closed to the West, Chinese immigrants to the United States came primarily from Hong Kong and secondarily from Taiwan. Both these islands are highly urbanized, industrialized, and Westernized. The residents have been exposed to the English language, to Western technology, and to American culture through publications and films. Therefore, the transition from Hong Kong to New York is not as great as for those who come from Mainland China. The latter have been highly insulated from Western culture. They have been imbued with an entirely different political ideology from the American one. The gap, therefore, is much greater for the Mainland immigrants to bridge, and the transition process will not be as simple as that reported in this study. The educational backgrounds and standards of the Mainlanders are lower owing to the excesses during the Cultural Revolution. They were taught to work for the common good rather than for individual advancement. They have been severely deprived in the way of material goods. Many were victims of abuse and persecution because of their ties to relatives in the United States. The trauma of these experiences may affect their coping abilities and stand in the way of their rapid adjustment.

Already the schools are discovering that immigrant children from the People's Republic of China are quite different from those who came before. The newest waves are not following in the footsteps of the traditional immigrants from more urbanized and more homogeneous cultural backgrounds, but they are injecting into the Chinese American communities greater diversity, hence greater complexity.

A study like this can only capture the situation within a short span of time. The picture is fluid and ever-changing, and the macro developments mentioned above could bring about sweeping changes throughout the Chinese American communities in this country. Some of these developments have already been set into motion, altering the scene even before we put the final period to this book.

APPENDIX TABLE A-1
Chinese Immigration to the United States by Sex, 1944-1984

Year	Male No.	%	Female No.	%	Annual Total
1944	10	29	24	71	34
1945	20	41	64	59	109
1946	71	31	162	59	233
1947	142	13	986	87	1,128
1948	257	8	3,317	92	3,574
1949	242	10	2,248	90	2,490
1950	110	8	1,179	92	1,289
1951	126	11	957	89	1,083
1952	118	10	1,034	90	1,152
1953	203	19	890	81	1,093
1954	1,511	55	1,236	45	2,747
1955	1,261	48	1,367	52	2,628
1956	2,007	45	2,443	55	4,450
1957	2,487	49	2,636	51	5,123
1958	1,396	44	1,799	56	3,195
1959	2,846	47	3,185	53	6,031
1960	1,873	51	1,799	49	3,672
1961	1,565	41	2,273	59	3,838
1962	1,916	42	2,753	58	4,669
1963	2,297	43	3,073	57	5,370
1964	2,597	46	3,051	54	5,648
1965	2,242	47	2,527	53	4,769
1966	8,613	49	8,995	51	17,608
1967	12,811	51	12,285	49	25,096
1968	7,862	48	8,572	52	16,434
1969	10,001	48	10,892	52	20,893
1970	8,586	48	9,370	52	17,956
1971	8,287	47	9,335	53	17,622
1972	10,437	48	11,293	52	21,730
1973	9,937	46	11,719	54	21,656

APPENDIX TABLE A-1 (Continued)
Chinese Immigration to the United States by Sex, 1944-1984

Year	Male No.	%	Female No.	%	Annual Total
1974	10,724	47	11,961	53	22,685
1975	11,179	48	12,248	52	23,427
1976	11,819	48	12,770	52	24,589
1976 qtr.	3,109	48	3,418	52	6,527
1977	12,176	48	13,220	52	25,396
1978	12,507	47	13,966	53	26,473
1979	13,242	47	15,141	53	28,383
1980	n.a.	—	n.a.	—	31,511
1981	n.a.	—	n.a.	—	29,858
1982	19,250	48	21,041	52	41,955[a]
1983	21,966	50	21,578	50	48,423[a]
1984	19,715	48	21,591	52	41,306

Notes: [a] Includes persons whose sex is unknown.

Fiscal year changed in 1976 to year ending in Sept. 30th.

Source: Immigration and Naturalization Service, *Annual Reports* and/or *Statistical Yearbooks* (Washington, D.C., 1965-1980).

Bibliography

ARTICLES

Abbott, K. and E. Abbott
1968   "Juvenile Delinquency in San Francisco's Chinese-American Community", *Journal of Sociology*, 4:45-46.

Abel, T.M. and F.L.K. Hsu
1949   "Some Aspects of Personality of Chinese as Revealed by the Rorschach Test", *Rorschach Research and Exchange Journal and Projective Techniques*, 13:285-301.

Arnold, M.
1970   "Teen-age Gangs Plague Merchants in Chinatown", *New York Times*, August 5.

Asian Week
1983   "Paul Chin Ning Wins Top Science Award", *Asian Week*, March 24. p.1.

Barnett, M.L.
1957   "Some Cantonese-American Problems of Status Adjustment", *Phylon*, 18:420-427.

Beels, C.C.
1976   "The Case of the Vanishing Mommy", *New York Times Magazine*, July 4.

Bonnett, A.
1980   "An Examination of Rotating Credit Associations among Black West Indian Immigrants in Brooklyn". In *Source Book on New Immigration*. Edited by Roy Simon Bryce-Laporte. New Brunswick, NJ: Transaction Books. Pp.271-283.

Brim, O.G., Jr.
1979   "Societal Influences on Children and New Actors in the Field", *National Council for Children and Television Forum*, Special Issue: "The State of the Child", 2(1):24.Winter.

Canal Magazine
1978   "Interview with Nicky Louie", *Canal Magazine*, Dec.8. p.1.

Chang, P.M.
1981   "Health and Crime among Chinese-Americans: Recent Trends", *Phylon*, 42(4):356-368. Dec.

Chang, S.
1974 "Mental Health in Chinatown", *Bridge*. Pp.34-37. Feb.

Charters, W.W.
1963 "The Social Background of Teaching". In *Handbook of Research on Teaching*. Edited by N.L. Gage. Skokie, IL: Rand McNally & Co.

Chen, T.H. and W.E.Chen W.
1959 "Changing Attitudes toward Parents in Communist China", *Sociology and Social Research*, 43(3):175-182. Jan-Feb.

Chin, A.
1948 "Some Problems of Chinese Youth in Transition", *American Journal of Sociology*, 51(1):7. July.

Chou, S. and C.Mi;
1947 "Relative Neurotic Tendency of Chinese and American Students", *The Journal of Social Psychology*, 8(2):155-184. May.

Dai, B.
1941 "Personality Problems in Chinese Culture", *American Sociological Review*, 6(5):688-696.

DeBary, T.,ed.
1960, 1964 "Introduction to Oriental Civilizations". In *Sources of Chinese Tradition*. Vol. I, Vol II. New York: Columbia University Press.

Dreifus, C.
1982 "LI Interview: Dr. Robert Coles", *New York Newsday*, Sunday Magazine. Pp. 15-25. Jan 3.

Doyle, P.
1976 "Gang Hacks Two Youths in Chinatown", *Daily News*, October 13.

Feinberg, L.
1981 "Asian Students Excelling in Area, U.S. Schools", *Washington Post*. July.

Fernandez, C., R.W. Espinosa, and S.M. Dornbusch
1975 "Factors Perpetuating the Low Academic Status of Chicano High School Students". Stanford, CA: Stanford Center for Research and Development in Teaching, School of Education. July.

Finn, S. and W.H. Kross
1972 "Child Rearing Attitudes of Chinese, Jewish, and Protestant Mothers", *Journal of Social Psychology*, 86:203.

Fong, S.L.M.
1973 "Assimilation and Changing Social Roles of Chinese-Americans", *Social Issues*, 29(2):115-127.

1970 "Sex Roles in the Modern Fabric of China". In *Sex Roles in Changing Society*. Edited by G.H. Seward and R.C. Williamson. New York: Random House.

1968   "Identity Conflicts of Chinese Adolescents in San Francisco". In *Minority Group Adolescents in the United States*. Edited by E.B. Brody. Baltimore: Williams and Wilkins.

1965   "Assimilation of Chinese in America: Changes in Orientation and Social Perception", *American Journal of Sociology*, 71:265-273.

Fong, S.L.M. and H. Peskin
1969   "Sex Role Strain and Personality Adjustment of China-born Students in America: A Pilot Study", *Journal of Abnormal Psychology*, 74:563-567.

Friedman, J.C.
1975   "Profile of Juvenile Gang Members", *Adolescence*, 10:563-607. Winter.

Friedman, J.C., F. Mann and H. Adelman
1976   "Juvenile Street Gangs: The Victimization of Youth", *Adolescence*, 11(44):527-533. Winter.

Golant, S.M.
1971   "Adjustment Process in a System: A Behavior Model of Human Movement", *Geographic Analysis*, 3:203-219. July.

Herzog, E. and C. Sudia
1968   "Fatherless Homes: A Review of Research", *Children*. Pp. 172-182. Sept-Oct.

Holsendolph, E.
1982   "Bilingual Funds: A Problem in Any Language", *New York Sunday Times, Fall Survey of Education*. Sec. 12. Nov 14.

Hong, L.K.
1976   "Recent Immigrants in the Chinese-American Community: Issues of Adaptations and Impacts", *International Migration Review*, 10(4):509-513. Winter.

1975   "Triple Stress: Some Special Social Psychological Problems of the Recent Chinese Immigrants in the United States", Los Angeles: California State University.

Hong, L.K. and R.T. Tsukashima
1980   "Asian/Pacific Americans", *California Sociologist* (special issue), 3(2). Summer.

Hsia, J.
1983   "Cognitive Assessment of Asian Americans". In *Asian and Pacific American Perspective in Bilingual Education*. Edited by M. Chu-Chung. New York: Teachers College Press.

Hsu, F.L.K.
1974   "Intercultural Understanding: Genuine and Spurious". Evanston, IL: Northwestern University. January.

1973   "Kinship Is the Key", *The Center Magazine*, 6(6). Nov-Dec.

1961   "American Core Value and National Character". In *Psychological Anthropology*. Edited by Francis Hsu. Homewood, IL: Dorsey Press.

1960   "Rugged Individualism Reconsidered", *The Colorado Quarterly*, 9(2). Autumn.

1959   "The Family in China: The Classical Form". In *The Family: Its Function and Destiny*. Edited by Ruth Anshen. New York: Harper and Bros. Pp. 123-245.

1943   "The Myth of Chinese Family Size", *American Journal of Sociology*.

"Chinese Kinship and Chinese Behavior". In *China in Crisis*. Edited by Ping-ti Ho and Tang Tsou. Chicago: University of Chicago Press. Vol. 1, Book 2. p. 583.

Hsu, F., B.G. Watrous, and E. Lord
1961   "Culture Pattern and Adolescent Behavior", *International Journal of Social Psychiatry*, 7(1).

Jacobson, M.
1977   "New York's Other Mafia: Part One: Young Warriors Fight for Their Place in a Changing Chinatown", *The Village Voice*, Pp. 12-15. Jan. 31.

1977   "Nicky Louie's Mean Streets: Tongs Strike Back in Chinatown", *The Village Voice*. Pp.18-20. Feb. 8.

Journal of Social Issues
1973   "Asian Americans: A Success Story", *Journal of Social Issues* (special edition), 29(2).

Kamm, H.
1979   "A Confrontation on Refugees", *New York Times*, June 28.

Kates, B.
1976   "Youth Gangs Are Ruining Chinatown", *Daily News*. Dec. 5.

Kendis, K. and R. Kendis
1976   "The Street Boy Identity: An Alternate Strategy of Boston's Chinese-Americans", *Urban Anthropology*, 5(1). Spring.

Kitano, H.
1964   "Inter and Intragenerational Differences in Maternal Attitudes toward Child Rearing", *Journal of Social Psychology*, 63:215-220.

1961   "Differential Child-Rearing Attitudes between First and Second Generation Japanese in the United States", *Journal of Social Psychology*, 53:13-19

Kitano, H. and S. Sue
1973   "The Model Minorities", *Journal of Social Issues*, 29(2):1-10.

Kunz, E.F.
1973   "The Refugees in Flight: Kinetic Models and Forms of Displacement", *International Migration Review*, 7:125-146.

Kuo, W.
1976   "Theories of Migration and Mental Health: An Empirical Testing on Chinese Americans", *Social Science and Medicine*, 10:297-306.

Lan, D.
1972   "Chinatown Sweatshops: Oppression and an Alternative", *Amerasia Journal*, 1:40-57. Nov.

Lee, R.H.
1956   "The Recent Immigrant Chinese Families of the San Francisco-Oakland Area", *Marriage and Family Living*, 18:14-24.

1949   "Research on the Chinese Family", *American Journal of Sociology*, 54(6):497-504. May.

Lee, S.C.
1953   "China's Traditional Family: Its Characteristics and Disintegration", *American Sociological Review*, 18:272-280.

Lewis, J.
1976   "Chinatown Spreads Out and Grows Within", *Daily News*, Nov. 28.

Lin, T.
1953   "Study of the Incidence of Mental Disorder in Chinese and Other Cultures", *Psychiatry*, 16(4):313-336. Nov.

Lindsey, R.
1982   "The New Asian Immigrants: Making Their Mark on America", *New York Times Magazine*, Pp.22-42. May 9.

Liu, W.T.
1966   "Chinese Value Orientations in Hong Kong", *Sociological Analysis*, 27(2):53-66. Summer.

1966   "Comparative Study of Refugee and Local Families", *Journal of Marriage and the Family*. August.

1965   "Achievement Motivation among Chinese Youth in Southeast Asia", *Asian Survey*, 5(4):186-196. April.

Liu, W.T.,*et al.*
1973 "Conjugal Power and Decision Making: A Methodological Note on Cross-cultural Study of the Family", *The American Journal of Sociology*, 79(1). July.

Lyman, S.
1971 "Red Guard on Grant Avenue: The Rise of Youthful Rebellion in Chinatowns", *Asians in the West*. Reno: Desert Research Institute.

_____
1968 "Race Relations Cycle of Robert E. Parks", *Pacific Sociological Review*, Pp.16-22. Spring.

Mairland, L.
1976 "Five Hurt in Chinatown Gang Fight: Flare-up Follows Month's Truce", *New York Times*, Sept. 10.

Marsella, A.J., D. Kinzie, and P. Gordon
1973 "Ethnic Variations in the Expression of Depression", *Journal of Cross-Cultural Psychology*, 4(4):435-458. Dec.

McCarthy, C.
1977 "The Government's – and the Family's – Obligation to the Family", *Washington Post*, P.A15, Jan. 29.

McClelland, D.D.
1963 "Motivational Patterns in S.E. Asia with Special Reference to the Chinese Case", *Journal of Social Issues*, 19(1).

McFadden, R.D.
1977 "Chinatown 'Mayor' Critically Injured in Knife Attack", *New York Times*, July 12.

Meade, R.D.
1970 "Leadership Studies of Chinese and Chinese-Americans", *Journal of Cross-Cultural Psychology*, 1.

Meadows, P.
1980 "Immigration Theory: A Review of Thematic Strategies". In *Source Book on the New Immigration*. Edited by Roy Simon Bryce-Laporte. New Brunswick, NJ: Transaction Books.

Mechanic, D.
1974 "Social Structure and Personal Adaptation: Some Neglected Dimensions". In *Coping and Adaptation*. Edited by G.V. Coelho, *et al.* New York: Basic Books.

Mitchell, J.
1976 "Warring Gangs of Chinatown", *New York Post*, Oct. 27.

Miller, W.B.
1958 "Lower Class Culture as a Generating Milieu of Gang Delinquency", *Journal of Social Issues*, 14(3):219-236.

Montero, D.
1979   "Vietnamese Refugees in America: Toward a Theory of Spontaneous International Migration", *International Migration Review*, 3(4). Winter.

Newsweek
1979   "Jimmy's Boat People", *Newsweek*. P.37. August 6.

New York Times
1978   "Chinatown Stabber Jailed", *New York Times*, March 7.

1972   "Study Discloses Wide Disparity in Crime and Police Efficiency", *New York Times*, Pp.1 and 16. Feb. 14.

Rice, B.
1977   "The New Gangs of Chinatown", *Psychology Today*, Pp. 60-69. May.

Richmond, A.H. and R.P. Verma
1978   "The Economic Adaptation of Immigrants: A New Theoretical Perspective", *International Migration Review*, 12(1):3-38. Spring.

Rosen, B.
1959   "Race, Ethnicity, and the Achievement Syndrome", *American Sociological Review*, 24:47-60.

Rosenthal, R. and L. Jacobson.
1968   "Teacher Expectation for the Disadvantaged", *Scientific American*, 218:19-23. April.

Schumach, M.
1970   "Neighborhoods: Chinatown Is Troubled by New Influx", *New York Times*, June 16.

Schwartz, A.J.
1971   "The Culturally Advantaged: A Study of Japanese-American Pupils", *Sociology and Social Research*, 55:341-353.

Scofield, R.W. and C.W. Sun
1960   "A Comparative Study of the Differential Effect upon Personality of Chinese and American Practices", *Journal of Social Psychology*, 53:221-224.

Sheppard, N., Jr.
1973   "Youth Gangs Involving 200 Members Become Growing Menace in Chinatown", *New York Times*, Aug. 18.

Sherif, M.
1969   "Reference Groups in Human Relations". In *Sociological Theory*, 3rd Edition. Edited by L.A. Coser and B. Rosenberg, New York: Macmillan Co.

Siegel, B.
1983   "New Immigrants about to Transform America Ethnically", *Chinatown News*, P. 3. April 18. Reprinted from *Los Angeles Times*.

Smith, M.E.
1957   "Progress in the Use of English after Twenty-Two Years by Children of Chinese Ancestry in Honolulu", *Journal of Genetic Psychology*, 90:255-258.

1938   "A Comparison of the Neurotic Tendencies of Students of Different Racial Ancestry in Hawaii", *Journal of Social Psychology*, 9:395-417.

Sollenberger, R.
1968   "Chinese American Child Rearing Practices and Juvenile Delinquency", *Journal of Social Psychology*, 74:13-23.

Sommer, J.
1981   "Public Education: America's Street of Gold", *American Educator*, P.25. Summer.

Sommerlad, E. and J.W.Berry.
1970   "The Role of Ethnic Identification in Distinguishing between Attitudes toward Assimilation and Integration of a Minority Racial Group", *Human Relations*, 23:23-29.

Stokes, H.S.
1979   "Ships Bound for Japan Avoiding Seas Traversed by 'Boat People'", *New York Times*, July 15.

Sue, D.W.
1973   "Ethnic Identity: The Impact of Two Cultures on the Psychological Development of Asians in America". In *Asian Americans: Psychological Perspectives*. Edited by S. Sue and N. Wagner. Ben Lomond, CA: Science and Behavior Books.

Sue, D.W. and B.A. Kirk.
1972   "Psychological Characteristics of Chinese American College Students", *Journal of Counseling Psychology*, 19:471-478.

Sue, D.W. and S. Sue
1972   "Counseling Chinese Americans", *Personnel and Guidance Journal*, 50:637-644. April.

1972   "Ethnic Minorities: Resistance to Being Researched", *Professional Psychology*, 3:11-17.

Sue, S.
1973   "Community Intervention: Implications for Action". In *Asian Americans: Psychological Perspectives*. Edited by S. Sue and N. Wagner. Ben Lomond, CA.: Science and Behavior Books.

Sue, S. and H. Kitano
1973   "The Model Minorities", *Journal of Social Issues*, 29(2):1-9.

1973   "Stereotypes As a Measure of Success", *Journal of Social Issues*, 29(2):83-98.

Sue, S. and D.W. Sue
1971   "Chinese-American Personality and Mental Health", *Amerasia Journal*, 2:36-49.

Sue S.,*et al.*
1976   "Conceptions of Mental Illness among Asians and Caucasian American Students", *Psychological Reports*, 38:703-708.

1975   "Asian Americans As a Minority Group", *American Psychologist*, 30:906-910.

Taft, R.
1979   "A Comparative Study of the Initial Adjustment of Immigrant School Children in Australia", *International Migration Review*, 13:71-80. Spring.

Teper, S.
1977   "Ethnicity, Race and Human Development", New York: Institute on Pluralism and Group Identity of the American Jewish Committee.

Thomas, W.I.
1930-31   "Relationship of Research in the Social Process", *Essays on Research in the Social Sciences: Papers Presented in a General Seminar Conducted by the Committee on Training of the Brookings Institution*, Washington, D.C.: Brookings Institution.

Time
1983   "Confucian Work Ethic", *Time*, March 28. P. 52.

Transaction
1968   "Why Chinatown's Children Are Not Delinquent", *Transaction*, 5:3. Sept.

Williams, J.
1982   "Young Suicides – Tragic and on the Increase", *New York Times*. P.10E. Apr. 25.

Wong, B.
1976   "Social Stratification, Adaptive Strategies, and the Chinese Community of New York", *Urban Life*, 5(1):33-52. April.

Wright, B.P.
1964   "Social Aspects of Change in the Chinese Family Pattern in Hong Kong", *Journal of Social Psychology*, 63:31-39.

Young, N.
1972   "Socialization Patterns among the Chinese of Hawaii", *Amerasia Journal*, 1(4):31-51. Feb.

Young, P.V.
1936   "Social Problems in the Education of the Immigrant Child", *American Sociological Review*, 1:419-429.

BOOKS

Abbott, K.A.
1976 "Culture Change and the Persistence of the Chinese Personality". In *In Response to Change*. Edited by George Devos. New York: Van Nostrand, 1976.

1970 *Harmony and Individualism*. Taipei, Taiwan: Orient Cultural Press.

Adamic, L.
1932 *Laughing in the Jungle*, New York: Harper Bros.

Allen, R.
1974 *Gang Wars of the 20's*. Chatsworth, CA.: Barclay House.

Almy, M.
1974 *Ways of Studying Children*. New York: Teacher's College Press, Columbia University.

Anderson, R.H. and H.G. Shane, eds.
1971 *As the Twig Is Bent: Readings in Early Childhood Education*. Boston: Houghton-Mifflin.

Blumer, H.
1969 *Symbolic Interactionism*. Englewood Cliffs, NJ: Prentice-Hall.

Boskoff, A.
1972 *The Mosaic of Sociological Theory*. New York: Thomas Y. Crowell Co.

Breur, H.
1972 *Columbus Was Chinese*. New York: McGraw-Hill.

Brody, E.
1970 *Behavior in New Environments: Adaptation of Migrant Population*. Beverly Hills, CA.: Sage Publications.

1968 *Minority Group Adolescents in the United States*. Baltimore: The Williams and Wilkins Co.

Bronfenbrenner, U.
1973 *Two Worlds of Childhood: U.S. and U.S.S.R.* New York: Basic Books.

Bulosan, C.
1943 *America Is in the Heart*. Seattle: University of Washington Press.

Chan, W.T.
1963 *A Source Book in Chinese Philosophy*. Princeton: Princeton University Press.

Chaney, D.C. and D.B.L. Podmore with A. Lu
1973   Young Adults in Hong Kong: Attitudes in Modernizing Society. Hong Kong: Center of Asian Studies, University of Hong Kong.

Chen, J.
1980   The Chinese of America. San Francisco: Harper & Row.

Chinn, T., ed.
1969   A History of the Chinese in California, a Syllabus. San Francisco: Chinese Historical Society of America.

Chou, C.
1970   My Life in the U.S. N. Quincy, MA.: Christopher Publishing House.

1969   Citizens' Survey and Fact-Finding Committee Report San Francisco: H.J. Carle and Sons.

Cloward, R. and L. Ohlin.
1960   Delinquency and Opportunity: A Theory of Delinquent Gangs. Glencoe, IL: Free Press.

Cohen, A.
1955   Delinquent Boys: The Culture of the Gang. New York: Free Press.

Cohen, P.S.
1968   Modern Social Theory. New York: Basic Books.

Coles, R.
1964   Children of Crisis. Boston: Little Brown & Co.

Cooley, C.
1918   The Social Process. New York: Charles Scribner's Sons.

Coolidge, M.
1909   Chinese Immigration. New York: Henry Holt.

Coser, L.A.
1956   Functions of Social Conflict. Glencoe, IL: Free Press.

Coser, L.A. and B. Rosenberg.
1982   Sociological Theory: A Book of Readings. 5th ed. New York: Macmillan Co.

Cronin, C.
1970   The Sting of Change. Chicago: University of Chicago Press.

Davie, M.
1936   World Immigration. New York: Macmillan Co.

Dillon, R.H.
1962   The Hatchetmen: Tong Wars in San Francisco. New York: Coward McCann.

Filstead, W.J., ed.
1970 *Qualitative Methodology*. Chicago: Rand McNally College Publishing Co.

Furfey, P.H.
1928 *The Gang Age*. New York: Macmillan Co.

Gallatin, J.E.
1975 *Adolescence and Individuality*. New York: Harper & Row.

Gee, E., ed.
1976 *Counterpoint*. University of California, Asian American Studies Center.

Glaser, B. and A.L. Strauss.
1967 *The Discovery of Grounded Theory: Strategies for Qualitative Research*. New York: Aldine Publishing Co.

Glazer, N. and P. Moynihan.
1975 *Ethnicity: Theory and Experience*. Cambridge, MA: Harvard University Press.

_____
1963, 1970 *Beyond the Melting Pot*. Cambridge, MA.: MIT Press.

Glick, C. and S. Hong.
1947 *Swords of Silence*. New York: McGraw-Hill Book Co.

Gordon, M.
1964 *Assimilation in American Life*. New York: Oxford University Press.

Handlin, O.
1962 *The Newcomers: Negroes and Puerto Ricans in a Changing Metropolis*. Garden City, N.Y: Doubleday, Anchor Books.

_____
1959 *Immigration As a Factor in American History*. Englewood Cliffs, NJ: Prentice Hall.

Haskins, J.
1974 *Street Gangs: Yesterday and Today*. New York: Hasting House.

Howe, I.
1976 *World of Our Fathers*. New York: Harcourt, Brace, Jovanovich.

Hsia, J.
"Cognitive Assessment of Asian Americans". In *Comparative Research in Bilingual Education: Asian-Pacific American Perspectives*. Edited by M. Chu-Chang. New York: Teacher's College Press.

Hsu, F.L.K.
1972 *Americans and Chinese: Reflections on Two Cultures and Their People*. New York: American Museum of Science Books.

1972   *Psychological Anthropology*. Cambridge, MA: Schenkman Publishing Co.

1971   *The Challenge of the American Dream: The Chinese in America*. Belmont, CA: Wadsworth Publishing Co.

1970   *Americans and Chinese*. New York: Doubleday, Natural History Press.

1969   *The Study of Literate Civilizations*. New York: Holt, Rinehart and Winston.

1963   *Clan, Caste, and Club*. Princeton, NJ: D. Van Nostrand Co.

1948   *Under the Ancestor's Shadow*. New York: Columbia University Press.

Hutchinson, E.P.
1956   *Immigrants and Their Children: 1850-1950*. U.S. Bureau of Census, Census Monograph Series. New York: John Wiley.

International Encyclopedia of the Social Sciences
1979   "Social Change", *International Encyclopedia of the Social Sciences*. New York: Free Press.

Kandel, D.B. and G.S. Lesser.
1972   *Youth in Two Worlds*. San Francisco: Jossey-Bass.

Kessen, W., ed.
1975   *Childhood in China*. New Haven, CT: Yale University Press.

Kim, H.C., ed.
1977   *The Korean Diaspora: Historical and Sociological Studies of Korean Immigration and Assimilation in North America*. Santa Barbara, CA: Clio Press.

Kim, I.
1981   *New Urban Immigrants: The Korean Community in New York*. Princeton, NJ: Princeton University Press.

Kramer, J.
1970   *The American Minority Community*. New York: Thomas Y. Crowell.

Kung, S.W.
1962   *Chinese in American Life*. Seattle: University of Washington Press.

Kuo, C.
1977   *Social and Political Change in New York's Chinatown*. New York: Praeger.

Kwong, P.
1979   *Chinatown, N.Y.: Labor and Politics, 1930-1950*. New York: Monthly Review Press.

Lang, O.
1946   *Chinese Family and Society.* New Haven: Yale University Press.

Lee, C.
1965   *Chinatown, U.S.A.* New York: Doubleday.

Lee, R.H.
1960   *The Chinese in the United States of America.* Hong Kong: Hong Kong University Press.

Lewis, O.
1968   *A Study of Slum Culture.* New York: Random House.

Lin, Y.
1935   *Chinatown Family.* New York: John Day Co.

Liu, W.T.
1979   *Transition to Nowhere.* Nashville, TN: Charter House.

Lowe, P.
1943   *Father and Glorious Descendent.* Boston: Little Brown & Co.

Lyman, S.M..
1974   *Chinese Americans.* New York: Random House.

Marden, C.F.
1952   *Minorities in American Society.* New York: American Book Co.

McDonald, M.
1970   *Not by the Color of Their Skin: The Impact of Racial Differences on the Child's Development.* New York: International Universities Press.

McWilliams, C.
1951   *Brothers under the Skin.* Boston: Little Brown & Co.

Mead, G.H.
1934   *Mind, Self and Society.* Edited by Charles Morris. Chicago: University of Chicago Press.

Miller, S.C.
1969   *The Unwelcome Immigrant: The American Image of the Chinese 1785-1882.* Berkeley: University of California Press.

Natanson, M.
1956   *The Social Dynamics of George H. Mead.* Washington, D.C.: Public Affairs Press.

Nee, V. and B. deBary Nee.
1972   *Longtime Californ': A Documentary Study of an American Chinatown.* New York: Random House.

1970   *New York Life Handbook*   (in Chinese) Vols. 1-3, New York: Chinese Scholars Service Corp.

Oakley, R., ed.
1968   *New Backgrounds: The Immigrant Child at Home and at School.* London: Oxford University Press.

O'Connell, D., *et al*
1977   *Research Relating to Children.* Chicago: ERIC Clearing House on Early Childhood Education.

Padilla, E.
1958   *Up from Puerto Rico.* New York: Columbia University Press.

Parsons, T.
1951   *The Social System.* Glencoe, IL: Free Press.

Petersen, W.
1969   *Population.* 2nd Ed. New York: Macmillan Co.

Ravitch, D.
1974   *The Great School Wars: New York City, 1805-1973: A History of the Public Schools As a Battlefield of Social Change.* New York: Basic Books.

Rubington, E. and M.S. Weinberg, eds.
1977   *The Study of Social Problems.* New York: Oxford University Press.

Sandis, E.E.
1973   *Refugees and Economic Migrants in Greater Athens.* Athens: National Center of Social Research.

Saville-Troike, M. and R. Troike
1971,1975   *A Handbook of Bilingual Education.* Washington, D.C.: TESOL.

Schilt, J.
1977   *Mental Health Programming for Chinatown: Issues and Options.* New York: Community Service Society of New York, Dept. of Public Affairs.

Segal, J. and H. Yahraes
1978   *A Child's Journey.* New York: McGraw-Hill Book Co.

Seward, G. and R.C. Williamson, eds.
1970   *Sex Roles in Changing Society.* New York: Random House.

Sherif, M.
"Reference Groups in Human Relations". In *Sociological Theory*, 3rd ed. Edited by L. Coser and B. Rosenberg. New York: Macmillan Co.

Sidel, R.
1973   *Women and Child Care in China.* New York: Penguin Books.

Sih, P.K.T. and L.B. Allen, eds.
1976   *The Chinese in America*. New York: St. John's University Press.

Simon, H.A.
1947   *Adminstrative Behavior*. New York: Macmillan.

Skinner, W., comp.
1979   *The Study of Chinese Society*. Essays by Maurice Freedman. Stanford, CA: Stanford University Press.

Stonequist, E.
1937   *The Marginal Man: A Study in Personality and Culture Conflict*. New York: Charles Scribner's Sons.

Stouffer, S.A., *et al*
1949   *The American Soldier*. Princeton, NJ: Princeton University Press.

Sue, S. and N. Wagner, eds.
1973   *Asian Americans: Psychological Perspectives*. Ben Lomond, CA: Science and Behavior Books.

Sung, B.L.
1979   *Statistical Profiles of the Chinese in the United States, 1970*. New York: Arno Press.

————————
1976   *A Survey of Chinese American Manpower and Employment*. New York: Praeger.

————————
1967, 1971   *Mountain of Gold: The Story of the Chinese in America*. New York: Macmillan Co., Collier Books.

Sutherland, E.H. and D.R. Cressy.
1939   *Principles of Criminology*. Philadelphia: J.B. Lippincott.

Tachiki, A., *et al.*, eds.
1971   *Roots: An Asian American Reader*. Los Angeles: University of California, Asian American Studies Center.

Taran, F.B.
1976   *Use of Neighborhood Health Services by Chinese Americans*. New York: Office of Planning and Research, Community Service Society.

Teggert, F.J.
1955   *Theories of History* As Quoted in *International Migration: The Immigrant in the Modern World*. New York: Ronald Press.

Thomas, W.I. and F. Znaniecki.
1918   *Polish Peasants*. Chicago: University of Chicago Press.

Timasheff, N.S.
1967   *Sociological Theory: Its Nature and Growth*. 3rd ed. New York: Random House.

Truzzi, M., ed.
1971   Sociology. New York: Random House.

Weiss, M.S.
1974   Valley City: A Chinese Community in America. Cambridge, MA: Schenkman.

Wheeler, T.C., ed.
1971   The Immigrant Experience: The Anguish of Becoming American. New York: Penguin Books.

Whiting, B., ed.
1966   Six Cultures: Studies of Child Rearing Vol. 3. New York: John Wiley & Sons.

Wilson, C.G.
1931   Chinatown Quest. Stanford, CA: Stanford University Press.

Wolff, S.
1975   Children under Stress. Harmondsworth, England: Pelican Books.

Wong, B.P.
1979   A Chinese American Community: Ethnicity and Survival Strategies. Singapore: Chopmen Enterprises.

Wood, A.L.
1974   Deviant Behavior and Control Strategies: Essays in Sociology. Lexington, MA:Lexington Books, D.C. Heath and Co.

Worchel, S. and J. Cooper
1976   Understanding Social Psychology. Homewood, IL:Dorsey Press.

Yang, C.K.
1974   Chinese Communist Society: The Family and the Village. Cambridge, MA: MIT Press.

1959   The Chinese Family in the Communist Revolution. Cambridge, MA: MIT Press.

DOCUMENTS AND MONOGRAPHS

Abbott, K.
1977   "Issues in Cross-Ethnic Psychotherapy". Northampton, MA: Smith College School for Social Work.

Bay Area Social Planning Council
1971   "Chinese Newcomers in San Francisco". San Francisco: Bay Area Social Planning Council, February.

Bernard, W.S., ed.
1972   "Immigrants and Ethnicity". New York: American Immigration and Citizenship Conference.

Chao, R.
1977   "Chinese Immigrant Children". Edited by Betty Lee Sung. New York: City College of New York, Dept. of Asian Studies.

Chiswick, B.R.
1977   "The Effect of Americanization on the Earnings of Foreign-born Men". Stanford, CA: Hoover Institution.

Department of Health, Education and Welfare Annual Reports.
Vital Statistics of the United States

Hurh, W.M. and K.C. Kim.
1980   "Korean Immigrants in America: A Structural Analysis of Ethnic Confinement and Adhesive Adaptation". U.S. Dept. of Health and Human Services, National Institutes of Mental Health.

Integrated Education Associates Staff
1972   "Chinese Americans: School and Community Problems".

International Ladies Garment Worker's Union Local 23-25
1983   "Chinatown Garment Industry Study of the International Ladies Garment Worker's Union".

Kim, B.L.
1980   "Korean American Child at School and at Home", U.S. Dept. of Health, Education and Welfare, Administration for Children, Youth and Family.

Lai, H.M. and P.P. Choy.
1972   "Outlines: History of the Chinese in America". Published by the authors.

Lesser, G., Fifer, G. and Clark, D.
1965   "Mental Abilities of Children from Different Social Class and Cultural Groups". Monographs of the Society for Research in Child Development, Serial No. 102, 30(4).

Llanes, J.R.
1980   "Human Enculturation within Group Culture-Clusters: Assimilation Patterns of Vietnamese Immigrants", Paper presented at International Conference on Communication, Human Evolution and Development.

Miller, W.B.
1976   "Violence by Youth Gangs and Youth Groups in Major American Cities". Washington, D.C.: U.S. Department of Justice, National Institute for Juvenile Justice and Delinquency Prevention Office, April.

National Indochinese Clearinghouse
1981   "Indochinese Refugee Education Guide, No. 22". Washington, D.C.: National
       Indochinese Clearing House, Center for Applied Linguistics.

New York City Board of Education Community School Profiles
1978   "Community School Profiles, 1976-77

1975   "Community School Profiles, 1973-1974". April.

New York City Planning Commission
1976   "Chinatown Street Revitalization". May.

1974   "Community School District Profiles". July.

San Francisco Department of City Planning
1972   "1970 Census: Population and Housing Summary and Analysis". August.

Sung, B.L.
1977   "Gangs in New York's Chinatown". New York: City College of New York,
       Dept. of Asian Studies.

U.S. Department of Commerce, Bureau of the Census
1980   Census of Population. New York State. (PC)1 B34.

1980   Social Indicators III, Dec.

1978   "Special Census of Lower Manhattan, New York City". Sept. 26.

1970   "Japanese, Chinese and Filipinos in the United States" PC(2)1G.

1960   "United States Census of Population: Non-White Population by Race".

U.S. Department of Health, Education and Welfare
1977   "Evaluation of the Impact of ESEA Title VII Spanish/English Bilingual Educa-
       tion Programs". Interim Report. April.

1976   "Asian American Reference Data Directory". Washington, D.C.: Rj Associates.
       March.

Annual Vital Statistics of the United States, Public Health Service.

U.S. Department of Justice, Federal Bureau of Investigation
1976   Crime in the United States. Uniform Crime Report, August.

Immigration and Naturalization Service. *Annual Reports.*

U.S. Department of Labor, Manpower Administration
1974 "Immigrants and the American Labor Market". Manpower Research Monograph No. 31.

U.S. House of Representatives, Committee on the Judiciary
1980 "Immigration and Nationality Act with Amendments and Notes on Related Laws". 7th ed. Washington, D.C.: Government Printing Office.

Yankelovich, Skelly and White, Inc.
1977 "Raising Children in a Changing Society". *The General Mills American Family Report 1976-77.* Minneapolis, MN: General Mills.

Yao, E.L.
1979 "School Teachers' Perception of Child Rearing by the Chinese". Paper presented at Asian and Pacific American Educators' Conference, San Francisco, April 27.

Yung, C.N.
1969 Chinatown Reports. Unpublished.

THESES AND DISSERTATIONS

Chen, M.K.
1964 *Intelligence and Bilingualism as Independent Variables in Study of Junior High School Students of Chinese Descent.* Ph.D. dissertation, University of California.

Kolm, R.
1966 *The Change of Cultural Identity: An Analysis of Factors Conditioning the Cultural Integration of Immigrants.* Ph.D. dissertation, Wayne State University.

Tam, T.
1978 "Chinese Suicide: An Investigation of the Problem in the Various Chinese Communities with Particular Emphasis on New York City". M.A. thesis, Columbia University School of Public Health.

Tan, M.G.
1968 *Social Mobility and Assimilation: The Chinese in the United States,* Ph.D. dissertation, University of California.

Tou, L.A.
1974 *A Study of Work Value Orientations: Chinese Americans and White American Students of the 7th, 8th Grades in Catholic Elementary Schools.* Ph.D. dissertation, Catholic University of America.

Voss, H.L.
1961   *Insulation of Vulnerability to Delinquency: A Comparison of the Hawaiians and Japanese.* Ph.D. dissertation, University of Wisconsin.

MAGAZINES, JOURNALS AND NEWSPAPERS

Amerasia Journal. Los Angeles: University of California Los Angeles, Asian American Studies Center. (1972-)

Bridge—The Asian American Magazine. New York: Basement Workshop. (1972-)

Chinatown News. Vancouver, Canada. (1953-)

Civil Rights Digest, special issue on Asian Americans. Washington, D.C.: U.S. Commission on Civil Rights, 9(1). Fall, (1978)

East/West, The Chinese American Journal. San Francisco.(1966-)

BIBLIOGRAPHIES

Cordaso, F.
1976   *Immigrant Children in American Schools.* Fairfield, NJ: Augustus M. Kelley Publishers.

Duphiny, L.
1972   *Oriental Americans: An Annotated Bibliography.* New York: Columbia University, Teacher's College, ERIC Clearinghouse, February.

Hune, S.
1977   *Pacific Migration to the United States: Trends and Themes in Historical and Sociological Literature.* RIIES Bibliographic Studies no. 2. Washington, D.C.: Smithsonian Institution.

Jayatimeke, R.
    The Education of Asian Americans. New York: Columbia University, Teacher's College, ERIC Clearinghouse.

Social Science Education Consortium of Boulder, CO.
1975   *Materials and Human Resources for Teaching Ethnic Studies: An Annotated Bibliography.*

1980 *Mid-Atlantic Directory to Resources for Asian Studies.*

Morishima, J.K., *et al.*
1979 *Handbook of Asian American Pacific Islander Mental Health*, Vol. 1. U.S. Dept. of Health, Education and Welfare, National Institutes of Mental Health.

1976 *Recent Immigration to the United States: The Literature of the Social Sciences.* RIIES Bibliographic Studies No. 1. Washington, D.C.: Smithsonian Institution.

U.S. Department of Justice, Immigration and Naturalization Service
1979 *Immigration Literature: Abstracts of Demographic, Economic, and Policy Study.* June.

Yashitomi, J., *et al.*
1978 *Asians in the Northwest.* Washington: Northwest Asian American Studies Research Group and the Asian American Studies Program at the University of Washington.

Index